A River of Hope

Amy Lynn

E/ergreen
PRESS

Mobile, AL

A River of Hope
by Amy Lynn
Copyright © 2007 Amy Lynn

ISBN 978-1-58169-249-5
For Worldwide Distribution
Printed in the U.S.A.

Evergreen Press
P.O. Box 191540 • Mobile, AL 36619
800-367-8203

Other books
by Amy Lynn

Hidden Castle

Seeds of the Heart

Bits of Heaven

When the Petal Falls

Each Moment a Gift

Dedication

To my beloved

Acknowledgments

First and foremost I must thank my Creator and King, my Savior and Redeemer, Jesus Christ who makes all things possible in my life including this book. He has indeed delivered me from the bondage of many trials and tribulations, positioning me with his loving support in a new place along my journey, where I can reach out on a deeper level than ever before. He continues to help me use my hardships to help others find comfort and healing. He inspires me to share my strength and hope.

Next, I would like to thank my family. My kids Amber and Alex are teenagers now. They have stood by their mother's side through thick and thin, no matter what. They have been challenged as well. It has not always been easy. Sometimes it has even been ugly, and yet they have been there to support and love their mother. Thank you, kids. You're great!

My parents are also awesome. Mom, Dad, you have always been there. Your love, support, and encouragement have been a steady pillar that I have been able to lean on for many years now. I would not have the courage, strength, or stamina to follow my destiny if it would not be for your unwavering and unconditional love. Thank you from the bottom of my heart.

And Ann, my dear sister. I love you. Words cannot even express the gratitude that swells in my heart for having you as, not only a sister, but also a best friend. God designed us so similarly, it is as if our very fibers are interwoven as one. You always know what to say and do when I am down or distraught. You see into my very soul. You are beautiful and special—the best sister God could have given me. I look forward to continuing our journey together.

Lastly, I would like to thank my husband. I believe God brings two hearts together to heal and grow. We have discovered this. We also learn at a much higher rate in relationships, and so I thank you for my lessons and experiences. You are helping me become who God wants me to be, one day at a time. You are strong and insightful. Thank you for your many gifts.

Introduction

So many women struggle these days. We are creative, intelligent, resourceful, and gifted; however, with our many gifts come numerous responsibilities and challenges. Some days we do not know where to even begin. We know that God created us to experience freedom and joy, but sometimes we feel lost and overwhelmed. We know there must be a better way, but what? This book is designed to help women find the way to peace and happiness.

Our emotional landscapes are complex. Feelings and emotions do not always come easy. Some of us are weighed down by the heavy chains of depression and anxiety. Others struggle with burdens like feelings of inadequacy and insecurity, low self-esteem, perfectionism, self-doubt, and fear. Whatever our worries may be, we can turn them over to the loving care of God. He holds each of us gently, delicately in the palm of his hand. We can learn to be as gentle and loving with ourselves.

Life is a journey in faith. Some days we grow. Others we slip back. It is the daily experience that keeps our souls vital and alive. We encounter hardships and pain, but we are also blessed by God's miracles and glory. Life is a delicate balance, and we can learn to trust and stay connected. It is our destiny. It is our hope.

Feelings/Release

Life provides a wide array of feelings that we can experience, express, and finally, release. Some of our encounters bring joy and others sorrow. We grow when we allow time and space in our heart for our feelings—both pleasant and not so pleasant. It is then that we discover our true identity.

Feelings mirror our choices. We can open our inner landscape to them, or shut the door. We can explore the wisdom they bring, for we create the garden from which they bloom. We might choose to turn the other way, but not without consequence. When we face them openly, they grace our path. We learn more about ourselves. We learn to love.

But there comes a time for tender release. Feelings can only be held for so long before we must let them go. Life is ever-changing and so are we. Each day we receive the opportunity to experience a new range of emotions, yet our ability to do so is dampened if we hold onto yesterday. Releasing the past creates room for light to shine into our future. We can move on.

Emotions are God-given. When we bow to the inner-voice, we are filled with peaceful guidance. Our path becomes clearer each time we pause and take personal inventory. We gain perspective during times of reflection. God is leading us toward serenity and life anew. Feelings bring us nearer to God.

Anger/Healing

Emotions help to guide us. Each one weaves an intricate thread through the tapestry of who we are. Anger is perhaps the strangest emotion. It makes some of us so uncomfortable that it stifles us. Women have a tendency to let anger fester. The time has come to recognize it, identify it, describe it, accept it, confess it, and let it go. Harboring resentment causes depression.

Locating anger can be difficult. Some of us do not know where to even start. Prayer is a good beginning. God will show us the source of our anger when we call upon his help. Identifying anger can also be challenging. We need to be specific. Vague attempts to find the source of our anger only inhibit the healing process. We can make a thorough and cleansing exploration. We needn't fear. God will hold us especially close as we seek to free our spirits from the shackles of resentment.

It is also beneficial to describe our anger. What is it that makes us mad about a situation or the person involved? Considering all of the dimensions of a particular event prepares us to focus on our part. It is easier to project the blame on others. And yet we know that healing begins with us.

Lastly, we need to confess our anger and let it go. We can lift our hearts to heaven and ask God to remove resentment from us. Anger steals precious moments from us. It prevents us from enjoying God's gifts. God will forgive; in fact, he is waiting for us to come to him.

JANUARY 3

Moving Beyond Decisions

Life is enriching and ever-changing. Each day hands us new situations that require choices. Each decision we make can bring us nearer to our destiny. We incrementally discover who we are. We grow to understand the depths of God's love for us. Choices help us live in this love.

But sometimes we make poor decisions. When we do, it can be especially hard to move beyond them. We will not always succeed. Although failure causes grief, we can learn to let go of the past and prayerfully attune our minds to the hope of the future. We will make many more right choices in our lifetime. We can praise God for our development and be kind to ourselves as we grow.

Letting go is the key to living healthily beyond past circumstances. The cornerstone is turning negative into positive. We can honestly and courageously admit and accept that we did some things wrong. When we feel the gentle pull against our heart, we can repent and move on. Every step we take, backward or forward, helps us arrive at where we are going. Each moment counts, even those we are not especially fond of.

For there is One who has a plan larger than we can imagine. He guides us through good times and bad. His love knows no bounds. May we forever appreciate His endless grace and mercy!

JANUARY 4

Choosing Happiness

Emotions are complex. They get muddled in our busy lives. Some of us get caught in the claws of depression for many days before even realizing it.

We may not even know why we are sad. It is refreshing to pause and realize that we can choose happiness, anytime and anywhere. We are all beautiful in our own way, wondrously and magnificently created to live joyful lives.

One ingredient necessary is daily quiet time. Moments in peace and solitude make room in our hearts for happiness to enter. We can plan ahead to ensure we have quiet moments. They will not happen automatically. We can schedule time for personal communion, reflection, and devotion.

Like colored pebbles along a rocky shore, these precious moments will collect to add beauty in our lives. They provide an opening for grace to touch and fill us. They build a healing bridge, arcing above depression and sadness, lifting us to walk above our troubles.

Happiness is a gift. It is not purchased or owned; it is free. Sometimes, it requires courage to experience. We might not feel worthy of its presence. We all deserve to feel the gifts of love and peace. True happiness blossoms in these realms. Centered in God, our joy becomes bountiful and everlasting.

JANUARY 5

Embracing the Unknown

We love to see our plans unfold as we expect. We are challenged emotionally and psychologically when things do not go our way. We also like it best when the end is in sight. It is hard to journey toward an unseen future.

The unknown stirs fear within us. When we are unsure of outcomes and solutions, we get scared. Thankfully, we can consider alternatives. Instead of surrendering to fear during uncertain times, we can trust in God's perfect guidance. We can surrender to love. God is moving us in the direction we must go. We can trust his care and inspiration.

Embracing the unknown is far better than running from it. The places that have made us comfortable are not necessarily the roads we need to follow. When we step into new avenues, even when we are unsure, it allows God room to work within us. During times of uncertainty, he can show us his ways. And his ways are so much better than our own!

We can even learn to treasure times of ambiguity. Instead of throwing up our arms in frustration, we can reach out our hands in faith. God sees the big picture. He understands and loves us completely. He designed the journey we travel. He handcrafted it especially for us, to bring us peace and joy. He will not let us down! Embrace him.

JANUARY 6

Unhealthy Behavior/Change

One of the primary ways that unhealthy behavior manifests itself is through a wide array of negligent acts. And they all have something in common—pain. All unhealthy behaviors eventually result in pain, whether physical, spiritual, psychological, or emotional. Thankfully, we can always decide to change. We can turn around wherever we are and walk in the footprints of healing. We are being led to a brighter place.

The first step is to face reality. It is easier to shut our eyes to personal characteristics that cause us shame. It is tempting to look upon the defects of others in order to try to camouflage our own. We must learn to view ourselves realistically—our weaknesses as well as our strengths. We can try to build upon our strengths and become ready to let go of weaknesses. We will begin to see that our greatest strength is God. He gives us the power to change. He is the ultimate transformer.

The second step is trust. We are so accustomed to our current behavior that the thought of changing can quickly turn us away from our comfort zone. We can trust that God will lead us to victory. He will reward us for righteousness. We can have faith in His unfailing love and direction.

Finally, we reach the time of change. Our intentions become actions here. Having prepared ourselves by facing reality and developing trust in God, we can embark on the path of healing. Courage will be our guide if we step out in faith. Negative behavior will be replaced by many positives. The great beauty that lies inside each of us will begin to unfold. We can add love to the world. We can help God unfold his destiny for us!

JANUARY 7

Searching/Discovery

Life is a spiritual search. We learn more and more about God and our precious inner spirit when we remain open to each event that happens along the way. We can search our souls to help determine our reactions and responses. We needn't act in haste. We can respond prayerfully and thoughtfully. This leads to a brighter tomorrow.

Searching involves truth. We can learn to be true to ourselves and honor God through our actions. We can embrace our creative seeds and contribute positively to life. When we continue in honesty, we will surely find our destiny. We will know why we are here. Our mission will be revealed.

Searching leads to self-discovery. We are born to discover great gifts. In this experience, we will come to know our life's purpose. Our days take on special meaning, and we no longer feel empty and void.

Awakening spiritually is not an overnight process, rather it is something that needs to be nurtured over time. It requires a continued willingness to learn and grow. We discover more and more about God, our relationships with others, and our inner landscape, paving the way to a wondrous journey ahead and opening the curtains to a brighter future.

JANUARY 8

Courage/Expression

One of the most important qualities that we can possess is courage. It takes courage for us to fully express ourselves. Women face challenges daily. People, situations, and events arise that test our confidence and faith. Courage equips us to face these difficult circumstances. It helps us stay true to our values as we act and respond.

Some of us are afraid to voice our opinions, beliefs, and values, especially when we know it will result in conflict. It seems safer and easier to go along with others and be agreeable. When the going gets tough, we bend. Our inner psyche becomes pliable, and we lose resolution. We will eventually suffocate. It is critical for us to freely express our feelings, emotions, thoughts, and ideas. When we compromise our values, we lose our soul. We become disconnected from our Source. This bears a high price tag, for without our Creator, we are nothing.

Courageous people bring light and love into the world. Each time we dare to stand up for what we believe in, we usher in a brighter future. We discover the strength of a spiritual way of living. This light spreads to others. It is contagious. We are helping others catch a glimpse of God.

JANUARY 9

Serenity/Becoming

Serenity is one of the greatest gifts on earth. We do not usually make it a priority. Some of us overwork, over-schedule, over-obligate, and overachieve until all traces of peace disappear. Praise God we can change. We can begin to honor serenity and hold this state of mind high. We can enter the hope of a new life.

Trust makes serenity possible. When we trust that God will provide, peace is ours to behold. Worry disappears. Fear devours trust and prevents us from walking God's path. We also lose trust when we settle for less than truth and love. These are the forces that bring us to serenity.

Holding the treasure of peace in the forefront of our minds helps us stay attuned to the many gifts that embody our days. Each moment becomes a special treasure. Quieting our mind, body, and spirit, we can enjoy them most fully. This is where the garden lies. It is a place of beauty and lasting satisfaction. It is a place of love and light.

And in the arms of serenity, our destiny becomes more visible. We are handed guidance for the future. We are empowered with the freedom to become. Our individual creation is genetically designed with infinite capabilities. If we relax and focus, we can experience our talent and purpose. Serenity allows us to be all that we are and leads us to become who we are meant to be.

❧❧❧

JANUARY 10

Vanity/Beauty

Vanity—a magnified focus on outward appearance—diminishes our ability to feel our inner beauty. We are robbed of true personal satisfaction and become dependent on the response of others. We lose self-love.

Insecurity gives birth to vanity. When we do not feel like we are enough on the inside, it magnifies our perception of the importance of our outward image. This fragments our spirit. The good news is that we can heal. We can step into the light of change.

We can learn to view beauty at a soul level. We can seek to appreciate the beauty around us and know that by grace we are part of God's great beauty. Life is more than hairstyles, nail designs, and fashion. Beauty is about love, and we are creations of God's wondrous love.

We can share this truth with others. We can be lights in a world of confusion and darkness. Our true beauty can shine through to brighten and bless the lives of others. We can show others how beautiful they are. We can be God's eyes for them.

The time has come for us to cleanse our hearts of vanity and embrace the pure beauty of our innocence. We are children of God. We can welcome the wholeness of spirit this revelation brings. We can kiss insecurity and misdirected effort goodbye. We can embrace the essence of who we are.

JANUARY 11

Stumbling/Becoming

We all stumble—some more than others—but, nonetheless, it is something we all have in common. We don't enjoy it; nor do we plan it, and yet stumbling is a necessary part of life. It helps us become who we are meant to be. It brings us closer to our destiny. Most importantly, it leads us nearer to God.

Although stumbling is inevitable, there are things we can do to gain discernment. One of the most effective means to clear away obstacles is learning to make good choices. The decisions we make all eventually lead to one of two outcomes—either positive or negative. We must make our choices carefully, holding our dearest hopes and beliefs in the forefront of our minds. Our choices ultimately determine who we become.

And becoming is what life is all about. One way or another, we will get there. We will discover the magnificence of who we are created to be. We are all children of God. We can spend our lifetime on earth living out His destiny. We can be lights where there is darkness and despair.

JANUARY 12

Ego/Forgiveness

The ego is an extremely fragile part of who we are and causes us to be sensitive to how people perceive us. It diminishes our spiritual health, especially when we allow it to control our thoughts and actions. When people affect us, our ego is often the first to respond. When they hurt us, we feel like lashing out in revenge. When they judge us, we assume the defensive. We do not want to look bad, no matter what. This insecure way of living costs us our most precious treasure.

Instead, we can learn to forgive and accept during the times when we struggle with pride. The best response might be silence and self-restraint. We can release egotism. We do not have to justify ourselves or even gain the support of those around us. Our greatest strength lies within. It is God.

God is love. Love heals all wounds in due time. The eternal story is unfolding. It will ultimately reveal the truth for all to see. It conquers inequity and brings justice to light. Forgiveness and acceptance help love shine in our lives. They are opposites of ego. They eradicate resentment and infiltrate kindness. They help us live better lives.

⁕

JANUARY 13

Patience/Surrender

We are all blessed with a wonderful journey. The Master Creator carefully designed each of our lives before the beginning of time. Patience is the key to discovering the great wonders of our creation. Our journeys will be beautiful, but beauty cannot be rushed. It cannot be forced. Love takes time.

A freedom of spirit is born when we develop a willingness to wait. We can surrender impatience, self-will, strife, and other control needs, and embrace our truest, deepest needs. We needn't worry. Our truest desires will be satisfied. Our plans may not progress at the rate we hope or expect, but we can rest, assured that we are progressing toward something even grander. We are growing in our understanding of God's love.

Surrender brings serenity and peace. Our spirit can be refreshed when we fully entrust our future to God. He holds great plans for us, and only he knows how to bring these spectacular wonders full circle. When we wait on his power, he surpasses our greatest expectations.

⁕

JANUARY 14

Appreciation/Blessings

We are blessed with so many gifts, but sometimes we fail to recognize them. We lack appreciation for the special things that God places in our lives: spouses, children, parents, and friends. We get wrapped up in what seems like important endeavors and make little time for what matters the most. Our hearts become empty and torn, and we wonder why.

Thankfully, we can nurture and grow a more appreciative spirit. We can respect, honor, and enjoy each and every gift God places along our paths. We can redirect our energy to spend time with the people that mean the most to us. Love matters more than anything else. We can tend to our relationships with care. Each one is valuable. They are God-given.

When we appreciate our blessings, we become more content. God enriches our soul. We move closer to him as we mature spiritually. When we discover that the journey is filled with joy, we can be deeply satisfied.

JANUARY 15

Happiness/Self-Love

Loving ourselves is an important part of happiness. It is hard to be happy if we are not satisfied with who we are. Acceptance leads to love. When we affirm our strengths and accept our weaknesses, we grow in self-love. We are free to discover our created abilities. We welcome life's teachings, even the hard lessons. We can learn that, no matter what, we will be okay.

Developing self-love takes time. It is a process. It does not develop overnight. It is linked to other fine qualities like self-respect, self-worth, and self-esteem. These qualities are all rooted in who we are in God's eyes. We are created in his image. When we try to see ourselves through the mirror of his love for us, it is easier to accept who we are. We can be happy.

One of the greatest gifts in this world is joy. When we accept who we are and love the person within, happiness abounds. We can quit comparing and judging, and instead be compassionate and kind. We can lower our expectations for ourselves because we know we too were not created perfect.

JANUARY 16

Regret/Confusion

There are times when past regrets grow out of proportion. If we are not careful, they can take on a life of their own, or at least severely interfere with ours. We all make mistakes. We are learning. Life is a series of decisions. Sometimes we pass; other times we fail. Each choice we make helps us become who we are designed to be. In fact, sometimes our wrongdoings lead us even closer to our destiny than all the things we do right. We find out who we are in a hurry!

Too often we find ourselves a victim of regret. We hold on to guilt and shame. We do not realize that we can brush the dust off our trousers and move forward. Life is too short for second guesses. We are rapidly becoming who God wants us to be, and looking back will only interfere.

Harboring regret eventually leads to confusion. We are unable to make crisp, clear decisions when we are psychologically subject to guilt. Thoughts become jumbled. It is difficult to move forward with trust. We do not want to fail. Fear prevents us from trying again. It tells us we must be extra cautious. But a life without risk is a life with little joy. We are not truly free.

It is time to let go of lingering regrets. Praise God he is forgiving and graceful. We can lay our burdens in his kind hands and move on. The journey is full of challenge, but God will see us through. He gives us all the chances we need. He empowers us to finish. He encourages us to succeed.

JANUARY 17

Unrealistic Goals/Depression

How high we set our goals! We plan to accomplish many projects and tasks simultaneously to achieve our dreams. Our causes may be worthy, but we must question the practicality of this method of operation. It is not realistic to expect that we will see all our plans unfold. In fact, there are some that are best left alone. Not everything we want is ultimately good for us.

Unrealistic goals lead to depression. When we set our mind on achieving something beyond our capability, it causes frustration and dismay. Instead, we can journey through life in smaller increments. We can strive toward reaching our ultimate destiny in small steps. Each day, we can perform some of the tiny tasks that will one day lead us there, living contentedly in the moment. A bright future is built upon many days of love and trust.

Just for today, we can know that God is moving us in the direction we should go. He hears our hopes and sees our dreams. When the time is right, we will be given the opportunities to make them come true. Bit by bit, we will achieve the goals that are meant to be ours. And, we needn't wait until they are behind us, to celebrate. We can embrace the joy found in each step along the way.

JANUARY 18

Reservation/Hugs

An invisible, yet impenetrable wall surrounds some of us. We need our space, or so we think. We feel uncomfortable and sometimes even violated when people cross this line and get too close, especially if we do not know them well. We are especially uneasy if we do not know them at all! It is difficult to let down our guard and let people get close. Yet when we do, our lives are enriched, and we receive love's finest gifts.

Hugs warm the heart. Instead of simply shaking hands, we can extend our arms and embrace one another. It is both encouraging and healing. We needn't fear reaching through our wall. Each hug we give, and receive, adds more love to the world. Lives are blessed. As we express our love, we experience joy.

Let's let go of our reservation and, instead, love with courage! We need to be ready to embrace family and friends with zeal and compassion. It is time to reach out to strangers with open arms. A hug might be just what they need to brighten their day. It is guaranteed the people God places along our path need a special touch. This is all part of the journey. We cannot truly live without it.

JANUARY 19

Miracles/Wonders

We are living proof that miracles happen. Some people chalk the unexplainable up to coincidence. Others attempt to theorize and philosophize. But, it is certain that miracles highlight our world! They grace humanity with the depths of God's love. Without the blessings found in miracles, some of us would not be who we are today.

Blessings come in many sizes. Some of the largest gifts are packaged in the tiniest ways. There is no rational explanation to fully encompass their magnificence; they belong to the realm of mystery, the order of the divine. These wondrous blessings occur in perfect symmetry, exactly where they belong. They grace us with the power that transcends the natural world. They may be extraordinary happenings, or may be as simple as a smile.

We can ask for miracles, and yet they most often coincide with God's divine timing. We are so grateful when they grace our lives! We can learn to be patient while we wait. We can accept that not all miracles are visible by the human eye. Great things are happening in the spiritual realm. Many of our prayers are answered in the heavens long before we see the results. We can trust the unseen power of God's care and love. He creates new wonders through our requests. We are part of His work.

JANUARY 20

Flexibility/Peace

Rigidity is deadly. It prevents us from being moved in the direction of God. It holds us back when we could be expressing our creativity. It squelches our talents and undermines our abilities. Rigidity is a byproduct of fear. It is empty and insecure.

When we become more flexible, our spirit is born anew. God can lead us along unexpected, yet glorious paths. His ways are beautiful. We can discover all the gifts He has to show us. Our hearts are stretched beyond physical limitation. We can do the things He wants us to do. We become free in mind and spirit to follow our destiny. Eventually, we will find that God's plans are far better than our own. His gifts exceed our greatest hopes and dreams. They bring us lasting inner peace.

Peace is a wonderful and priceless gift. Letting go of predetermined goals and opening the heart to the spontaneity of God's guidance are liberating and enlightening. It is within our power to change. God gives us the strength we need daily. We can overcome rigidity and learn to be open to the many blessings we will encounter along the journey.

JANUARY 21

Humility/Empowerment

Some of us are accustomed to feeling "more than" or "less than." We either feel above or below those around us. We long to be comfortable with who we are. How nice it would be to feel good about ourselves, not because we are better, but just because we are. We especially dread our feelings of not being good enough. There must be a midpoint between these two polarities! Can we learn to be content in the knowledge that we are simply children of God? This ushers in the light of true empowerment.

Humility is the midpoint where we find peace along the journey and feel satisfied with who we are, treating others and ourselves with love and respect. Humility is not feeling less than. It is seeing and accepting our value and purpose in God's eyes. Through this enriched outlook, we are empowered to share our many gifts. We are not ashamed; rather, we are inspired. And through our work, we can help God show others the hope in his love.

Each one of us makes a difference. We are all designed uniquely to fulfill our part of God's great destiny. We can be confident in our ability to affect people in a positive way. We are no better or worse than they are. We can be helpful to those around us and interact with them in ways that make us stronger.

***

Boundaries/Destiny

We do not always recognize when people violate our personal boundaries. Some of us may have not even established boundaries in the first place. This process requires self-awareness. It requires time and effort. Developing boundaries is not an easy task, yet it paves the path to serenity.

Developing boundaries requires an understanding of who we are and what we want our life to look like. Boundaries reflect the intensity of our desire to live out our destiny. They require strength and courage. Praise God we can call on him to help! He will hold us close along the journey of self-discovery.

At times, our boundaries are tested. Someone or something will cross our path and challenge who we are and what we believe. This can be frightening. We want to please everyone and have each situation run smoothly, despite the cost, even if the price is self-love. We must remember that love is all we really have. It is the beacon of light within our soul that ensures the hope of eternity. We can not give it up for anything or anyone!

God created each and every one of us with special talents and abilities. We all have a miraculous destiny. Boundaries are the tools that get us there. They help us walk within God's gifts. They secure us in the depths of his love. We are protected from evil and sheltered from the many storms that come our way. What a blessing to be part of God's wondrous tapestry.

***

Insecurity/Freedom

We spend little time showing others who we really are. We mask our deepest convictions with superficial facades. We are afraid to be ourselves. What if we are not accepted? Worse yet, what if we put forth our most precious ideas, and they are rejected? Would we survive?

Insecurity is one of the greatest plagues of modern times. Thankfully, it can be overcome. We can develop the courage to be incredibly, totally ourselves! We can nurture a willingness to express our opinions and ideas, no matter how well they are received. We can courageously contribute the best of who we are in a world that is rapidly changing. It is our spiritual responsibility.

Living fearlessly ushers new freedom into our lives. When we exchange self-doubt for self-confidence, we help to open the doors to a better world, a new heaven on earth, a place where everyone comes to love. We enter the outer realms of the restoration of paradise. We are approaching the gates of eternal freedom.

⁕

JANUARY 24

Communication/Expression

Communication is the key to maintaining healthy relationships. This is true at home, at work, in the community, and everywhere we travel. When we fail to communicate, we fail to love. When we hide our feelings, we hide the most important part of who we are. When we mask our thoughts and ideas, we are flinging our lives away. We are shortchanging the journey and robbing ourselves of God's most glorious gifts.

We all have the ability to change. If we have been reluctant to tell others what is on our minds, for fear of rejection, we can turn the corner and dare to express ourselves. We can trust our thoughts, emotions, ideas, and inspiration. They help us touch the hearts of others. Failing to express them is denying our precious spirit and suffocates the soul.

Openness and expression build bridges, connecting two souls that would otherwise remain apart. These virtues allow us to experience the fullness of relationships. We can understand others and be understood. We can contribute to life without holding back. We are helping God affect the world in this way. We are helping the splendor of his love shine brightly!

⁕

JANUARY 25

Fantasy/Reality

Fantasy is an escape. It is intoxicating, alluring, and intriguing. It is a way out of negativity. It allows us a passageway out of a world full of anger and sadness. It is especially attractive when our inner landscape is shadowed in the wings of despair. As life hands us tough situations, we can forget for awhile. We can pretend that everything is all right—or can we? It is only a matter of time before we are forced to face reality.

Problems seldom disappear on their own, and although fantasizing may bring temporary relief and, in some cases, comfort and pleasure, it is not lasting. Situations left unattended only get worse. Healthy living requires facing our circumstances, as they are, with open eyes. Spiritual well-being requires that we embrace reality. Viewing situations clearly helps us take necessary action. We will not be lost in the oblivion of denial or rationalization.

The courage to change is found in reality. We need not be afraid, for this is God's world. God is perfect reality and truth. He does not exist in fairy tales. He is pure light and our brightest hope. In his power, we can overcome any burdens. Obstacles are crushed. The need to escape disappears because he helps us find answers to our problems. He is the solution to all our troubles. Hallelujah!

JANUARY 26

Motivation/Satisfaction

Let's face it. There are tasks, responsibilities, and jobs we would rather not perform. No one likes everything he does. Some of us dread beginning chores or tasks that will take a lot of time and energy. We procrastinate rather than tackle big projects. We dread small, tedious work. If only we could have a foretaste of the relief and satisfaction that come when we complete our goals. We feel good about ourselves and our accomplishments when we are motivated to finish.

We can enjoy our free time even more when we take care of our obligations first. We might even find joy in our work. There is no need for a grim face while we are in the process of tending to business. We can choose to be happy in the middle of any difficult task. The mind is a powerful tool that has the ability to influence the body and spirit. When we foster positive thoughts in the midst of a taxing situation, we can rise above it and be victorious!

There is joy and satisfaction in a job well done. We can sit back and be proud of our work. We can rest and play knowing we have handled our duties. Satisfaction feeds the soul. It helps us thrive spiritually. It leads to lasting happiness. It is the dawn of peace of mind.

JANUARY 27

Relationships/Care

Relationships are fragile. They take so long to establish and are so easily torn apart. That which takes years to build can be torn apart in seconds. Sometimes, we take friendships for granted. We falsely assume they will always be there. It is heart wrenching to discover we are wrong. Relationships need love and attention and require forgiveness and compassion. We need to handle them with great care.

The best things in life are delicate. We cannot take children, family, marriage, and friends for granted. Sometimes we do not realize this until it is too late. We need to do everything possible to nurture our bond with others. We can show care and concern for the needs of others by letting go of selfishness and placing the welfare of others before our own. This helps love grow and flourish.

So let's reach out and show those around us how much we care! Our lives are enriched when we foster loving relationships. We become better people. Friendships add meaning and depth to an otherwise lonely world.

JANUARY 28

Belief/Healing

The power of healing is real! There are so many hurts and there's so much despair in the world. We can all identify loved ones who suffer from physical, emotional, or spiritual burdens. The power to heal is within our reach. By tapping into this source of strength and trusting in its power, we can change lives.

Healing begins with belief. We feel helpless all too often. We become discouraged and wonder why life must be so unfair. Instead, we can turn our minds toward faith and love. In God's grace, all things are possible. When we earnestly request and honestly seek his healing power, it becomes ours to share. We become conduits of his illumination.

We can help God accomplish great miracles through our small actions, in faith. We can believe in his love and extend his compassion to others. We are tributaries of his mighty river of hope. Our hearts and minds can help his love flow within us and across the world.

JANUARY 29

Love/Faith/Grace

Love is splendid. It is spectacular! It warms our inner being and uplifts our spirit. Where love flourishes, fear and depression cannot exist. Love highlights the golden way of faith. It is the messenger of eternal joy and happiness.

All good things are born out of faith in God, including love. Love can only flourish in faith. In its absence, love is comprised and eventually suffocates. Faith gives us the wings to fly with love. It grants us the courage to reach out to others and helps us care unconditionally.

God's grace is the essence of love. His great love gave birth to our destiny. We see its rich beauty as his love is mirrored across the many wonderful dimensions of this universe. It touches the tiniest cell with infinite energy. It does not cease or even pause. As he holds each flower carefully in the palm of his hand, he holds us as well. We are his precious creation, an expression of his love. Today, I will embrace the love that God so freely gives.

JANUARY 30

Silence/Power

We have lived our lives believing in will power for so long. "If only I can find the will power, I can change. If only I had enough will power!" Sound familiar? When we surrender our self-will to the silent and sheer omnipotence of God's true and lasting power, our lives begin to change.

Silence can help us relax and let go of will power. It is an awesome gift that reaches deep within the soul and repairs our broken spirits. Silence brings us near God's heart. When we clear our minds and hearts of restlessness and debris, we receive mercy and grace. When we empty ourselves of all that stands between God and us, we feel utter joy. It showers upon us like eternal jewels. We begin to understand the mystery of God.

Moments of silence give birth to the infinite power within. This differs from will power, self-seeking, and personal power. It is the pure power of eternal love within us. We are filled with God's energy, the miraculous power that lifts us above any burden, obstacle, or challenge. We can embrace heaven, for it is found in these moments.

The power of silence is infinite. Clearing the mind and resting the heart makes room for the Almighty to enter in and affect us. When we are quiet and still, we can hear God speak. His guidance is clear and not distorted by our perceptions. The inspiration we receive is rich and flawless. Experiencing his power brings ecstatic joy to the soul.

JANUARY 31

Memories/Stepping Stones

The past occasionally captures our attention. We replay memories in our mind, some of them good and others bad. We wish we could reshape our negative experiences and recreate the good times. We need to realize that memories are mere stepping-stones. Each one lays another golden segment of the path that will one day lead us where we are meant to go.

It is wonderful to glance back across our journey and see how all the pieces of our past fit together nicely. It is even better when we can let go of our past and understand that each step we took is now a valuable part of who we are. We have grown along the way and become strong. We are caring, compassionate, intelligent, and enlightened. Each memory has helped us arrive here.

And as we continue to move forward, we create tomorrow's memories. We live each day anew. We make better choices, leading to wonderful experiences that we can savor in our years to come. We will have the courage to continue striving toward our goals because we have confidence in what the future holds. We will not let the days gone by wear us down. We have hope.

FEBRUARY 1

God's Guidance/Empowerment

There is no limit to what God can do through us. His power overflows from within as we extend our hands to those in need. There are so many needs all around us. The world is starving for things like love, friendship, companionship, understanding, and compassion. The journey helps us discover that as we offer these gifts to others, we will find them increase.

God wants to work deeply in our lives. Some of us question his power because we lack faith and trust. When we develop the courage to surrender our personal quests and embrace God's guidance, great things come to pass. We can participate in his miracles firsthand. We are one of them.

We cannot let anything interfere with our destiny. We all have a mission in life. Our destinies are to love—it is our highest calling. Love nudges us to reach out and help others. It inspires us to add beauty to the world. It encourages us to be our best. It empowers us to show others the strength that we have found.

❧

Criticism/Positive Reinforcement

We can be so critical of others and even of ourselves! We know we must learn to love ourselves unconditionally, but how? Surely this must involve loving others too. The time has come to shift our focus from weaknesses to strengths. Instead of zooming in on our shortcomings and the downfalls of others, we can look at the talents and gifts God gave us all. We can quit scolding and begin praising.

One tool that helps us change our perception from the negative to the positive is an exercise called positive reinforcement. When we reach a goal or even another stepping stone, we can pause and appreciate our success. We may be accustomed to diving into the next project or task and seldom take the time to rest and replenish. It is not conceited or selfish to do so because we build confidence in this way and become more fruitful.

Positive reinforcement replaces self-criticism with peace of mind and helps us become better people. Our strengths are enhanced, and our weaknesses fade. When we place our focus on the good, we begin making a more positive impact on the world. God sees the beautiful creation each of us is becoming. He knows who we are and who we will become. When we see how much he loves all of his children, our praises come more naturally, brightening our lives and the lives of those around us.

❧

Balance/Joy

Some of us struggle with balance. We try too hard in some areas, and not hard enough in others. One particular arena of life might absorb all of our precious time. Nothing is worth that much! When we narrow our vision and magnify a small portion of our lives, we lose the opportunity to experience the rest. And sometimes, the rest brings the most joy.

We are most successful when we balance our time. We discover a fresh energy, an infinite source of inner strength that helps us effectively accomplish all our tasks. We are inspired in new ways. We gain a sense of confidence, which gives us the diversity to broaden our focus across many areas of responsibility, instead of just one. We maximize our many gifts.

We can experience joy in all we do and feel the peace and satisfaction of knowing that all our responsibilities in life are truly gifts. We are blessed with many opportunities to accomplish God's purpose for us: raising children, homemaking, visiting an elderly friend, shoveling snow, raking the lawn, reading a book, or completing a large project at home or at work. Each thing we do holds special importance. God has created our responsibilities to fulfill his purpose for us. They all lead us along life's beautiful journey.

FEBRUARY 4

Prayers/Blessings

God has a way of providing us with exactly what we need, even when we do not ask. Sometimes we receive unexpected blessings, far beyond what we ask for, which shows us how intimately God knows our hearts. He knows us better than we know ourselves, and his care for us is compassionate.

So often, we plead with God that he will grant our wishes because it seems unlikely there would be any other way to resolve a situation. We narrow our vision and focus on what we think should be, failing to consider the eternal dimensions of our future. Our perspective is finite; God's sight is infinitely flawless.

But even when we neglect to ask God to disclose his will to us, he graciously provides. He gives us answers to prayers that are left unasked. He satisfies our deepest needs. Our wants are lessened as our true needs are exposed. We begin to see how meager and imperfect our vision is. God's providence exceeds our greatest hopes and expectations. It's time to trust him.

FEBRUARY 5

Selfish Outlook/Compromise

There are many solutions to each problem. Some of us get caught up in what we feel is the only way. It is empowering to consider there may be more than one answer to a single problem. We might be viewing a situation from a self-centered perspective. We tend to believe we are always right and others are wrong.

It takes courage and faith to reach beyond our self-centered notions into the realms of compromise and healing. Life is give and take. It is a journey of discovery. We are sometimes wrong, even when we think we may be doing what's best. Right and wrong actions weave together intricately to lead us in the direction of our destiny.

When we learn to compromise, we make room for love in our hearts. We can give up perfectionism and welcome the presence of peace. We can quit fighting life's battles and embrace our purpose in the world. We can seek the energy to work our mission. This is our ultimate destiny and the reason for our birth. It brings happiness and peace to our days.

FEBRUARY 6

Relationships/Effort

Relationships are crucial to our spiritual well being. It is impossible to live a full life without the encouragement of friends and family. When we acknowledge just how important they are, we begin to cherish our loved ones. We place their well being above our own. This is the wonderful beauty of healing and wholeness, the bright dawn of love.

The best relationships require much effort. Close friendships do not develop overnight. It takes time, patience, and avid attention to reap the fullest benefits of any personal encounter. Even existing bonds can be enriched with extra attentiveness and care. A little effort can go a long way!

Sometimes the effort it takes to make a relationship successful is beyond our power. We give it our best shot, but a hole still exists deep within. Thankfully we can trust in God's healing power and guidance. He can accomplish great miracles when our own strength is depleted. He can help our relationships succeed and flourish.

Anything we turn over to God becomes good. When we wonder how we can make it happen, we can lean on him. The wisdom that we lack will be given to us one moment at a time. God will see us through until the end. He loves us that much! He wants us to be happy.

FEBRUARY 7

Confidence in the Path

God gives us each an individual road to travel. It is designed especially for us. We need not expect others to understand our path, for it is uniquely and personally ours. We might feel alone and misunderstood. We may long for approval. Yet, we can develop an inner fiber of faith that will allow us to travel in confidence. We experience our destiny on an intimate, spiritual level. We know deep down what is right.

Life throws us twists and turns with each passing day. There are many times we question the journey. We lose heart and fall short of our true purpose. Regaining confidence helps us along the way. We can remember the real reasons for our lives. We can reflect on love, forgiveness, mercy, and grace. We are born to understand and develop these virtues. We are created to grow in our God-given image.

When we have confidence in the path, we see the higher ground. We live above criticism, ridicule, judgement, and the need for approval. We know that life is difficult, including many of the decisions we make. Many times, we are the only ones who understand our obstacles and subsequent actions. We ask God to guide us and we follow his calling on an individual level. Our journeys are unique. We are the only ones who can accomplish them. God, please give me confidence and strength to walk my path.

FEBRUARY 8

Misunderstanding/Support

Some of us feel misunderstood. If only others could see our situations and problems from our perspective! We feel alone and isolated. We think that having the support we need and deserve would make the journey easier and help us get through. Sound familiar?

There are tender burdens that occur in life. At times, we will not have the complete support and understanding of everyone in our circle. But, we can still rise above in victory one day at a time, sometimes even one moment at a time. We can deepen our faith in God and trust the guidance he pours down upon us daily. He is sufficient to support us through any burden or obstacle. His strength and love are empowering and sustaining.

When we seek our Creator and fully open our hearts and minds to his channel of compassion and inspiration, we can shift our thoughts away from our need for support and approval into the higher realms of hope and healing. God transparently views what is at the heart of each of our needs. He knows our personality and understands our concerns like a perfect parent. He is the Lord of understanding, the Maker of all that is good and true and lasting. He will lead us toward restoration when we hang onto his unfaltering sustenance. He is the key to overcoming; he is the key to heaven.

<hr />

Norms/Sanity

Society revolves around norms. Many of us are surrounded by conformity and predictability at the office, in the community, and in outside engagements. We are ruled by status quo. We learn to behave in ways that allow us the comfort of fitting in. It takes courage to act in ways that set us apart. Self-expression requires bravery. We all want to be accepted, but sometimes, in trying to fit in, we give up who we are. This can cost us our peace of mind. We are robbed of knowing we are participating in a journey that God created for us to fulfill.

So much of what we see today is false. We live in a materialistic era, and within it, there is a superficial void. Many characteristics and attitudes, which people consider normal, are harmful to our inner landscape. We have come to accept many situations and behaviors as being alright, even when we know deep down they are fundamentally wrong. We move further and further from God.

When we embrace God's light and live within our soul's guidance, we are guaranteed to not fit in. Thankfully, we are also promised peace and satisfaction. True emotional wellness lies far above norms. We can develop a strong confidence in our knowledge and practice of truth. We might feel alone, but we are not. God's presence fills our souls when we are living in spiritual reality. We experience the lasting joy of his love there.

<hr />

Pain/Relief

Life hands us episodes of severe pain. Accidents, disease, and grave situations surface, and we suffer the symptoms of adverse health, whether it is physical, emotional, or spiritual. Many times nothing can be done to cure our ailments. We pray for healing, but also realize that recovery takes time. We can find hope in the comfort that the pain will eventually pass.

Relief begins when we focus on the positive, even in the midst of pain. The recovery process speeds up when we place our mind on the hope and assurance of God's healing power. The mind and body are intimately linked. A positive attitude paves the way to good health.

Pain challenges us to strengthen our practice of gratitude. We can deeply appreciate life's many gifts when we are well again! We need to thank God abundantly for our many blessings, including our restoration to wholeness. His love and grace are the foundational fibers of healing and bring us lasting comfort and relief.

FEBRUARY 11

Overwhelmed/Increments

Do you ever wonder where to start? Sometimes life throws us a curve ball or special assignment that might seem insurmountable. Everything swirls in the haziness of stress and anxiety. We are afraid to begin what appears to be a steep, uphill journey. We want to move forward but how? We long for order and direction.

The impossible task can be handled smoothly in increments. We do not have to dive in and accomplish everything at once. We needn't rush to reach the end of the road. Instead, we can separate the journey ahead into stepping stones, and we can walk toward our goals one step at a time. We can even celebrate each time we accomplish another segment of the journey. We can affirm our thoughts and efforts so we will not become discouraged in the process. Nothing of great value is achieved overnight. The best that life has to offer requires time and patience to realize.

When we diligently attend to each necessary step along our way, we will, one day, reap the rewards of honest and faithful effort. If we dare face life's many facets, success becomes ours to appreciate. We needn't give up or be afraid. We can tackle each phase with confidence. The road will soon be filled with dreams come true. We will see a guiding light shine through our mind. We will see God in this light because he is close by our side, every step of the way.

FEBRUARY 12

Poverty/Riches

We are so blessed in this country! Few of us know what it is like to hear the constant horror of gunfire, to wonder where we will sleep, or to feel the pangs of hunger before falling asleep at night. There is a wide variety of poverty among the many states and nations of the world. Although more oppression and economic hardship occur in foreign lands, there is also misfortune right here at home. We are not all blessed with equal gifts.

Most of us look down on poverty. We sometimes even do questionable things for fear of becoming poor. But how about considering poverty in a different light? Instead of viewing it as substandard, we can consider the riches it provides. Some of the poorest people in history have led the richest lives and have been the richest in spirit. Poverty carves a place in the heart where we can deeply appreciate God's abundant and simple blessings—gifts that are easily taken for granted. More is not always better, and materialism destroys the heart and spirit.

Our greatest gifts cannot be bought or sold. They are free. When we have little, we realize how much the simple things in life are really worth. They are as beautiful as holding the fragile, warm hand of a child, hugging a friend, even smiling at someone in need of love. These tiny blessings all add together to give us true wealth. They enrich our soul!

FEBRUARY 13

Loosening our Grip

We hold the things we love so very tightly. After all, if we let go we might lose touch, or at least we would be relinquishing control! Our lives have consisted of carefully manipulated maneuvers and actions. What would happen if we change? For sure we are risking abandonment! This thought is scary. It is too much!

Anything we grasp too tightly, whether it is a relationship, possession, idea, or dream, is suffocated and eventually dies. A bird in too small a cage will lose its magnificent beauty. So it goes with the things we try to cage in life. We may think we need to control certain outcomes, inflexibly plan our careers, or even manipulate our loved ones so they will conform to our expectations. Our journeys will not flourish in this way, and we are certain to inhibit the journeys of others.

When we loosen our grip, our minds and hearts open to the unexpected and spontaneous blessings of the divine. Our spiritual and emotional landscapes expand. We are better able to see alternatives, solutions, and hope. We can allow our loved ones the precious space they need to discover, learn, and grow. We can let situations become, and unfold, according to God's plans. We can relax and observe the wondrous miracles that abound in the lives of those who simply let it be. We can believe in the power of divinity!

FEBRUARY 14

Love Bravely

Valentine's Day marks each year with the precious moments that we spend celebrating love. As we reflect upon the years gone by, some of us might discover that, somewhere through the hands of time, we have lost the courage to love. We have become passive and complacent. Thankfully, it is never too late to rekindle love's zeal. We can let go of negative experiences in our past, of inhibitions, walls, and other reservations, and recapture love's illuminant passion. This is the essence of our spiritual well being.

Some of us wonder where to begin. It has been a long time since we have loved fluently and freely. Others have never dared to love at all. We feel our souls stirring and want our relationships to be vibrant and fulfilling. We know that the things we do and the people we affect along our journey all contribute to a destiny far beyond our most incredible dreams. It is incomprehensibly beautiful, yet it is within our reach. We are all part of God's plan. He is pure love.

We can dismantle our walls and dare to embrace our loved ones unconditionally. We can have faith that God is working through all our relationships and encounters. Each person in our lives needs us as much as we need them. We help one another grow. God expands our souls in this way.

So let's giggle and laugh and cry and really talk with our family and friends! We can even reach out and make new friends. We can risk rejection and expose our needs. We all need each other.

FEBRUARY 15

Failure/Strength

Sometimes we journey through a series of failures. We become frustrated and hopeless. We might even plead with God that we not fail anymore! Life seems difficult and grim. Are there any answers? How can we go on?

And yet, each failure brings us nearer to God. When we try and try, by our own will, to accomplish and succeed at anything, whether it is parenting, a relationship, a project, a career, or some other challenge, we are continually disappointed. We do not have the power to truly flourish in any category of life by our own effort. We can only succeed by God's power and strength.

We will experience many hard knocks, broken dreams, and unfulfilled wishes. We are sure to make countless mistakes and learn many lessons. Our total experience enriches our path with the strong fibers of a new consciousness. We begin to see how dependent we are on God. With him, all things are possible, but when we try to rely on our own plans and strength, we are let down time and time again.

When we are faced with failure in the future, let us search for hope instead of giving in to grief. This is our golden opportunity to open our hearts and let the healing light of God fill us with grace, love, and guidance. It is a precious time when we can let him mold and shape us into the wondrous person that he designed for us to become along our journey.

❦

FEBRUARY 16

Doubt/Inner Faith

Some of us have been hurt many times over. After a while, it is difficult to believe in anything. We begin to question and doubt everything. We are unable to accept our blessings or take advantage of opportunities. We become afraid to make decisions. Our journeys stagnate in ruin.

And yet, hope shines through the most treacherous obstacles. A divine light is present to guide us through the worst despair. We can develop the inner faith to overcome doubt, bewilderment, and uncertainty. We can step away from delusion and confusion into the brilliant radiance of faith. We can trust in God. He will bring about strength and clarity. He can help us change our path from disillusionment to optimism.

The deeper our inner faith, the better we are able to overcome all obstacles, including doubt. The essence of our being is blended and fortified by the grace of God. We gain the ability to make healthy decisions and choices. We no longer believe that life is a road that ends in despair. We can see the rich threads of eternity woven before us through each step we take, forward and backward. And we feel ourselves drawing nearer to God. He is the hope we seek. He is the light we experience. He is the love we long for. His presence expels darkness and confusion and fills us with confidence and peace.

Resistance/Acceptance

Life is full of opportunities for growth and development. We receive many opportunities to make healthy choices. But occasionally, we resist the very things that are good for us. Whether we are used to experiencing pain and suffering, or it has become comfortable, we might be afraid to do what's right. We might not even know what "right" is.

We are resistors by human nature. We gravitate toward the familiar and secure and avoid new horizons, even though they might be illuminating and beautiful. Some of us have lived in darkness so long that even the faintest tinges of the light burn our eyes. We try to take cover, or even panic and turn away. And yet, the longer we resist, the longer it takes to begin healing. We must accept where we are as a first step.

Acceptance is the key that opens miracles. It helps us move away from the stagnation of character defects and into the dawn of a bright new day. We can open our clenched fists and release to God the problems we have cultivated and nurtured for so many years. We can begin nurturing our inner landscape instead, where the garden of hope is endless. This special place of communion with God, deep within our spirit, brings peace and leads to lasting love.

Attitude/Success

Success is closely linked to attitude. It is hard to accomplish anything of real value when we focus on the negative. When we feel hopeless, we become depressed. When we doubt our intellectual abilities, we do not try as hard as we can. When we feel defeated, we become defeated. Our thoughts lead to actions, and everything we do one day unveils the road we are travelling. It can be full of purpose or pompous circumstance. The choice is ours, and attitude determines the outcome.

When we work to maintain a positive attitude, we can succeed along any path. We can believe in what we are doing and commit to make a difference in all that we do. There will always be situations and people that bring us down. We can react whichever way we choose. We can take heart in the knowledge that we are valuable creations, placed on earth to offer our many gifts and talents; or we can curl up and doubt the most precious treasures of the heart.

We succeed by keeping our chin up, even when circumstances challenge the very fiber of our inner being. We can try to maintain a positive outlook, even if our emotions are hanging by a thread. There are many seasons in life. Some are much harder than others, but we can move through them in faith. God does not present us with challenges beyond our abilities. He designed us to find the answers.

<hr />

FEBRUARY 19

Loved Ones/Space

Many of us were abandoned at an early age, at least emotionally and spiritually. Broken homes resulted in frustration and pain. We lost and lost and lost some more. Just when we saw a ray of light on the horizon, our hopes were dashed once more. The only thing we were used to was chaos and loneliness. Our closest relationships were far from ordinary; some of them were even bizarre.

We *can* mature beyond our old thought patterns and behaviors. And, as we are growing and changing, it is important to realize that we must give our loved ones space. This can be hard when we deeply care for someone. We might be under the false impression that the tighter we hold something, the less likely it is to slip away. But, in fact, the opposite is true. When we squeeze our relationships and grasp them too tightly, we suffocate the people we are so desperately trying to love. True love is not insecure. It will not blow away if we open our hand. It is constant and steady like the evening tide. We can have faith in its presence and endurance.

It is not easy to give up control and turn our relationships over. The very thought of letting someone have the space they need might be frightening. What if they never come back? What if they quit loving us, or worse yet, what if we never see them again? These are just some of the irrational thoughts that can quickly prevent us from making the brave decision to give our loved ones the space they need and deserve. Without it, love is comprised. But with space and time, love can flourish.

FEBRUARY 20

Energy/Priorities

The universe is filled with energy and so are we. There is a divine component to everything we see and feel. Our own personal energy is so very precious. It freely flows through us so that we may express our most inspired thoughts and beautiful ideas. Sometimes life can weigh us down, and we begin to feel our energy slip away. We become tired and lose the vibrancy of our spirit. We know—deep down—something must change.

When we feel our energy waning, it is time to examine our lives and reprioritize our days. So many of the activities in which we involve ourselves are senseless. Some of us take on more and more responsibility to the point where we become frustrated. We fragment our souls. We don't know how to say no. We willingly volunteer for any job or responsibility, even at the expense of our precious moments in prayer and meditation. We don't always see the value of caring for ourselves. We don't recognize the priceless gift of spending time with God.

When we pause and search our souls, we find the answer. Busy days that once seemed like a vicious maze become clear and purposeful. Placing our spiritual well being above all else paves the road toward a more peaceful journey, and we become filled with joy!

FEBRUARY 21

Affection/Attention

It is impossible to express true affection without giving someone our full attention. It is easy to pretend as if we care. We can tell others we love them, but it is what we show them that really matters. They can trust that we mean what we say. They will know we are sincere.

Not all of us are able to freely show affection. Some of us have been hurt in the past, which has caused us to shut down and isolate. It takes time to learn to trust in love again. Old habits are hard to break. It is natural to carry forward the unhealthy cycles of generations past. We may not realize that it is within our power to break negative patterns. In fact, it is up to us.

Affection begins with devoted attention. We can turn our thoughts toward others and focus on their needs. We can let go of our insecurities and have confidence in building relationships. When we substantiate our love for one another through caring action, we are giving each other our very best. We are learning love's greatest secret. We are daring to be vulnerable. We are embracing life's most wonderful gift.

FEBRUARY 22

Relaxation/Answers

Life is filled with mystery. We search for answers, but more often than not, they evade us. We look for solutions to our problems, and yet sometimes we feel as if we are chasing the wind.

Life is a journey in faith. Destiny is disclosed in small portions day by day. There is a divine reality. We can trust that God is lovingly guiding us along the path we are created to travel. We can pause to rest and embrace the gifts in each moment.

The journey is seldom easy, but it can be beautiful if we relax and let the answers come freely. We can surrender our need to know outcomes and allow God to fill us with his wisdom. As soon as we accept a situation and let go, our spirits are washed in peace. Anxiety departs; solutions flow in.

Life contains many seasons, and each one can be as beautiful as we make it. Through the many uncertainties they contain, we learn more and more about who we are. We see the purpose of our journey unfold in greater proportions. Most importantly, we can discover how very special we are in God's eyes! Today, I will relax and trust that the answers will come.

FEBRUARY 23

Hope in the Present

Many of us hope for the future. We make plans and entertain dreams that will someday lead us where we want to go. Sometimes in the midst of our expectations, we forget to enjoy the present. We miss the essence of life. Our greatest hope lies within the moments before us.

We can ask God to help us live out this hope day by day. Instead of scattering our thoughts across an unseen future, we can place our attention in the here and now. There are infinite possibilities in any given moment. We can be attuned to these opportunities and treat them as gifts. One by one, they contribute to a brighter tomorrow.

All good things require time and patience. When we quit leaping forward, we can appreciate the blessings in front of us. Each day contains endless miracles. We can stop and appreciate the treasures of the present as we nurture our understanding of tomorrow. Together, they make hope shine!

FEBRUARY 24

Struggle/Victory

Sometimes our struggles defeat us emotionally. They test our faith and challenge our spiritual strength. We might feel like giving up or at least wish life could be easier. We can take comfort in the thought that struggles are an intricate part of the journey. They add substance to our personalities. They help us mature and grow along our way.

As we face each struggle and work our way through the pain, we eventually discover victory over despair. We are given the confidence and grace to overcome all obstacles. At each and every corner, victory is at hand. We can reach toward it. It is not as far as it might seem. In fact, it lies within.

Our lives are filled with many tough circumstances. In facing our challenges and accepting our burdens, we are equipped to begin on the road to victory. These are the first steps. We can see the hope that forever flickers in the distance. We can fan it to flame and embrace the light of its presence!

FEBRUARY 25

Inner Wholeness

Some of us are insecure. We feel fragmented as if something is missing. It is hard to be comfortable when we are alone. We might fear abandonment, as if we are stranded on a desert island with no food or water. We begin starving, and worry sets in. What is it we need?

Perhaps the greatest gift we can encounter in this life is a feeling of inner wholeness. We need to gain an ability to be content with who we are. We can rest in the presence of solitude. We let peace wash over us in our moments alone. We needn't fear if we bask in God's love. We are inspired when we trust God.

This does not happen overnight. We can incrementally work toward reaching an inner state of peace. We can nurture our spirit and care for our soul. We can make the choices that are necessary to provide the time and space to grow. All beautiful things follow a process, including us. We can surrender and embrace this healing reality.

FEBRUARY 26

Self-Expression

We sometimes get so preoccupied with how others perceive us. Some of us are hypersensitive to the responses and reactions of others. It is empowering to discover that our own belief systems and values are what matter most. We must remain true to our innermost being because it is critical to our spiritual and emotional health.

We can have faith in ourselves, apart from the opinion and influence of those around us. We do not have to conform to a mold that does not fit our most precious convictions. Following the crowd can create extreme conflict. We will know when we are out of step with who we are, because it hurts.

At times, remaining true to our self involves taking risks. It requires courage. It demands self-confidence. It is not easy to express our thoughts, feelings, and ideas when we are going against the grain of social pressure. We might feel uneasy, but we can have faith. We are paving the road to self-expression.

FEBRUARY 27

Humility/Replenishment

Life is difficult. There are seasons when the journey becomes treacherous and painful. We may not realize it, but our hearts can harden during challenging times. Our souls become dry and wither in the dust of broken dreams. Like a sun-crisped flower, our petals shrivel and fade. We silently long for new growth.

During times like these, we can embrace the gift of humility. We can get on our knees and let the tears flow and wash us in a new beginning. When our hearts soften, our soul is replenished. We are enlightened by the healing touch of God and renewed by his strength.

The journey is filled with many trials and much tribulation. We are led through the darkest valleys so that we can better appreciate the brilliant light that shines vibrantly on the other side. Each time our hearts become weary, and we lose hope, we can remember our ever-present source of restoration. We can bow in the arms of surrender and lift our minds to heaven. We can hold the hand of peace, where healing begins.

Silently, carefully, God works miracles in a humble heart. We begin by giving our troubles to him in sincere need. He opens the window through which his light and power are shed upon us. Admitting that we cannot travel alone places us on an easier, softer path. We are lifted above the mire and back into the higher realms of faithful living. Here, we can experience the joyful treasures of the divine. We can rest in the miracle!

FEBRUARY 28

People Pleasing/Destiny

Some people grow up with a "Cinderella syndrome." Somewhere along the line, we are convinced that we must do everything everyone asks of us. We have not learned how to politely say "No." We have forgotten our own needs. Perhaps we have never even given them the time to develop.

When we fall into the trap of doing what everyone else wants, we are falling into the pattern of neglecting the inner self. We think we are being helpful. Perhaps we even feel like we are serving God. Unfortunately, when we are overly busy doing for others, we have little time to nurture our true purpose in life and compromise our destiny.

Learning to say "No" is not easy, so let's practice. We needn't say it in anger or haste. We can carefully consider whether what we are being asked to do is truly a task that we are responsible for. If the answer is no, we can kindly decline the request. We are freeing up precious time to serve a higher calling. We are tending to the garden of our destiny. We are being true to ourselves.

MARCH 1

Blame/Reality

Blame gets in our way. Sometimes we get so caught up in who is right and who is wrong that we are paralyzed. We are unable to move beyond the problem. Black and white thinking prevents us from dealing with reality. It robs us of our ability to reason and solve problems. It blurs our vision.

With some things, there are no easy answers or simple explanations. Pointing a finger does not help; in fact, it delays the healing process. Realizing that blame does not contribute toward any good solutions is a huge step forward in dealing with the real issues; it begins the process of restoration.

What freedom is found in letting go of blame! We will see how much it weighs us down and holds us back. It prevents us from achieving our full potential. When we leave it behind, we can effectively work on the problem at hand. No one can do it for us. With God's help we can move on.

MARCH 2

Anxiety/Peace

We are wound up some days! Situations and events hurl our way and at times it seems like they have all been heaped on top of us. It feels so very heavy. We fear we cannot continue to carry the load. We are sinking. We might remain silent, but our hearts are kicking and screaming! Deep down, we long for a better way, an easier, smoother path. We grow weary.

Anxiety, like all other emotional wounds, can be soothed and healed. We do not have to fall into its trap. We can make a conscious decision to let go. We can still our hearts and rest our minds until our inner landscape calms, allowing the river of hope to run through us. These waters bring freedom and release. They lead us to peace.

Cultivating a deep sense of inner peace relieves almost any anxiety we encounter. There will always be times when we are tested, yet when we focus our energy on the presence of God within, we can move through emotional challenges. He will see us through.

MARCH 3

Self Doubt/Courage

Some of us are plagued by self-doubt. We lack confidence in our ability to succeed. Fearing that we will be unable to perform a task or accomplish an event, we might not even try. "Better safe than sorry" is our motto.

But when we find the courage to try new things, we grow by leaps and bounds. We soon realize that we can do much more than we ever realized. When we ask God to accompany us and help us accomplish that which we fear, we are empowered. He grants us the ability to succeed.

Let's step out in a new confidence today. It is time to say goodbye to self-doubt and embrace our talents and God-given abilities. We are created to complete an incredible journey. We all have a unique and valuable purpose here on earth. We are finely designed to be an intricate part of God's destiny. We can show others his love.

Joy/Experience

We are not always joyful. Life hands us many tests and trials, and it is not easy to keep a positive outlook. Sometimes the harder we try, the further we drift into discouragement and depression. Perhaps we try too hard. Grace comforts the still and quiet heart. It leads us to joy.

Joy adds depth to our experience in life. It helps us appreciate our many blessings and gifts. God places tiny miracles around us, each and every moment. They are ours to enjoy. When we are conscious of his infinite wonders, our journeys are enriched. Our experience becomes deeply satisfying.

A joyful outlook will even help us through times of trial. When we praise God, even in the midst of pain, our hearts are filled with hope and healing. We are delivered to a place where our days become more comfortable. We experience the light at the end of the tunnel. We see God's promises coming true.

Grief/Acceptance

Acceptance is the key to spiritual and emotional health. It is the pillar of positive living. However, sometimes acceptance is initially accompanied by grief. It hurts when we are finally brought to the point where we realize what must be done. When we are faced with saying goodbye to lingering dreams or hopes that will never be realized, we move through a grieving process. It might feel like a part of us has died. This is normal. We are letting go of what we desperately hoped might some day be.

Thankfully, we can develop the willingness to walk through grief. We must acknowledge and feel it, but we needn't let it make a home in our hearts. We can continue moving forward. If we do not, we are not able to make healthy choices in the future. Our vision becomes distorted.

Acceptance gets easier the longer we journey along God's path. We eventually discover that a lack of willingness to embrace reality costs us valuable serenity. The price is far too high. Let us face the facts and feel the loss, and then let it go. For every door that closes, God opens a window of hope.

MARCH 6

Organization/Effectiveness

Good organization leads to effectiveness. Some of us procrastinate, letting things pile up instead of handling tasks right away. When we are prompt in handling our affairs, we are more efficient. Our days are more successful, and we reach our goals.

Organization also helps us maximize our time. It lessens feelings of anxiety and defeat. There is not enough time to get things done some days, or so it seems. We experience frustration, which further contributes to our inability to complete a project. We might even toss our goals out.

And yet, when we take a large task and divide it into smaller steps, we regain hope and perspective. Each day we can strive to accomplish another segment of the journey. There are many days when we will not have the end in sight, but we can affirm our progress. We can reward ourselves for remaining dedicated. We can rest in the assurance that we are reaching our goals one day at a time. May God grant us the gift of organization and help us discover that our grandest dreams can be accomplished in small steps.

MARCH 7

The Power of Faith

Faith can move mountains! When we believe, and more importantly, act upon our beliefs, we can move mountains. We can turn the most hopeless situations around. No matter how deep the valley or dark the tunnel, faith is the light that sees us through. It is the power of God!

Faith gives us the ability to affect the world in awesome ways. We can have the confidence and security to put forth our bravest, boldest thoughts, ideas, and efforts. We can impact the lives of others, showing them the power we have found within. It is the source of all good things, and yet it is available to each and everyone personally. When we cleave to this truth, it becomes our infinite hope and carries us through any storm.

It is time to search our souls and discover the seeds of faith that lie waiting to blossom and grow. We have remained slaves to society for too long. We do not need to compromise, settle, or even shy away. We have been empowered to work through any situation. We are equipped to share this strength with others. We can witness God's power to change lives. We will see that true hope lies in his hands.

MARCH 8

Grace/Wisdom

God carefully holds the smallest flower, sheltering it from the wind and rain. His touch reaches above the highest star, stretches across the widest field, and embraces the depths of the deepest sea. He is near and far. His love embraces the universe.

Recognizing the magnitude and power of God's grace is the beginning of wisdom. When we see his magnificent works of love, we view the world in a new light. The frustrating and confusing appear calm and clear. The darkest clouds are etched in shining silver. Rainbows emerge from storms. Life is transformed from somber gray to radiant colors. Grace brings us to rebirth.

Life is a journey toward wisdom. As we move through this life, we discover God's love first hand. We encounter his merciful providence as his grace leads us through the journey. It picks us up when we fail so we can begin again. It is our greatest hope.

MARCH 9

Trust/Courage

Our trust in God is dependent upon courage and requires faith. It cannot be established on remnants. It flourishes only on a solid foundation—one built with the lasting materials of love, forgiveness, and healing. It is not simply earned or given; it is consciously constructed.

There is no magical formula that leads to trust. There are no easy remedies. We can bravely make a decision to begin working toward this gift. We discover it by putting one foot in front of the other each day and eventually reaching the place where we feel our burdens lift. Our minds become weightless and our spirits free when we are no longer trying to be in control.

Courage is an enduring trait. Our level of trust varies because life is ever changing. When we are handed situations that test our faith and challenge our beliefs, we are often tempted to try to regain control. And yet, we can reclaim the courage to allow God's power to work within us. We can remain in his loving arms. He is the true source of our security, a river of hope.

MARCH 10

Helplessness/Simple Action

Feelings of helplessness often lead to defeatism. Our emotions waver. Actions freeze. We might not dare to step forward out of fear that our efforts will not succeed. Hope fades. We lose heart in our dreams.

We do not have to lie dormant in these unclear thoughts. Hope is our greatest friend, and maintaining faith in ourselves helps God guide us through our destiny. Instead of succumbing to fear, we can brush the dust off of unmet expectations and begin moving forward again. Simple action is the key to restoration and happiness. It frees us from the dark bondage of inaction. It helps us overcome.

Prayer is always at our disposal if we need help getting started. God knows our hearts like no other. He holds us in the palm of his hand. He sees our burdens and weaknesses transparently. Turning our inability to act over to his power transforms us. We are filled with the energy to journey ahead. Hope will return! We will see the dawning of a better tomorrow.

MARCH 11

People/Partnerships

It is sometimes necessary to call upon others to help us accomplish certain goals. God created us to work together. We cannot do everything alone. It is amazing how God brings people together to achieve his purpose. Our destiny intertwines with others'.

Many of us struggle with the need for independence. Others are hindered by pride. No matter the stumbling blocks, when we lay them aside, we bridge the gap toward becoming more effective. We all have special talents and gifts. We are designed, by God, to work with one another in harmony.

Most importantly, partnership can lead to friendship. Working toward mutual goals helps relationships flourish. We can show others we care enough to be who we are and allow them the same. This leads to true success. May God show us how to partner with others in a positive way.

MARCH 12

Melancholy/Enlightenment

Feelings of sadness are natural, especially after events that cause us grief. Loss is always painful, whether we have suffered losing a job, a loved one, or even a hope or dream. A period of time follows when our hearts and minds are burdened. We do not have to shut the door on sorrow.

And yet there comes a time when we have cried long enough. If we remain melancholy over an extended period, we may fall into the throes of depression. At this point we need to turn our thoughts away from sadness, upward toward the light that will lead us back to happiness and peace. Lifting our hearts to heaven brings healing and enlightenment. God recreates our thoughts, turning us from disillusionment to hope. His love flows through us like an endless river. It fills us with the knowledge of his grace and is the source of lasting joy.

So let's release pain, anger, and sorrow so that we can open our arms and embrace the life that awaits us. It is a life of happiness and peace. It can be ours today!

MARCH 13

Patience/Rewards

Patience is the virtue that allows us to experience life's finest gifts. It comes to those who wait. My, what a chore waiting can be! Some of us are frightened by the quiet and the stillness. Being anything but busy is uncomfortably foreign. And yet each time we pause and wait upon God, we are blessed beyond proportion!

When we are patient, we see and feel the tiny miracles that surround and fill each of our moments. We can listen to our children with caring attention. We can respond to the needs of others with intuitive kindness. We can let the sounds of nature fill our spirit with peaceful renewal. These are just some of the small, yet mighty, rewards that come with patience.

Trust makes patience possible. When we believe deep down that our Creator will care for our every need, it becomes easier to wait. We can rest in this reality. It is true. It is lasting. May the Lord lead us beside the quiet stream.

MARCH 14

Anger/Misunderstanding

Anger is a misunderstood emotion. It is hard to identify. It is not easily explained and often suppressed, festering into depression and associated feelings of defeat. We seldom know why we are even mad. Perhaps the cause of our anger is a simple misunderstanding? If we pause and look carefully within, we can find the beginning of the solution. We can evoke restitution and healing.

Misunderstandings can be easily resolved. Chances are, the other person involved does not even know we are hurt. We can dare to openly and honestly express our thoughts and feelings concerning the situation. We can let others know where we really stand when they have misinterpreted our position. We can try to help them understand our point of view. This promotes peace and friendship.

When we leave anger unattended, it leads to resentment. Resentment moves us away from the spirit of God. It severs our lifeline. It destroys the soul. Instead, let us embrace empathy, kindness, and understanding. These great things enrich the journey. They lead us to love.

MARCH 15

Dare To Be Different!

We love to fit in. Life is so comfortable when we get along. We find security in agreement. We don't want to rock the boat. We are content with the norm. And yet what about our beliefs, values, and convictions? How do we respond when our dearest desires are challenged?

It takes courage to step outside the crowd. We can dare to be different! We might feel out of step, and yet we know that spiritual and emotional health belong to those who are true to their values. God helps our spirits to be sound and our minds illumined. We can be grateful for these gifts and preserve them.

Daring to be different involves trying new things. We will walk uncharted territory and journey through new corridors. But we can trust there is one who will be with us all the way. Even when we are scared and feel alone, this friend is right by our side. He is proud of our courage. We are his children of light.

MARCH 16

Being Kind to Ourselves

Women are compassionate. We graciously care for the needs of family, friends, community, and co-workers. Given the opportunity, we will even care for strangers. However, some of us find it difficult to be kind to ourselves. It is hard to turn our love inward. And yet, we know we must.

Self-love is an important foundation upon which we can truly love others. We can begin by caring for our basic needs like rest and proper nutrition. As we grow, we can be kind to ourselves in other ways. We can try not to push ourselves too hard or have unrealistic goals and expectations. We can accept where we are at any given point along our journey. We can be grateful for who we are and the many gifts we have.

Kindness and gentleness go hand in hand. We can take it easy and breathe deeply. God loves us—each and every one. When we focus on his love, we begin to see ourselves through His eyes. We see our special qualities and spiritual needs. We come to know what really is. We discover that we are precious in his eyes, which is all that really matters. Let's rest in the reality that God loves us and begin learning to love ourselves.

MARCH 17

Joy/Presence

Joy is found in the presence of God. When we calm our spirits and empty our minds of worry and strife, God enters our hearts in a peaceful, yet profound way. He fills our hearts with true and utter joy. We experience feelings of happiness that surpass all understanding. This joy exceeds our greatest hopes and dreams.

Spending quiet time with God produces enduring satisfaction. He touches our souls and brings us near his love, where life is full of beauty and grace. In this special place, we are inspired to do his will. We can exchange thoughts with our Creator for he listens to everything we say. When we are silent in his presence, he enlightens us.

In God's presence, heaven becomes visible. We catch glimpses of how glorious it will be. We grow to understand a little more about how amazingly and wonderfully God cares for us. We are his greatest love.

MARCH 18

Choose Happiness

Depression is not a state of powerlessness. We do not have to remain in sorrow and sadness for prolonged lengths of time. In fact, it is unhealthy. Our spirits must breathe. We need to laugh because it is crucial to our spiritual well being.

It is refreshing to discover that we can choose happiness wherever we are, whatever we are doing. Making a conscious decision to appreciate our many gifts is the beginning of positive change. We can let our burdens go and embrace friendship and fun. Sadness will disappear, and the world becomes brighter.

Choosing happiness takes courage and willingness. Some of us have become comfortably discontent. We become complacent. For some of us, a smile feels foreign. It's okay. Change does not occur overnight. But we can patiently practice laughter. Before long, it becomes contagious. We can share this great gift with others!

MARCH 19

Blessings/Gratitude

We are surrounded by blessings, both big and small. They grace our paths. Sometimes we take them for granted. Our health, safety, and security are just a few of the gifts we seldom notice. But as we recognize and appreciate our many blessings, they grow. We grow!

This is the magic of gratitude. We become content with life, through the ups and downs of it. Our perspective turns away from focusing on what we don't have, to truly appreciating all we possess. Children, family members, and friends are just a few examples.

We are surrounded by the beautiful treasures of nature. The universe is held in the loving hands of God. He places each star to shine through the dark of night and causes the sun to rise and usher in a new day. His grace and mercies are endless.

With hearts of gratitude, we cannot go wrong. The waters of God's peaceful river flow through our mind, body, and spirit. The Lord can work through us when we are thankful. He lifts us in peace and grants us serenity.

MARCH 20

Diligence/Quality

We are well accustomed to multitasking. We seldom specialize or focus on just one area. We juggle many tasks and assume multiple responsibilities. We think we must! There is so much to be done. The road ahead is long, and we must hurry if we are to arrive at our destination. Sound familiar?

We are empowered when we realize that this kind of thinking is irrational. We are created to specialize in one area, and to work that job well. This helps us achieve our best performance. It is impossible to produce quality when we muddle through overly packed agendas and overextended projects and deadlines. Quality requires time and diligence.

We can gently turn our minds toward healing this anxiety by slowing down. Then, we can ask God to grant us a spiritual perspective. We will soon discover what is most important to us and, at the same time, corresponds to God's plan for our life. We can make a decision to work out our destiny with diligence. It is our highest calling!

MARCH 21

Tiredness/Rest

We are occasionally caught in performance traps and work so hard to achieve our goals. For some of us, the more we accomplish, the higher our goals escalate. This can be both good and bad. It is good to realize our full potential, but it is harmful if we do not occasionally rest and enjoy the blessings we have received. And our accomplishments are just that.

Our need to achieve can become insatiable. When we lose gratitude for each step along the way, we enter a danger zone. We want more and more. It can become a vicious cycle. It is hard to see what is truly best. We are not turning our will over to the care of God. He holds our greatest needs close to his heart. We can trust in his plans.

Rest helps us regain perspective. We can find the courage to take a nap, take a stroll through the park, or enjoy a warm bubble bath. When we ease our mind away from the vicious cycle of overwork and sink our soul into the healing light of rest, we are recreated. We are born anew. The world becomes luminous and rich, and we enter God's peaceful universe.

MARCH 22

Old/New

Sometimes we must let go of the old to make room for the new. We become accustomed to holding onto the familiar, even when it hurts. It is difficult to consider letting go. This opens the door to the unknown. It advances the reality of change.

But when we finally let go of whatever it is that's holding us back: old habits, negative behaviors, past emotions, painful memories, grief and sorrow; we are able to embrace the new. Our hearts are free to experience the refreshing joy of change. Our minds can be vibrant and creative. God can work through us. He will equip us to affect the world in miraculous ways. We can utilize the power of his love.

Life can be viewed as a series of recreations. We leave mistakes and regrets behind. We move beyond doubt and disbelief and receive grace and forgiveness. We are formed anew. We are reborn.

MARCH 23

Overcoming

God can lift us from the pit of despair. He reaches down with his loving arms of grace and mercy and empowers us to overcome the worst tragedies. Our Maker is truly awesome!

There is no wound too deep or tender that God can't repair it. He sees the frayed fibers of our hearts, even the secret places that we are unaware of. He formed us in our mother's womb, designing each of us with splendid potential. He longs to restore us. He created us to shine in happiness.

We can give praise because we know that God is at work in our lives, molding and shaping our futures to be magnificent. He weeps when we hurt. His heart bleeds when we experience pain. He lovingly holds us and comforts our spirits until it has passed. We can trust he is right by our side. We can rest in his love and have faith.

MARCH 24

Self Discipline/Satisfaction

We do not always choose to do what is best for us. Life presents many options. God has given us free will and with this comes the ability to select our own path. Self-discipline helps us choose the right path. It leads us along the road of destiny.

Self-discipline is a learning process. It comes only after we have spent many days choosing to follow the good. It is developed through hard work and a strong inner motivation to grow and mature spiritually. In time, we will flourish. We can simply dedicate some time to God's guidance and direction each day.

We are not alone in any endeavor. In each obstacle we face, along every new avenue, in each project we undertake, even between tasks and responsibilities—God is with us. He affects our hearts, minds, and spirits in each passing moment. His presence enhances our journey. It gives our lives a deeper meaning and higher purpose. He illumines the mind with the colors of heaven. His inspiration turns our deeds into wonderful blessings.

MARCH 25

Natural Balance

We don't have to push ourselves to give, do, or perform. Sometimes, our mind, body, and soul need time to heal. There are seasons for giving and receiving. We can seek healing. We need to maintain our natural balance of energy. We can learn to care for our spirits.

This supports our happiness and well being. We can listen to our body and soul to discover what we need and when we need it. If we are uncertain about what we need, we can ask ourselves. We can pause and listen to the sound of our breathing, feel the muscles of our body, or hear the beating of our heart. We can tap into the strength of our soul.

These are all clues that help us know if we are in balance. They help us know how we are doing. We nurture and care for ourselves best when we stay attuned to these internal signals. God, help us stay balanced.

MARCH 26

Change/Acceptance

Our journeys take many twists and turns. We flow through the changes of life like a river meanders around many channels and banks, gracefully winding toward its final destination. Many of the turns life takes are unexpected. We do not always know where we are headed.

Acceptance allows the heart to flow gently and peacefully like a stream. When we run up against a bank or an unexpected turn in life, we can re-channel our thoughts and energy to synchronize with our changing circumstances. We needn't resist in fear. Instead, we can follow freely in faith.

God holds us carefully and lovingly. He will not let us drown. He is watching over us and protecting us as we journey toward our final destination. Accepting his perfect love and direction opens the door to faith. It helps us face and endure any change, good or bad. It lays the foundation upon which we can accept what comes our way.

⁂

MARCH 27

Perfectionism/Perspective

Some of us have extremely high expectations for ourselves. We try to do everything perfectly. We are swept away by the illusion that we could have or should have done better. Isn't it time we admit that we cannot do everything flawlessly? God is the only omnipotent being. We can simply do our best and leave the rest up to him.

We can translate this truth into our daily activities. As we work, complete a project, or accomplish any task, we can keep the question in mind, "Did I give it my best shot?" This helps us realistically move forward with no regrets. Regrets are counterproductive. They rob us of our ability to live life fully and effectively.

A healthy, balanced perspective is the key to emotional and spiritual wellness. When we let go of perfectionism, we can achieve this balance. Our lives become serene. We can accept ourselves for who we are and be satisfied with what we do. After all, "We gave it our best shot!"

⁂

MARCH 28

Humility/Grace

Humility is seeing who we are in God's eyes. It is not feeling more than or less than others; rather, it is appreciating our true role in life. We spend too much time trying to be people who we are not. We long for approval and acceptance. Humility helps us realize that we are one of life's unique treasures. We can be ourselves.

When we find humility, we enter the realms of grace. We see the mighty wonders of God surrounding us, and at the same time, we feel his presence deep within. His love shapes our hearts and minds so that we can affirm all we are in his world. From this eternal viewpoint, we are neither big nor small. We are one of a vast creation and yet we possess the power to move the universe in love. In God's grace, we can share our gifts with others.

God's grace synchronizes each particle of matter in perfect harmony. Nothing happens apart from his wisdom and mercy. This applies to our lives as well. Each event in which we participate, everything we achieve, and all our accomplishments are gifts from our Creator. Realizing this is the essence of humility, we can live in awe of God's power. He is the source of all we are. We can embrace his sovereignty.

❦

MARCH 29

Despair/Evaluation

It is hard to maintain inner strength and emotional well being during times of great tragedy. We might be devastated by the loss of a loved one, an unexpected change in financial stability, a natural disaster, or the end of a marriage. The list of life's trials is endless.

Tragedies are multidimensional. They affect each area of our lives and touch every fiber of our emotions. We may get swallowed in feelings of hopelessness. It is helpful to identify our fears and burdens as a result of our misfortune, and to thoughtfully sort out those that are rational and those that are unrealistic. Not every problem we think we are facing truly exists. Some of the worst things that happen are actually blessings in disguise.

Carefully evaluating our dilemma helps us find solutions to help us cope. We are able to view our situation clearly, which creates a path toward recovery and hope. Each day, we can take one more step toward dealing with the real issues. We are freed from the bondage of despair!

❦

MARCH 30

Spiritual Gifts

There are gifts that exceed all forms of earthly riches. And yet, sometimes we get caught up in the busyness and clutter of life. Our minds are unwittingly trapped in materialism and worldly success. We see where we must go, and we work very hard to get there. It is refreshing to pause and consider where "there" really is. It is even more enlightening to consider whether or not we actually want to go there.

Exploring the spiritual realm leads us to deeper, truer realities. We might discover that we are heading in the wrong direction. We may have been so busy we couldn't even see the light God reveals. He is constantly pouring his gifts upon us. He incessantly works to show us his treasures. He wants to share them with us because he loves us so!

When we loosen our grip on the material and open our hand to the spiritual, God's gifts rush in to fill our broken hearts. Every crack, each tiny crevice, and every single mar and scratch within our inner landscape is healed. God blesses each moment with eternal joy. Our only real job is to open the door and let him in.

MARCH 31

Self Will/Letting Go

We are intelligent, resourceful, and creative. We can do anything we commit our mind and energy to, which can be both good and bad. There are negative ramifications associated with some quests. We were not born to conquer in all life's arenas. The challenge becomes seeing clearly those things we are meant to pursue in our lives, and letting go of the opportunities that do not belong to us.

Sometimes it takes more courage not to do something than to do it. We are used to seeking courage to help us undertake new responsibilities, assume more duties, and build opportunities. But how about when the small voice of our soul whispers, "It is time to let go." There are paths we are not meant to travel.

It is hard to let go without first abandoning self-will. We need to gently, yet firmly, surrender our ideas and expectations of how our lives should be and embrace the merciful reality of how beautiful God can make our lives when we lean on him. We can turn our plans, hopes, and even dreams over to his perfect direction and care. His will far exceeds our grandest wishes and desires; his blessings put our own simple plans to shame. We will discover this over time.

Letting go brings peace of heart. As hard as it is to give up control, we must do so to truly live. We enter a deeper, more radiant plateau of existence when we surrender to God's will. His ways are spectacular. His guidance is unfailing and leads us to the hope of a new dawn.

Foolish Choices/Trust

Some of our lives have been marred by foolish choices. For one reason or another—perhaps through fear, maybe to please others—we have done things that are not good for us or others. We have fallen away from our path.

It is not easy for some of us to assert our convictions and values. We might follow the advice and guidance of others instead of doing what we know is right deep down. We feel pressured. We judge ourselves based on the reactions of others. And yet it is time to get back on track. We must return to what is in our heart.

There is a place in the heart that speaks the truth. It is our guiding light. We can learn to follow this, instead of being swayed by others. God knows what is best for us. He quietly whispers the divine inspiration that we need to pay attention to and trust.

Life becomes simpler and more beautiful when we begin acting upon the guidance we receive from God. We can learn to make choices based on the wisdom we receive when we seek to do his will. His inspiration and guidance are truly remarkable.

Fear/Forgiveness

No matter how much work we have done in the area of self discovery, no matter how committed we are to healing, there may be a part of us that still feels frozen, frightened, hopeless, and abandoned. Certain situations still challenge us. We are not delivered yet.

During times of challenge and fear, we can learn to be gentle, kind, and compassionate with ourselves. We can forgive ourselves for being so frightened. We can embrace our weaknesses and frailties. Then, we can lift our hands and let them go. It is time to grow up.

We are slowly moving toward an easier, softer way of living, one that is free of shame and fear. We can be patient with ourselves along the way.

APRIL 3

Silliness

Silliness is rejuvenating. We are so serious. We think we must maintain an intellectual aura if we are to succeed in this world. Or perhaps depression and sadness weigh heavily on our hearts. But we were made to live free of heavy burdens. We were created to enjoy the journey!

Children can help us be silly. Just watching them play brings the child in us to the surface. Joining in their play is even better. We can giggle, dance, and be carefree. All we need to do is let our guard down.

Laughter and fun brighten the day. They help us focus on the positive and not be overly critical, especially of ourselves. The more we try it, the better we become. Before long, it becomes an important aspect of who we are. Each moment spent in happiness is a gift.

Today, let's dare to be silly! We are brave and smart; we can muster up the courage to let go of social norms and the doldrums for a little while. Let's play in the park, run through a forest, swim in a pond, or ride a bike along a winding trail. Whatever road we take to laughter will be well worth our while. It will lead us to our truest selves. It will lead us to peace and joy.

APRIL 4

Negative Surprises

Many surprises are exciting and appreciated, like birthday parties, flowers, and unexpected visits from old friends. This is not so with negative surprises, the ones that, without a moment's notice, turn a day from good to bad. We usually want to run and hide from them. Negative surprises cause instant anxiety and throttle us into the vicious claws of insecurity. There must be alternatives!

We can quickly choose to center our minds on things above when challenging circumstances arise. We can lift our thoughts to God for answers to our problems, even if at first we only listen. Often listening is enough; in fact, it is the best thing for us. When we focus our hearts on seeking God's guidance, we discover love, faith, hope, and understanding—all virtues that help us overcome our obstacles. We gain healthy perspective. We see them as small compared to the more important things in life.

Life is full of surprises, both pleasant and dreadful. Keeping faith—even through difficult times—is the key to spiritual comfort and growth.

Thankfully, we are all born in faith. We are never alone. We can tap into the source of life each day, each moment.

Clarity

Many of us struggle with clarity. We try so hard to prove ourselves and to please others that our strongest values and finest qualities get lost in the shuffle. We lose sight of who we really are and what is most important to us. We forget that we are worthy and beautiful, separate from our social status, our surroundings, or the level of acceptance we feel from others. We lose sight of life's most precious component—love.

A lack of clarity causes our priorities to fall out of line. We are reluctant to take the time that's necessary to develop relationships while haphazardly chasing superficial and shallow endeavors. We might even get stuck in relationships that were never meant to be. We sacrifice tender hopes and dreams in a fruitless effort to achieve temporary success. We give up the best of who we are, to try to become who others expect us to be. We deserve so much more than this!

Nurturing our spirits helps return us to clarity. Taking some time alone to gently reflect on the details of our lives leads to hope for tomorrow. We can recall and reclaim what is most important to us, and let go of all that blocks our true destiny. Confusion will dissipate, and we will once again surely know our way. Our way is love and peace. It can light a path for others to follow. It leads us home.

Good Judgment

Praise God for opportunities. In this modern era, we are blessed with the freedom and gifts to do many things. We can choose what we want to do. We can also be mindful of what not to do. We can learn to use good judgment as we travel along life's paths. We gain discernment that is critical to our well being.

Good judgment comes through a developed conscience. Deep down, we all have a true sense of right and wrong, good and bad. The key is to become aware of our purest senses. Spiritual nudges can guide us through tough situations. When we make a conscious effort to seek God, we are filled with the empowering feelings of satisfaction, security, and direction. When we deny our conscience, we wind up apprehensive and confused. We make bad decisions. And eventually, poor choices can destroy us.

We can practice good judgment daily. Before long, our whole experience is changed. We are reinforced by the positive actions that result from letting our spirit guide us. When we do what's right and avoid activities that are detrimental to our souls, we are given one more day of inner comfort. Discernment brings peace of mind.

Making healthy choices is not always easy, and yet using good judgment and listening to the conscience ushers in the dawn of serenity. No matter what happens around us, love will dwell within. Love is everything. It is perfect direction and total peace and comfort. It is the beacon in the storm. It is God's presence.

<hr>

APRIL 7

Failure/Growth

No one likes failure. We enjoy success. It hurts when we cannot accomplish something that we set out to do. We usually end up feeling like a failure. It is enlightening to look upon these situations simply as outcomes that did not go our way. Our misfortune does not have to become us. There is an easier, better way to live.

We can learn to view failure as a self-defining experience. It is unrealistic to expect that we will achieve every goal. Failure helps us discover our true talent. It encourages us to exercise our natural abilities and gifts. Failure shows us which way to go and, more importantly, which way not to go next time.

Failure also keeps us honest. We develop a healthier perception of who we are and where our capabilities lie. When we reach the end of a road, there is no other way but to turn around. We come closer to the path we were meant to travel from the beginning. We learn to admit our weaknesses along the way. We identify shortcomings and develop spiritual strategies to avoid allowing them to overcome us in the future. We mature.

When we learn to deal with failure, we grow immensely. In looking back, some of our toughest times have brought forth the most light. Even through the darkest tunnels, God's wisdom and guidance permeate our surroundings. He shows us the way and leads us to a better future.

APRIL 8

Sickness/Healing

No one likes to be sick. Sickness distracts us from the things we want to do. It slows us down. We need treatment and rest in order to heal. Some of us suffer from disease. It can feel like a curse, especially when we do not understand the purpose. Sometimes there seems to be no logical reason at all.

Let's view our ailments in a new light. Illness often begins in the soul and, from the core of our existence, infects our spiritual, emotional, mental, and physical makeup. We are accustomed to treating the physical symptoms, but how about adopting a holistic approach? We can use the time when we are resting and recovering to explore the deeper causes of illness, such as overwork, depression, anxiety, and other forms of stress. Healing begins when we focus on the root cause of sickness.

Moving through sickness helps instill valuable attributes. We learn the fine quality of endurance. It is not easy to deal with physical pain, especially when it is prolonged or takes us away from the things we enjoy in life. We also gain understanding and empathy. We learn about others and the struggles they go through, as well as recognize and accept our own limitations. From here, we can develop boundaries that help us avoid future struggles.

But the best part of sickness is the gratitude it provides. We can delight in our recovery and praise God for his healing hand. Without pain, we are incapable of fully knowing joy. We need both sickness and health in our lives to achieve balance and stability. We can rejoice in this journey!

APRIL 9

Forgiveness

Life can be unfair. For example, there are those who take advantage of us and cause us great harm. We can become bitter and resentful toward them. It is hard to see beyond our anger and hurt. But there is a way.

When we feel violated and victimized, we can look outside of our pain and try to understand and sympathize with those who have hurt us. We are all born to love. No one truly wants to cause others grief. People fall into traps, vicious cycles that perpetuate over time and through generations. They are usually incapable of viewing their actions honestly and openly. Their vision is warped. They are captives of their own despair.

When we acknowledge the burdens that have led others to behave the way they do, forgiveness becomes easier. We open the door to healing. Letting go of anger and resentment frees us to continue the journey. We are no longer held down. We become the beautiful creatures we are designed to be. Our lives are enriched and become better than ever before.

APRIL 10

Doubt/Self-Confidence

We are not always sure of our God-given gifts or even ourselves, especially when we haven't been spending enough time in prayer and meditation. Doubt disrupts the journey. It unravels the spirit. It pulls the mind away from our destiny.

Developing self-confidence diffuses doubt. When we are confident, we believe in our talents and abilities, goals and dreams. We dare to present our ideas and exercise our gifts. We have the courage to embrace our purpose and live it out day by day.

Self-confidence is not gained overnight. It takes time and practice. As we encounter trials and tribulations, as we face tough choices and meet conflict and uncertainty, we can respond and behave with confidence and maturity. It is not always easy, and yet, it becomes more natural each time we act upon our convictions and values.

We need to develop self-confidence to reach our full potential. Without it, we are subject to the whims and temptations of insecurity and distraction. This valuable trait can make our most precious dreams a reality!

APRIL 11

Thoughts/Temptation

The mind is very vulnerable to temptation and its subsequent anguish. It is like a battleground at times. We try to stay positive. We count our blessings and still we are faced with doubt, disillusionment, and fear. Does the battle ever cease? There must be an end!

Unfortunately, we will need to struggle to keep our thoughts above the mire our entire lives. This is the story of Genesis, the rapture of the garden. But, there is hope. For every temptation and each negative thought, God offers us a solution. We are never alone. He has given us the promises of a new day. We are almost there!

APRIL 12

Kindness/Happiness

Being kind leads to happiness. It is easy to be kind on the surface. We are naturally cordial at work and with acquaintances. We greet those who cross our path with a smile or a handshake. But what about our closest friends and loved ones? Are we also kind to them? This is the kindness that matters most.

When some of us are stressed, we take it out on those nearest to us. We may lash out at them. We feel safe to vent our anger on our loved ones, and yet the ramifications can be devastating. We hurt the ones we love thereby hurting ourselves deeply.

Let's make an extra effort to be kind to those we love. This leads to happiness for everyone. It enhances the journey.

APRIL 13

Joy Will Find Us

It will happen somewhere along the journey. We will relax and then quietly, imperceptibly without knowing it—joy will find us. We will begin enjoying ourselves, accepting ourselves, and accepting life. It will happen. It will seem effortless because it will be a gift.

Joy is a gift. It appears suddenly, without warning, like the morning sunrise creeps in and etches brilliant highlights upon the dark horizon. If we keep doing the activities that bring healing and growth into our lives, it will happen just as predictably. We can keep loving ourselves and it will come. It is already knocking at the door of our hearts waiting to enter. Keep walking. Continue loving. It is time to receive.

APRIL 14

Learn to Heal

Sometimes we trick ourselves. If we feel unhappy, troubled, or scared, we grab for things that we think will make us feel better. We grasp for something, anything that will stop our pain. We are desperate. We think if we get one thing or another (a new job, a new relationship) then we will be happy, and our pain will stop.

It is refreshing to learn that we cannot heal pain from outside of ourselves. External circumstances do not make internal emotions disappear. We cannot heal without having the strength and courage to face our emotions directly.

The only way to heal pain is to feel it and release it. It is personal. It belongs to us. God will help us on our journey. He is right by our sides, loving and caring for our deepest needs. God, help us release our pain.

*

APRIL 15

Shifts

Just as nature shifts and moves into new shapes and forms, so do we. Sometimes our shifts happen suddenly. Other times they take years to manifest. As we become more aware of ourselves and our reactions, we will become more aware of our shifts. We will know when they are taking place.

During stressful times when we feel sudden shifts taking place in our hearts and lives, we can lean on God in prayer to help us through. He is forming a new shape within us. We can trust his handy work. The more flexible we become, the easier it will be to endure these times. We can work with them rather than against them. These moments are natural. They are how we evolve. We can let the shifts happen and trust the new shape and form of our world. We are trusting God.

*

APRIL 16

Talent/Creativity

We each have special abilities and strengths. Some of us discover our talent early in life. Others discover it later or not at all. No matter the timing, it is important for us to search out our gifts and abilities.

Creativity leads to uncovering our talents. We are not used to spontaneity. Some may think it is a waste of time. Not all of us dare to be creative. It takes courage to make time for the precious things in life, and this is no exception. It requires exercising self-love.

Discovering and developing our talent are two of the greatest gifts we can give God and ourselves. Talents and abilities are God-given and help us achieve our created purpose. They show us destiny. They help us catch a glimpse of heaven on earth. Being creative paves the way to helping others in ways that no one else can. We spread inner beauty. Let's all dare to be creative today. Let us resolve to share our talents with the world. This world is so hungry, so lonely, and so afraid. And yet, it is slowly returning to love. Let's be part of this great movement!

<hr/>

APRIL 17

Sadness/Joy

We would prefer never to experience sadness. We try desperately to avoid it. We shun pain. When it rears its ugly head, we shut the door. We close our eyes and move forward. But, the question remains, are we really moving forward?

We need to work through sadness to reach the dawn of healing. We can walk through it step by step, creating a beautiful trail that will lead us to the point where we can truly progress freely, uninhibited by the dark etching of sorrow. When we honestly and openly deal with grief, we begin to heal.

And, healing brings joy. The finest quality of pain is that it carves a special place, deep within the soul, where joy will one day flow. Times of sadness can ultimately lead us to true happiness. Trying times can work in our hearts to show us a brighter direction for the future.

Joy is a great gift. It is an amazing personal principle to accept that sadness can bring us closer to lasting comfort. We needn't run or hide. We can embrace each emotion as a friend and guide. The choice is ours: walk through or shut the door; heal or continue suffering.

<hr/>

APRIL 18

Stress/Serenity

We often find ourselves boggled in stress. The events of the day seem crazy. We encounter challenging situations. We perceive a lack of cooperation from those around us. All these things lead us into a state of frenzy. We are on the edge of exhaustion. We are consumed with negativity and intolerance. There must be an alternative!

To overcome stress takes a combination of faith and attitude. We can consciously lift our minds above the mire and confusion. We can focus our energy on the divine synergy that lovingly hovers above our disillusionment and despondency. We can escape and relax in the presence of his peace.

When we lift the mind above stress, we discover serenity. We enter the sacred place of healing where the colors of the sun and sky flow like a river. This place is found anywhere and everywhere. It is simply that precious moment in time when we meet God. He restores us to emotional strength. Tranquility fills us. Worry seeps away.

Today, despite commotion and turmoil, let us turn our hearts toward heaven. Let us leave stress behind and enter the luminous gates of peace. May sunshine flow in and through us, and may it dance in our hearts.

APRIL 19

Consequences

The decisions we make in life are always followed by consequences. The choices we make today become tomorrow's reality. Our behavior forms our future. The things we do and don't do both contribute to the consequences we later face. They become valuable tools for spiritual maturation.

When our choices create difficult obstacles along the path ahead, it is tempting to run. It is hard to admit that we have contributed to the construction of the barriers we encounter. It is easy to turn the other way and blame others. It is only after we develop the personal strength to face consequences head on that we grow.

Embracing the reality of the effects of our decisions requires acceptance and humility. Entertaining the notion that we may have been wrong ushers in the illuminant dawn of a new understanding. It is the beginning of change. It is the light at the end of the tunnel. It leads to the hope of a brighter tomorrow.

Working honestly through consequences moves us closer to our created image. We discover destiny. We gain wisdom. Each experience in life teaches us more and more. When we are open to the reality of our behavior, our journey toward peace and serenity quickens. They stand together at the other side of every conflict. They pave the way to love and restitution.

APRIL 20

Nervousness/Contentment

How often we end our day with another series of meaningless events. We get caught up in one thing after another, and before we know it, the day is gone. We are nervous. Fear seeps in. We do not make a habit of carefully considering tasks and obligations, evaluating which ones truly belong in our lives. It is time to begin.

Each day is a gift and can be filled with as many blessings as we let in. When we open our heart, inspiration shines to enlighten our activities and actions. We find contentment. We develop the inner courage to step off the roller coaster of anxiety and enter the peaceful realms of knowing, deep down, that all is well when we lift our minds to heaven. God is there.

Discovering deep contentment is one of the treasures we find along life's path. Turning our daily activities over to the guidance of God and seeking the gifts that lie along the way paves a new avenue toward freedom and happiness. Nervousness and strife become burdens of the past. We embrace the dawn of wisdom and hope.

⁂

APRIL 21

Greed/Kindness

Greed is so ugly! It mars the beautiful reflection of who we really are. It destroys the spirit and weakens the soul. When we let it control us, our thoughts and actions fall out of harmony with our created purpose. In the blind fury of the quest for more, we lose the true gifts of the journey.

An antidote for greed is kindness. Instead of pursuing selfish interests, we can open our minds and hearts to the enriching mosaic of caring for others. Before long, our self-centered needs disappear and unconditional love pours in. When we nestle our hearts in kindness, the insatiable battle of greed subsides.

Just for today, let's release our longing for more and embrace the satisfaction of harboring a kind and generous spirit. May our thoughts and actions be a reflection of the person God wants us to be.

⁂

APRIL 22

Endurance/Discernment

Endurance is one of the finest strengths we develop along the journey of life. Each challenge we face prepares us to bravely maneuver through the difficult circumstances we encounter along the path ahead. We learn as we go if we are patient and willing to grow. Our vision is sharpened. Our thoughts and ideas gain depth and clarity. We acquire wisdom.

We become willing to endure. We can trust that God is at work in our lives—forming and shaping our beliefs and actions to help us achieve his ultimate destiny for us. With endurance comes the gift of discernment. We discover a higher state of existence. We experience divinity. We develop an understanding of the purpose of our lives. And there, we see a glimpse of heaven's grace.

We will not always know the reasons for the trials that life holds. The journey is seldom easy, but our destination can be incredible when turned over to God. He is the author of a better tomorrow. We can let him inscribe our hearts with perseverance and faith. We can trust him to guide our way!

APRIL 23

Limited Scope/Big Picture

We often get stuck in narrow-mindedness. Human instinct positions us to view situations from a selfish, limited perspective. We hone in on how things affect us. It is refreshing to expand our vision and consider that there is a much bigger painting being created in and through our lives. There are things far more important than the trivial pursuits that generally occupy our thought patterns.

When we open our minds to the big picture, we embrace a higher state of living. We become more effective and creative. Everything that happens in our lives eventually evolves to form a miracle. We will begin to see this through our own experience. We can see how problems, turned over to the care of God, are resolved better than we could have ever imagined.

God is painting a destiny for us that is beyond our wildest dreams. We do not always see the beautiful strokes of his brush, and yet we can trust that his masterpiece will one day be unveiled in vivid beauty. We do not have to let life's troubles bring us down. We can keep our eyes on faith and the knowledge of a heavenly process that is not yet revealed. God is omnipotent and will not let us down. He is the Creator of light, the Author of eternity, and our greatest companion and friend.

APRIL 24

A Step in the Right Direction

Change is not easy, especially when it deals with changing old behaviors. We grow accustomed to acting and responding in certain ways. It can be harder yet to change negative behaviors, even when we know we are causing ourselves and others harm.

Sometimes all it takes to begin on the path of change is a step in the right direction. Many of us are perfectionists. We operate under the false assumption that, if we cannot correct a problem completely, then we should not even bother. This illusion prevents us from trying, which is the pivotal beginning to any lasting change. As a result, past behaviors continue to resurface and eventually consume us. They destroy the best of who we are.

But when we break away and take a step in the right direction, we begin the journey toward solutions. We see things get better as our actions improve. Life is more joyful and less troublesome. This does not mean we will never step back again, and yet we can seek to continuously move forward in small steps and ultimately be transformed.

APRIL 25

Life/Lessons

Life is a never-ending series of lessons. We have the opportunity to learn as we go. The key is to remain observant. We can attune our minds to the meaning of daily events. We all make mistakes. When we realize we are wrong, it is empowering to recognize and admit it. This will pave the way toward making better choices in the future.

Each lesson we discover in life helps us become who we are meant to be. We are evolving. The further we journey, the more teachable we become. We discover hope when we are able to integrate past experiences and relate their outcomes to our strategies for a brighter future. As we learn and discover today, let us remember how far we have come. This will help us change.

APRIL 26

Inner Pain/Healing

Pain runs deep. Some of us have felt the agony of loss devour our very soul. It has been a long time since we have experienced peace or serenity. We may even have forgotten what it feels like to be happy. Some of us cannot ever remember being content, perhaps not since we were children.

It is curious to consider why we hold onto pain. After a while, we become used to feelings of sorrow and self-pity. It is almost like we are afraid to let go. It is familiar and, therefore, offers a false sense of security. We can do better. We must do better! We can let go of many of the burdens we carry if we simply give our grief to God in prayer.

Taking a moment to reach deep within the heart can disclose the beautiful dawn of healing. We can ask the Lord to uncover that place deep down where pain manifests itself and to heal us. We needn't continue in the same way. We will be okay when we let go and move forward. In fact, we will be recreated. We will be happy, joyous, and free!

APRIL 27

Savoring the Moment

Our attention is so easily diverted. There are so many things to cloud the mind, whether they are work-related stresses, personal conflicts, or underlying fear and anxiety. Sometimes it is hard to appreciate the many gifts that surround us in the moment. Many of us take our blessings for granted.

The mind is enlightened when we consciously pause and increase our awareness of the gifts in our surroundings. We rise above the turmoil and the strife we fight against and are suddenly and miraculously saved. Simplicity seeps into our spirit as we listen to the precious sounds in the environment. Serenity graces the soul as we open our eyes to a new world, one that is in a higher realm. Trouble and worry dissipate. Peace begins to flow through us.

We all possess the power and insight to escape the stress of life and join the gifts of the moment. We are replenished in this special time. We discover a new strength and a renewed spirit. We can return to the tasks at hand more effectively and with a better outlook. Most importantly, we gain a deep sense of comfort. We trust in the future. We come to believe in hope.

APRIL 28

Trust/Honesty

Honesty is the best policy, but some of us feel trapped in dishonesty. We don't always have the courage to be honest. In fact, depending on life's circumstances, some of us dread asserting our deepest beliefs and emotions like the plague. Fear is paralyzing and debasing. There may be people in our lives that are over-controlling and scare or shame us for expressing our thoughts and feelings. It is not long before we retreat. It becomes a means of emotional survival.

We develop the courage to be honest as we learn to trust in God and in our most precious inner beliefs and values. We learn that there is life-giving sustenance in the phrase, "To thy own self be true." Affirming the inner self, and asking God for the strength to express ourselves, ushers in a bright new dawn. We are released from the bondage of fear and dishonesty. Faith and trust in our higher power becomes the beautiful reed that replaces the horrible chains that have bound the most precious part of who we are. God gives us the confidence to be true to ourselves and express our best thoughts and ideas. We are free to share our inner vision with the world.

Today, let us begin on the challenging, yet healing journey of letting fear and dishonesty go, so that we may become confident and honest with others and ourselves. If we hold on to God and brave the stormy waters, we will eventually encounter the peaceful river through which God's wonderful grace flows. It is well worth enduring the raging tide that is trying to prevent us from being fully alive. Those who are still trying to control us will eventually have to accept that we are beyond their stifling grip. We are now forever in the loving hands of God.

APRIL 29

Stillness/Presence

It is phenomenal to become so still that we feel God's mighty presence. What a blessing it is to consider that, in any given moment, we can be silent and calm long enough to feel the awesome power of God embracing our spirit, holding our very soul in complete peace and solace. We can absorb God's love in this place. We can feel it soothe each and every fiber of our weary body, mend our frayed thoughts, heal our torn emotions, and renew our lives. We long to be in this place and don't want to leave there. God is preparing us. He is forming and shaping our spirits so that we can touch others with the gift of his love and saving power.

When we take time to be still in God's presence, we are enlightened and transformed. There are no words in human language to describe how good it feels to be connected to God. It is both supernatural and, at the same time, the most natural relationship we will ever experience. We were born to discover God. We were created to encounter his journey of love.

Empowered by his spirit, we can live wondrously! Love's energy radiates around us and works through us in a way that encourages others. Our days become brighter. We are made happy and whole. We find that heaven begins right here on earth. It surrounds the entire galaxy, but is also found in a tender place deep within. When we connect with this silent, yet profound space, we enter the presence of peace.

<hr/>

APRIL 30

Self Pity/Value

Pity is self-defeating. When we convince ourselves that we are "less than," we are sabotaging our future. We are destroying our chances to succeed, and even more significantly, we are surrendering happiness. We might feel as if we do not deserve peace and harmony. When we feel this low, we are turning our back on the beauty of the journey.

We are all created with an important purpose in life. We cannot let self-pity steal us away from our destiny. We can affirm that each one of us is born with unique talents and abilities—strengths that God has already seen work wonders in heaven. We must believe in ourselves! We must embrace the power of God within us. The time has come for us to spread our wings and fly.

Letting go of harmful emotions lifts the spirit to higher realms. We reach the pivotal place where we find our true value. We see all that we are in God's eyes, and we are satisfied in this ultimate vision. We catch glimpses of the miracles that God works in and through our lives. These are tiny prisms of our destiny as it unfolds, our greatest dreams coming true. God reveals his love through our actions when we open our minds and hearts to his will. He is bringing us to hope.

<hr/>

MAY 1

Hope/Despair

There are seasons in our journey that lead us through dark valleys. Circumstances arise that challenge our faith and rob us of the joy we find in living out our destiny. Perhaps we have been in the valley so long that we have forgotten what our destiny is, or maybe we have never seen the light of love. We may have never searched for our purpose here on earth. When we are caught in despair, our destiny can be hard to see and discover.

But we can turn despair to hope when we raise our thoughts to heaven and realign our mind and spirit with God's purpose for us. We are pulled from the dark valley by the mighty hand of God. Our vision is enlightened and we can regain the priceless gifts of freedom and happiness. Salvation descends upon our hearts. We are made new.

Thankfully, there is no limit to the number of times our hearts and minds can be recreated along the journey. Our paths wind us through many dark valleys, but we can see the spectacular peaks when we reach the higher points in life. There is space and time here on earth that is eternal. Divinity interweaves her merciful hands of grace in and through each of our days. Despite our present circumstances, we are constantly given small, yet miraculous opportunities to rejoin the work of our heart, the core of our destiny. This keeps us living in hope rather than despair. It is the way of lasting happiness.

⁂

MAY 2

Behavior Traps

Even the best of us have our fair share of negative behaviors. We do not always respond positively to challenging life events. The day becomes difficult, and before we know it, we are caught in a rut. We panic. Things are not going the way we expect or plan and a barrage of negative behaviors is unleashed. How can we stop this vicious trap? It is not easy to shut feelings off once they have been turned on!

And yet we can pause and turn our minds to heaven when we feel caught in negative behavior. We can stop just long enough to let the tender light and love of God warm our minds toward new ways of thinking and behaving. It is never too late to change our patterns and recreate the day. We can turn things around in any given moment. We can always begin again.

The path to peace and happiness is beautiful, but it takes effort. Leaving old behavior patterns behind is not always easy; they will periodically return to haunt us, especially when life gets rough. Be prepared, not disappointed. We can break free each time we lift our hearts and minds to heaven. There we will experience and feel the Maker of peace, the Giver of love, and the answer to all our troubles. There we will find God.

MAY 3

Walking Through/Running Away

It is tempting to run away when life gets tough. The road before us seems too treacherous and long. We quickly jump to another path, a different time and space, one we think might be easier. We hate conflict. We desperately try to get back to a place where everything is easier, softer because we can't stand the pain. Our present circumstances may engulf our very soul, and there seems no way out but to run and run fast.

The journey is designed for our souls to mature. Trials in life season our spirit. We grow to one day comprehend more than just what is here on earth. We learn to look beyond life's circumstances through the eyes of our soul. Our attitude and vision begin to include the divine. Although our journey ahead might seem difficult, and fear is telling us we cannot handle it; walking through our present circumstances can lead to spectacular outcomes. We don't always know what blessings and joy lie waiting for us on the other side of the turmoil. It is well worth our while to hang in there.

The next time we are faced with a series of events that seem insurmountable, let's not run. Instead, let's pause and consider the benefits of walking through this difficult time. If it seems overwhelming and fear seizes our spirit, we can reach up for God's help. He is constantly willing to offer his strength. He will carry us through.

MAY 4

Commotion

Life is so hectic that we find it hard to relax and enjoy. We are busy making key decisions in the board room, working hard in our careers to prove ourselves worthy, spending time with our husbands or wives and children, keeping the home in good order, entertaining friends and family—our list of duties is endless! We feel the pressure to please everyone. We think if we could make everyone else happy then we would be happy.

Our lives have become like kaleidoscopes. We have twisted and turned them many times over to make our days beautiful, yet we miss that which lies beyond our limited scope of vision and narrow sense of perception. The busier we are, the more commotion we create. We miss the truly beautiful. We miss God and all the precious treasures he tucks within each day.

The good news is it is never too late to stop the commotion. When we are consumed by stress, when demands exceed our human strength, or if we simply feel overwhelmed and scared, we can take time out and pray. We can ask God to fill us with his love and guidance, thereby renewing our strength. We are then able to review our priorities more clearly and watch as our lives fall back into place.

Life is about choice. We can choose to remain in the maze of commotion or break free to the innermost realms of freedom. We are not victims. This is the beginning of a peaceful, happier life. It is the beginning of hope.

MAY 5

Releasing Resentment

Resentment is a deadly character defect. It eats away at peace and serenity until all that is left is a painful hole. Sometimes it is hard to tell how our feelings of resentment even began. Before we know it, hate sweeps us away, and with it, goes our precious spirit. We cannot lose this. It is all that we are. There must be a way to release these negative feelings.

One way to reverse the downward spiral of resentment is to pause and pray. Whenever a situation, person, or event angers us, and we feel our blood pressure rising, we can stop and ask God to remove our unhealthy attitudes. It is amazing how quickly he comes to the rescue when we ask for help. Our spirit is washed clean and our minds refreshed. We can let go of those people and things we don't agree with and move on. It is wonderful!

MAY 6

Surrendering Judgment

This world is filled with judgmental people. At times, we may even catch ourselves joining in this bandwagon of destruction. It is not healthy to give our opinions where they do not belong. We all have a special journey, and many of us are doing the best we can. When we judge others, we are interfering with the flow of energy. We are disrupting the stream of life, whether we realize it or not.

The good news is we can surrender our own judgmental behaviors and attitudes. Instead of asserting what we feel is right or wrong about others, we can welcome the unique personalities of everyone we meet. We learn a little something from each person who crosses our path. We are born to enrich one another. As we live and communicate in openness and understanding, we grow and develop. We evolve along the path of destiny. We become who we are meant to be.

We can also learn to ignore those who judge us harshly. We are all incredible people. We are divinely inspired, hardworking, and diligent. No one is perfect, and yet we can be confident that we are the best we can be right here in this moment. When we feel torn and weighed down by the negative attitudes of others, we can choose to affirm our inner spirit. We know deep down that we are okay. We can move forward and upward!

❦

MAY 7

Peace in the Present

We waste much of our lives reaching forward and falling backward. We look toward the future to solve our problems when the answers lie in the present. We struggle with past burdens. Some of us do not know how to let go. We hold on to yesterday and all its sorrow, wondering if someday it will be better. It is time we realize that "someday" is now, and our life as it is today is a precious gift. We can learn to treasure the moment.

Drawing our attention to the present takes practice. Thought patterns are ingrained through life, and dwelling in the past or future may have become our means of escape. Perhaps fear is involved. Maybe there are things that must change about our present circumstances so we can be more comfortable with today.

When we redirect our energy flow and focus on the present, we experience a complete change of psyche. Problems that seem too big to solve, mountains that loom along our path, fear of what might happen or not happen, all will disappear. We find tools to deal with the here and now. The past no longer burdens us either, but simply becomes a stepping stone upon which we have learned many good lessons.

Best of all, we find peace in the present. When we let go of the worry that surrounds our current time and place, serenity can flow in. It flows like a river of hope through a dry and thirsty land.

Busyness/Numbness

Our lives can be very hectic! New opportunities and responsibilities pop up here and there. Before we know it, we are swept away. It is hard to resist the drive to succeed because, after all, there is nothing wrong with success. But what happens when our motivation to get ahead takes full control? When we look at our ambitions and desires, do we see materialism? It doesn't leave room for our precious spirit, nor does it lead to happiness or satisfaction. Many times over, it only leads to defeat.

We become numb when we are continually busy, especially when we have allowed our schedules to get overwhelming. This does not necessarily happen right away, but over time, the spirit gradually numbs. We lose depth and perspective. Fear, doubt, and insecurity begin infecting emotional harmony. What's worse is we probably don't even care. We have lost our perspective so we don't notice. We die emotionally and spiritually.

It is refreshing to realize that we can revitalize our inner landscape if we simply take a break from the busyness, even if it is only once per day. If we can put our pressing deadlines on hold for a moment and open our minds and hearts to be illumined from within, we are spiritually renewed. The numbness and emptiness we have experienced throughout the hectic schedules of our week can be filled by the electrifying grace and love of the divine power in our lives. And when we return to work, our efforts are better directed. We are more effective when we are reconnected to the channel of faith and love.

Accepting the Journey

Life hands us ups and downs. It is easy to enjoy our path in life when things are going smoothly or at least according to our expectations. But how about when the going gets tough? How do we react when circumstances change for the worse, or even when tragedy and hardship strike? Do we run for cover? Do we scream and shout? Do we pout or hide? Or, could we consider adopting a new attitude to help us through?

When we learn to accept our journey as it is, our lives become more joyful. We can funnel all the precious energy we have wasted through worry into hope and gratitude. We will soon realize that things will get better if we focus on the positive. This new outlook will transform our way of dealing with problems. We will be happier and more effective.

Accepting the journey is the key to life's greatest treasures. It is the passageway to psychological freedom, security, and usefulness, and our destiny. It is the cornerstone to discovering our purpose or higher calling in life.

MAY 10

Choose Joy!

Life can be difficult. At times, our circumstances may seem overwhelming, perhaps even hopeless. The good news is that even when we feel hopeless, we are not helpless! We do not have to let life stress us out. Instead, we can learn to overcome the obstacles that bring us down. We can reach beyond whatever it is that causes us grief and trust that God will see us through. We can choose joy.

Thoughts are powerful! Our mindset is an intricate part of emotional well being. Thoughts lead directly to feelings. If we are depressed, scared, lonely, tired, or nervous, chances are we are allowing negative thoughts to penetrate our mind. We can learn to stop this downward spiral of thinking.

Most importantly, we can choose to experience joy anytime, anywhere, despite our problems. Amidst challenge, we can redirect our thoughts to the many blessings we have in life. We can focus on the good! When we choose joy, life becomes wonderful. The journey is lightened and the load is lifted. Our spirit rises to a higher realm, a place of freedom and happiness.

MAY 11

Conformity/Regression

We want to fit in at work, in family circles, and with friends. We all have a deep inner need to be liked and accepted. We like to go with the flow. We get more affirmation this way. We don't always remember that the most enriching form of emotional reinforcement comes from within. After all, how important is fitting in? Is that desire causing us to compromise our highest values and truest convictions? In an effort to conform, what sacrifices are we making, and are the costs higher than we are willing to pay? You cannot begin to put a price on spiritual health and happiness.

Conforming to the attitudes and expectations of those around us can lead to regression. Goals and dreams we once held high may soon disappear in the rat race to be someone we are not. When it is more important to us to be accepted rather than expressive, we are in trouble. Self-expression keeps us vital and creative. It opens the door to future opportunities.

Breaking the cycle of conformity is not always easy, but ultimately, it is the key to spiritual development. It is refreshing and empowering to be who we are with no reservations or inhibitions. Instead of following the crowd we can be open to the guidance of divine direction. We may feel backward. More times than not, it might even feel as if we are now bucking the crowd, and yet we can have the peace and confidence that passes all understanding.

MAY 12

Outcomes/Letting Go

Life can be confusing! It is easy to become scattered in our thinking. We might have several opportunities directly before us. We are not sure which ones to take advantage of. It is difficult to prioritize with so many things going on. We may not even know which of our tasks is most important.

Much of the confusion and frustration we experience in life comes from our illusion that we must know the outcomes of our actions. We can refresh our outlook by simplifying our ideas and plans. Instead of feeling scattered, we can focus our attention on doing what we can in each situation and leaving the outcomes to God. He will direct our attention to those opportunities that are present to enrich our lives. He will shut the door to others. We can learn to trust him in this process. He is unfolding our journey and leading us toward a brighter future.

Letting go of our desire to know outcomes is liberating and empowering. We can devote new energy to living each day the best we can. There will always be the stress of uncertainty. We will never have all the answers, but we can learn to trust the One who does. That one is God. Unlike our plans, his direction and guidance are infallible.

Amy Lynn

MAY 13

The New and Exciting

Some of us get caught in ruts. We are comfortable sticking to what is familiar to us. The thought of trying something new or doing something different can be frightening. It is important not to be overcome by a reluctance to try new things. When we are asked to do something challenging, even though it might scare us, we can muster up the courage to try.

In fact, some of the very events in which we hesitate to participate could be exactly what we need at this particular time in our lives. It is truly amazing how people affect our journey. Some of our acquaintances are like angels. They are messengers who guide us in the right direction. They tell us what we need to hear and coach us to do things that will be good for our character. They encourage us to develop along our chosen path.

Although avoidance might be our first reaction when presented with a new challenge, let's try to be more open to it. Assuredly, our lives are enriched when we meet each unique opportunity with a willingness to participate. We gain in maturity, develop self-confidence, and discover wisdom.

MAY 14

Victimization/Choices

Some of us feel controlled by outside variables in our lives. We may let others make decisions for us, even if they are not the best. Deep down, we know what we want and need, yet we compromise in an effort to make peace with our friends and loved ones. At other times, we may feel overwhelmed by the challenging circumstances that we face. It is important not to get stuck in the illusion that we are subject to the people and circumstances that make up our days. We are not victims!

As we grow, we come to realize that we influence our journey. Our thoughts, feelings, and actions all combine to lead us toward positive or negative outcomes. We can build our character, trust our ideas and values, and assert our hopes and plans; or we can let life's difficulties and problems swallow our courage. The choice is ours. The only reason we are victims is because we do not dare step outside this role.

Small steps will help turn our path in the right direction. We can begin taking responsibility for our choices and actions one day at a time. When we feel circumstances consume us, we can consciously turn our thoughts toward heaven and rekindle our spiritual life. As others try to take over and tell us how we should think, feel, or act, we can kindly, yet firmly say no. We can hold on to our inner strength and knowledge. We can remember that the journey is ours, no one else's.

MAY 15

Freedom From Regret

We are not exempt from mistakes. Failure is innate to humanity. Unfortunately, mistakes often lead to deep feelings of regret. Regret is not only a useless emotion, it is damaging to our spirit. In its extreme, it can be mentally disabling. When we harbor negative thoughts and feelings about the past and ourselves, we withdraw from experiencing the full beauty of life. We are distracted from the possibilities of new opportunities. We are unable to appreciate the many gifts that comprise each of our days.

Thankfully, we can all find a place to begin anew. We can ask God to enlighten our thoughts and emotions. Hope lies in discovering freedom from the lingering sadness from our past. We can draw a line and make a conscious decision to let go of the situations and circumstances that bring us down. We cannot change what has already been. We can only work positively toward a new and brighter future. If we don't let them go, past experiences repeat themselves. We get caught in the same negative cycles and are unable to grow along the journey.

We can willingly let go of what is now behind so that we may embrace the rest of our journey. Freedom from regret elevates us to a place where we can live richly and meaningfully. It is amazing how much energy arises when we release the heavy weight of our burden. We will find new space in our hearts for love and creativity to flow. We become more aware of the blessings and inspiration that God provides to each and every one of us. We experience a truly awesome way of life!

MAY 16

Clarity

Many people struggle with issues of clarity. We try so hard to prove ourselves worthy and please others that our deepest values and best qualities are blurred along the way. It is easy to lose clear sight of who we really are and what is most important to us. We forget that we are intelligent, beautiful people; separate from our social status, attire, surroundings, or the level of acceptance we feel from others.

As our vision blurs, our priorities fall out of place. We might become reluctant to take the time necessary to develop needed friendships. Worse yet, we might haphazardly choose hurtful relationships that were never meant to be. In an effort to be someone we are not, we sacrifice precious hopes and dreams in a fruitless effort to achieve temporary satisfaction. We give up the best of who we are to become the person others expect us to be.

Nurturing ourselves helps us to regain clarity. Hope and solutions are found when we take the time to reflect on the details of our lives. We can recall and reclaim what is most important to us, and let go of all that stands in the way of our destiny. Confusion dissipates as we rediscover our way. Our way is love. It lights the pathway that we can follow in order to live each day to the fullest. It leads us to success.

MAY 17

Choose the Positive!

Thoughts are so powerful. They affect our feelings and behaviors. Our feelings plummet when we choose to remain in a state of negativity for very long. We spiral down in depression, anxiety, and fear. Eventually our behavior is affected as well. We are immobilized. We become indignant, withdrawn, and critical. It is impossible to do anything of true value.

The good news is that our thoughts are a matter of choice. We can change our mindset at any given time. Instead of cultivating negative thoughts, allowing them time and space to grow, we can turn our attention to that which is good. We can expand and enlighten our vision to appreciate and embrace the many blessings and opportunities that come our way. There is always something positive we can focus on if we look hard enough. Searching for our gifts rather than dwelling on misfortune is life-changing. It is the beginning of a fresh and fruitful journey.

So let's chose the positive today! It is the light shining at the end of a dark tunnel. It is the antidote to fear, frustration, and sadness. We are reshaping our inner landscape. It is not an easy process, but it is well worth the effort. We are discovering a better way of thinking and, therefore, living. We are beginning to experience joy and peace.

MAY 18

Happiness

What do we need to be happy? This is a question we often forget to ask ourselves. We can pause and consider what it would be like if we were happy. What would it take? What could we do?

Most of us have not asked ourselves these questions enough if even at all. Instead, we diligently search for our path, a way through our lives, through our current situation or circumstance. We never take the time to consider what would make us happy or what would feel good to us. Then we wonder why life is so hard.

Discovering what would make us happy can help us through any difficulty. It is a simple question with a profound impact. It leads us to a path that is in our best interest. It eases the burden and brings joy.

MAY 19

Clearing the Path

There are often obstacles on our path. Sometimes these roadblocks are telling us we are moving in the wrong direction because they are not letting us through. We can find another way that works better for us.

Other times they indicate that the road we are going down is special. We can try harder to make things happen. We will have to focus and push forward to make our dreams a realty.

The path will clear in good time if it is meant to be. When the obstacles become too large and the going is tough, we can pray and meditate. God will reveal the answers. He will help us discover the path that is truly ours to enjoy.

MAY 20

No One Can Do It All

Do you try as hard as you can to do what others want you to do, yet somehow end up feeling inadequate? Do you feel like, no matter what you do, it is not enough? Are you overwhelmed? You might realize that you are in way over your head, but refuse to ask for help. We think people might realize that we do not have all the answers and are afraid they will call our bluff! This would destroy our illusion that we can do it all.

Peace and serenity flow into our lives when we learn to accept the fact that we cannot do it all. We cannot always accomplish everything on our lists, nor can we make everyone happy. Our lives become even better when we dare to ask for help. No one has all the answers. We are created to depend on one another. The universe is interdependent, from the smallest particle of matter to the mightiest mountain. What makes us think that we are exceptions to the law of nature?

So, today, let's take life one step at a time. Let's remember that we cannot do it all at once. Firmly based in this reality, our lives will be enriched. We will see greater results from our efforts. We can expend less energy, and yet watch as some of the things we have been struggling with miraculously work out. We will come to know true satisfaction and release from worry.

MAY 21

Celebrate!

We get so bogged down with our troubles. We might awake in a good mood, but before we know it, life seeps in to steal our serenity. Happiness does not come naturally for some of us. Perhaps we are more comfortable with worry and despair. These are feelings we are used to. The thought of being truly happy seems foreign. Will we ever dare to let go and experience joy?

These self-searching questions are good tools toward opening the door, but we can begin celebrating right now. It is transforming to realize that we can celebrate, instead of fretting, through each and every day of our lives! We do not have to wait until our lives are perfect. That will never happen anyway. Just as soon as one problem is solved, a new one will arise. The challenge of life is a continuum of obstacles for us to overcome. We can view frustrations for what they are and learn to be happy anyway.

Celebration is a state of heart that we can all enjoy if we consciously place our mind there. No matter what happens, good or bad, we can find something to celebrate in each and every moment. Turning our attention to the light of our many blessings, we will develop a better disposition. We become the people we were born to be. We see the dawn of a new destiny—handcrafted just for us—and we can share our discoveries with others.

MAY 22

Holding Tight/Letting Go

We want what we want so badly! We hold on to solutions that may or may not be realistic or good for us. We chase the answers we want to the problems we face in life. We develop tunnel vision. We see what we want and put up walls to block out the rest.

Learning to follow God's guidance, on the other hand, brings about the peace and happiness that many of us deeply desire. When we are holding on too tightly to anything in life, it is our will and not the will of God. His vision for us is much broader than the small things we cling to. He has an awesome plan for each and every person. The first step in discovering his guidance is to open our minds and release the things that we are holding tight. We can begin to enter the freedom of his love and care for us.

Ironically, the things that God wants to show us are more spectacular than we could ever imagine. When we let go of our insecure ideas of how our lives should be, we are truly graced by an evolution of the soul that will lift us to new realms. We can begin experiencing some of the joy found in heaven here on earth. We become viable creations in the hands of a mighty and kind Creator. We will never be sorry—only thankful—and relieved to have left behind a way of life that doesn't really work. We can trust Him.

MAY 23

Beating Around the Bush/The Direct Approach

We try so hard not to hurt anyone's feelings. We do not want to be a bother or rub anyone the wrong way. After all, everyone should like us, right? Wrong! These thoughts create a fantasy world in which our expectations and ideas are unrealistic. It is impractical to believe that we can please everyone. Our focus is best directed by doing those precious things laid before us by our Creator. This does not leave room for beating around the bush while trying to appease the people around us. It requires a direct approach to living.

When we beat around the bush in our daily relationships, we are only postponing the inevitable and delaying the spiritual process. We cannot follow the straight and narrow path of destiny. But we can change our ways. It is as simple as embracing the gifts of courage and faith.

Today, let us begin our new lives by being direct—saying what is on our mind and not beating around the bush. Let's let go of the fear that we harbor about the potential reactions of others. In its place, let us hold on to the faith that passes all understanding, the trust we have in the things yet unseen, and the power in our lives that is leading us to a better way of life.

MAY 24

Frailty/Inner Strength

Life is a journey, and our journeys are designed with many challenges. During our lifetime, we experience many different seasons. Some of them are good; others can be excruciatingly difficult. We might feel as though we would rather give up and throw in the towel. We succumb to the negative emotions of depression and anxiety. Answers and solutions slip beyond reach. These are the times when we feel weak and frail.

And yet, through utter frailty and feelings of defeat, we are able to begin the process of restoration. We are able to clear away imperfections and build true inner strength. We can let go of our illusions. We can surrender false pride, perfectionism, self-will, and ego. In turn, we can embrace all that we are truly meant to be. We are children of love and grace—beautiful, marvelous creations of a master Creator who will never let us down. He never gives up, even when we do.

And through our frailty, God works mighty wonders. Our Creator will help us build unshakable inner strength when we accept our weaknesses and remain in our fragility without running the other way. We can develop a quality of character that does not break or bend when the road becomes rocky. Eventually, we learn to hand our emotions to God, so that when we encounter challenge, He can remind us of the way, the truth, and the light. His way is truly awesome, and we can trust in his guidance. He will continue to reveal more of his truth as we journey in faith.

MAY 25

Materialism: The Unquenchable Thirst

Some of us are under the false impression that "things" can fix our emotions. We acquire more and more stuff: clothes, shoes, jewelry, knick-knacks, collectibles, videos, dishes, and fine silver—the list is endless. We fall captive to the illusion that the material can heal the spiritual, when in essence, the opposite is true. Healing is born within the spiritual realm. We can only mend torn emotions by reaching inside ourselves.

The temptation is always to circle around our problems by busying ourselves in other ways. Unfortunately, we spin further and further away from our center when we live compulsively. We delay the resolution to our problems. We must stop and refocus our energy. We can embrace the light within that satisfies and makes us whole.

We can all put an end to material desire and relax as our lives become more magnificent than we could ever imagine. We can slow down and reach out for God who heals, restores, and redeems. In embracing the spiritual essence of our very being, we are satisfied to the point that the vain and superficial disappear. In this light, all that we have is enriched and edified. Who could ask for more? Our lives become all that we truly need!

MAY 26

Taking Care of Ourselves

We love success! Some of us chase accomplishment like we are chasing the wind. As soon as we reach one goal, it is on to another. Our ambition has no limit. Unfortunately in striving to accomplish too many things, we lose sight of our need to care for ourselves. We fail to take the time we need to rest and replenish between tasks. We certainly don't remember that we are also important on the list of items to be taken care of!

Ironically, when we take care of ourselves, the things we have been struggling to accomplish have a way of taking care of themselves. They just work out. The events of our day unfold with a symmetry far smoother and more effective than we had planned. We are amazed to see just how easy life can be when we remember the simple task of caring for our inner being. We are less tense. We radiate kindness and ease. We become better people.

Let us remember today how important it is to take care of ourselves. When we feel life swirling out of control, let's pause, take a deep breath, and remember to trust the one who unfolds events miraculously. Let us practice putting our faith in God rather than our own meager blasts of exertion. Omnipotence resides far above our trivial affairs. It binds the universe together and can solve our problems. Our only job is to let it happen.

MAY 27

Loving Loosely

Some of us hold on to everything tightly, including our loved ones. Perhaps out of fear, but certainly out of concern, we grip those we love with such strength that sometimes they cannot breathe. It is impossible to find serenity when we hold on with all our might. It is time to relax our grip and feel the breeze of change.

It is not surprising that our loved ones are also happier and more serene. It feels good when we display trust in our affection. Our relationships are enriched. We no longer cling in fear, but care in faith. It becomes natural for others to reciprocate this unconditional compassion. In turn, they give us the space we need (whether we realize we need it or not). We all need space for love to breathe. Without room, it cannot grow.

Most importantly, when we love loosely, we find the time and energy required to tend to our spiritual needs. When we make space for us, it creates an empty cup that God can fill with his wondrous love and mercy. He inspires us in these special moments. Here we discover who we are truly created to be. This is the foundation of love. It is the platform from which we can love others most intimately and purely. It is where we can experience our loved ones with pleasure and unselfishness. It is where I want to be!

⚜

MAY 28

Let's Play Dress Up?

There is a powerful, false illusion that runs rampantly through the lives of women. We think that what we wear makes us feel better. We choose clothes that will make us prettier, sexier, smarter, or more powerful. We feel ugly on the inside; therefore, we attempt to dress to fit a different perception. We fail to realize that we each have the gift of inner beauty. When we discover this precious truth, we no longer need clothes to make us who we are. We make everything we wear, and all that surrounds us, shine!

Discovering our inner beauty is a process, like finding all other treasures along the journey. Although it requires time and patience, it is well worth the effort. When we reach deep within, down to the very core of our existence, we begin to experience the light of healing. We expose our fears and disappointments so that we can deal with them and move on. We can place love and self-respect where the empty void once was. This lays the foundation of an enduring sense of emotional satisfaction.

And with this wholeness and sense of well being comes our consciousness of the beauty that lies deep within. We discover God. We radiate. We no longer need the material and artificial to express ourselves. We become expressions of something far greater and much richer. We shed the light of creation, and in this light, all is made beautiful. It is the light of love.

❦

MAY 29

Love/Ego

It is easy to get caught up in egotism. Many factors support its development like our careers, accomplishments, opportunities, and even our circle of friends. It is crucial to remember that love and ego are complete opposites. It is impossible for them to coexist. Ego is selfish; love is selfless. When we live egocentrically, our journeys are comprised. Our vision is narrowed from the truth that shines from heaven. We miss the possibilities of freedom and happiness.

When we commit our journey to love, a whole new world appears. The eyes of our hearts open to God and the many opportunities he presents each day for us to embrace and enjoy. Our thoughts, feelings, and actions gain infinite strength. Eventually we will discover that all the things to which our ego tries so desperately to cling are not really important anyway. We see the need to engage in deeper pursuits. We catch a glimpse of destiny.

Today, let's surrender ego. Let's empty our spirit of selfishness and pride, making precious space for God to fill us with love, guidance, and grace. We will see a brighter future, for our tomorrows will get better.

❦

MAY 30

Humility/Letting Go

Some of us are held down by burdens. We read, listen, learn, attend lectures and seminars; and still it seems the harder we try, the larger our problems become. Are we moving backwards?

The answer is humility. The problem is we have tried everything in our own power to change. The time has come to surrender our weaknesses to a power greater than ourselves—God. It is time to let go.

82

We begin healing when we fall to our knees in prayer. We can open our hearts to the Lord, venting our frustrations, exposing our downfalls, and surrendering our defects. We can surrender all the stumbling blocks to a peaceful journey. God knows our hardships before we utter a word. He desperately wants to give us peace.

So, let's surrender. The struggle is over. We have reached the other side of turmoil, the end of ourselves. God, we offer ourselves to you.

MAY 31

Doubt/Self Confidence

Many people are plagued by doubt. Not many of us are sure of ourselves or our God-given gifts. Feelings of doubt and insecurity increase when we do not spend enough time in prayer and meditation. This is tragic. Doubt kills the spirit. It pulls us away from destiny.

Developing a deep sense of confidence in God's love and his desire to help us succeed is the only way to truly relinquish doubt and fear. This leads us to believe in our talents and abilities, even reach for our dreams! We gain the courage to express our ideas. We become funnels of inspiration. We begin to embrace a destiny far greater than we could ever imagine, and we dare to live it out one day at a time.

Confidence is not gained overnight. It takes time and practice to flourish. As we encounter trials and tribulations, as we face tough choices, and as we meet conflict and uncertainty head on, we receive opportunities to react and respond in confident and mature ways. It is not always easy, but it becomes more natural each time we act upon our values. These decisions become our future, and our future is very important.

We need confidence to realize our full potential. Without it, we are bound to fall short of our destiny and purpose in life. Thankfully when we exercise it in our daily activities, we can make our wildest dreams a reality. The sky is not even the limit. Our journey climbs to heaven.

JUNE 1

Redemption/Freedom

Some of us carry heavy burdens of guilt and shame. The past has not always been our friend. In fact, some of us have experienced horrendous tragedies that we do not care to even remember, and yet, we are seldom able to forget. Unfortunately, we sometimes equate negative happenings with who we are. Our personalities are tainted with things of which we are ashamed. In this way, we are slowing dying. Instead, let's remember that we have been redeemed.

Redemption is not easy to understand, and yet it is as real and beautiful as the sun that rises and sets. It is the flower that opens the petals of the heart to feel the warmth of inner freedom. No matter what mistakes we have made and despite any pain we have caused others or ourselves, we can embrace the light of God's forgiveness. We do not have to live in the past. We can release the burdens that have chained us.

Let us make a new beginning. God suffered long ago so that we may journey forward in peace and happiness, regardless of our history. We are redeemed! We can believe in redemption. It is our truest hope!

JUNE 2

Boundaries/Courage

It can be so hard to enforce our personal boundaries! Some of us may not even have boundaries in place at all! If we take an honest look at our past, we might discover we have never thought about developing a structure for living. Perhaps we do not understand how important this is. Maybe we have not loved ourselves enough to deem them necessary. Oh, but they are! Without knowing what is right or wrong for us, we are bound to get hurt, time and time again. Then we are stuck, and our lives do not get better.

Boundaries define a better future. They are an intricate part of the road map that leads us to becoming who we want to be. We can begin by reflecting on those things that are most important to us, and then make a list of what it will take to preserve our values in the days ahead. It is not an easy process, but the results are incredibly wonderful!

The key is courage. It is nearly impossible to develop and enforce personal boundaries unless we are brave. We can trust deeply that God will care for us as we make the necessary decisions. He will give us the strength we need to stick to them. He will comfort us through the transition from pain to joy. We can make a new beginning.

JUNE 3

Trusting the Flow of Life

Have you ever felt like you are swimming upstream, or worse yet, drowning? So many of us struggle to keep our head above water, or so it seems. We need to consider simply moving in harmony with the flow of life. God moves the quiet and still. He works miracles when we are least resistant. The journey does not have to be arduous because God has designed it to be light and free.

We discover just how many blessings flow around us when we loosen our grip on the world. We are delighted to notice the small gifts tucked away in nature. Perhaps we can take the time to get to know a stranger a little better or meet a new friend. The possibilities are endless when we surrender to the flow of life. We find peace and comfort at last.

JUNE 4

Doubt/Destiny

Some of us are plagued with doubt. We fail to seize opportunities when they come our way. We do not believe in our talents or abilities. We nullify the fact that we are capable of accomplishing anything we commit our hearts to. This does not make us bad. It simply means we can learn to follow a new path. There is a better way to live, a higher realm along the journey, which exists beyond doubt. When we reach this special place, we begin to see our destiny!

Remaining in doubt makes it impossible to embrace the depth and beauty of our creation. We are unable to see and, more importantly, believe in the wonderful plans which God has for us. We are all created with an incredible purpose in life. When we release doubt and dare to believe in all that we are, we can discover the meaning of our journey. We begin to see our lives more clearly. After a while, there will be no doubt at all! We are here for a reason. We are valuable pieces of the Master's plan.

This new way of thinking leads us to our destiny. We can discover the magnificence of who we are meant to become. The chains that have held us back are now broken, and we can move forward in trust and freedom. We will discover that we can be successful at anything that has been placed in our heart, whether it is writing a book, rearing a family, reaching out to a group of less fortunate, or beginning a new career. Removing doubt removes all limitations. The possibilities are infinite!

Rest/Replenishment

It is not always easy to use the cherished moments in which we need to rest. Rest is healing, replenishing, and inspiring. During times of rest, we are prepared for effective action. We can open our minds and spirits to love. Our best efforts are love-based. Rest brings us to the precious place where love is born. We discover the magnificence of the quiet and experience God.

Fear blocks our ability to rest. We are accustomed to being in charge, running the show, and getting where we need to be in half the time! The thought of letting things go, even for a minute, can be frightening. Our heart rate increases. Our palms become sweaty. Perhaps we will pull away our security blanket (called "busyness").

Even deeper attitudes that block us from rest are shame and low self-worth. Some of us possess a deep-seated belief that we are not worthy of personal time. We do not realize that we are all born to discover God's mercy and peace. He made us to lie down in green pastures and walk beside quiet streams. Rest brings us closer to his great glory.

Small steps help us overcome these obstacles. Changes in personality and behavior do not materialize overnight. We can just be glad we are striving to find reprieve. Rest, like water, is a necessary ingredient in life. During these sacred times, we are cultivated and strengthened. God speaks to us in quiet moments. We catch glimpses of his destiny for us. We are equipped to live in the center of this destiny. God's heart warms us with a mercy and grace that we have never known. We feel the gift of eternal peace.

Dare To Believe the Best

What a challenge! So many of us are prone to highly negative thoughts. We wait for the next shoe to drop. We feel that surely someone will pull the rug out from under us at any time. We lose hope and fear the worst.

It is refreshing to change our outlook. Instead of dreading our future, we can re-frame our minds in the light of God's truth. We can hold onto his promises. We can have faith in his undying love for us. This gives us strength to dare to believe the best.

God created each of us to experience his love and grace. He longs to show us his endless mercies. We can rest in his shelter. Our futures will be as bright as we "let" them be. We are the only ones holding us back. It is time to believe and be happy. It is time to embrace our many blessings.

❦

JUNE 7

Greed/Unselfishness

We live in a greedy society. So many things are at our fingertips! We are used to instant gratification. This can be dangerous if we are not careful. We develop false needs and think they should be satisfied. Our desires spiral out of control. We lose sight of the truly important. We miss the eternal.

Greed damages the soul, perhaps more than any other negative characteristic. When we are consumed with wanting more, we are selfish, and selfishness collides with love. Although it may appear as though things are going our way, we are slowly rotting. Greed robs us of the precious gifts of the journey.

We can become less greedy by practicing the art of unselfish living. The best way to begin is by shifting our focus to others. We can learn to place our thoughts on giving to others rather than getting for ourselves. Our lives will be blessed abundantly. We will discover that it is in releasing our wishes and wants, our true needs will be met. We will long for nothing!

❦

JUNE 8

Jealousy/Contentment

If only I were smarter, younger, prettier, skinnier, richer—sound familiar? Occasionally, we get caught in the trap of wishing we were someone else. This is a vicious cycle of destructive thinking. It gets us nowhere fast! The good news is we can learn to stop. We can find true contentment.

Learning to be content is a process that requires patience and understanding. We are all created differently. Each person has a unique array of strengths and weaknesses. It is wondrous to discover that we are all beautiful in a unique way. Heaven gifts us all differently.

When we catch ourselves wishing we were more like someone else, let's

87

immediately stop and reflect on something we like about ourselves. We can hold our mind in the positive until we find contentment with who we are. We are priceless works of art, designed by the master Sculptor. We are beautiful, just the way we are. Let's never forget this!

JUNE 9

Regret/Freedom

Some of us are lost in regret. We are stuck in the past and its disappointments and failures. We are consumed by the negative things we have done. We yearn for all that we had hoped to accomplish along the way. The journey seems unfinished. We have lost hope. We forget that each day is a new beginning.

We can all let go of regret and embrace the mercy and kindness of God. He provides an endless amount of opportunity for us to succeed. No matter how many times we have failed, he will lift us up to try again, if we are simply willing. He has great hope for us. He created our journey to be filled with joy and fortitude. We can believe this truth. We must!

We find freedom in the arms of this beautiful revelation. Self-forgiveness fills us with wonder and passion. We can do great things! There is one who paid the price for every mistake we make and will make in our future. He bore the burden of our transgressions. He was bruised and crushed for our freedom and hope. He carries the guilt and shame of our heavy, painful past. We can simply let it be. It is the miraculous path that leads to higher ground. It is the fiber of reality and truth. It is our hope. It is our salvation.

JUNE 10

Fantasy/Reality

It is tempting to live in fantasy. It is more comfortable there. Many of us are dissatisfied. We are unhappy with our lives (the way they truly are) and so, we attempt to escape. We pretend things are different. We might dream of the day we are no longer working so hard. We might disappear in grand thoughts of being rich, powerful, or even beautiful. We block out what we do not like about our personality and environment. We are playing games.

These games can become dangerous. When we escape into a world of unreality, we lose our ability to truly change what we do not like about our lives. Although we might feel more comfortable, we are caught in an illusion of distraction that is not enduring. It is only a matter of time before we will have to face the consequences. The game will end. It always does.

We cannot fear reality! We can learn to embrace our lives as they truly are, and utilize the many blessings we have. When we quit fantasizing and direct our valuable energy toward molding and shaping our true world, we begin to make our grandest dreams a reality. We will no longer want to escape, for we will be well pleased with our developing lives. It is hard to imagine all that God has in store for us. We cannot even begin to grasp the vastness of his plans for our future. He is trying to show us a reality that puts our wildest hopes and dreams to shame. We can find this now!

JUNE 11

Happiness

How often we find ourselves thinking, "I will be happy when..." Let's fill in the blank. I will be happy when my house is clean and orderly, when I get that promotion, when I go on vacation, when my husband does this or that, or when my problems are finally solved. We chronically postpone joy. We do not realize that we can choose to be happy in any given moment, despite our circumstances. There is never a time when all our problems will be solved.

Perfectionism contributes to this dilemma. Somewhere along the way, we have developed the idea that we must earn the right to be happy. We are rigid with others and ourselves. We think we must live up to the standards we have set. We certainly cannot simply feel good. After all, our goals are at stake! Unfortunately, sometimes they are also unrealistic. No one is perfect.

So let's quit postponing happiness. We can let go of thoughts like "if only" and "I will be happy when..." The time is now. It is here. We are far from perfect, but we can celebrate anyway. It is our gift.

JUNE 12

Beginning Each Day

It is an honor to begin a new day. Some of us miss this sacred moment. We awake in a panic. We only have one hour to get to work. The kids are not even up yet! We must hurry to get them ready for school and prepare for work ourselves! Help! We are caught in frenzy. We miss the wondrous gifts of dawn as they stretch out to illumine the colors of our day.

It is good to develop a morning routine that promotes serenity and peace, rather than stress and worry. We can set the alarm clock a bit earlier and take some time to stretch and pray before getting out of bed. We can read uplifting literature while drinking coffee. We can pick up a meditation guide, a devotional, or even the Bible. The book of Psalms is soothing. This is well worth our time. We will be inspired to live the day more fully.

Taking precious time in the morning to start the day out right builds a healthy spirit. Our thoughts begin in a positive light, leading us to an edifying day. We will feel a peace and certainty in the hours ahead that guide us to make good choices and accomplish marvelous things. We are equipped to succeed. We are prepared to make the very best of our day!

JUNE 13

Don't Worry

It doesn't help to worry! Worry prevents joy. It snuffs out happiness and peace. Our worries flow from fear. We think we must wait to relax and enjoy until we have worked all our problems out. This is self punishment. It is a form of not forgiving ourselves, not loving ourselves, not trusting.

God can help us to trust. When we are trusting, we release our fears, confident that he will provide us with what we need. We also know he will enable us to get through the troubles and hardships when they come our way. Lord, help us not worry. Give us peace.

JUNE 14

Thoughts/Actions

Thoughts are priceless. They are a valuable part of our journey. They steer us in the right direction, or lead us down the wrong path. Eventually, our thoughts lead us to where we end up. They pave the way to our destiny or turn us away. When we focus our minds on love, we usher love into the world. When our minds are dark with pain and despair, we move further away from the light of joy. Each good thought we have brings us closer to God. He is pure light and joy!

Thoughts lead to action. Loving thoughts breed compassion. Unhealthy thoughts lead to destruction. We can learn to set our minds on one or the other. We can choose our frame of mind. Our behavior is sure to follow. We can work to share love with others or waste our lives creating hardship.

Let's begin changing our thought patterns with simple ideas. Some of the smallest thoughts are the most pure and powerful. So often, simplicity precedes joy. Let's take some time today to dedicate our energy to nurturing our basic gifts of friendship, family, and reaching out to others.

Behavior mirrors our personality, and personality is governed by our intellect. When we invest our attention on heavenly, spiritual values, our actions spur blessings in the lives of others. We are lifted to a higher realm of living. We can embrace happiness and release sadness and despair. We mirror God's love to the world. We make a difference!

JUNE 15

Selfishness/Kindness

We are selfish by nature. We make decisions and weigh outcomes based on how things will affect us, but we limit our opportunities in this manner. There is a much more magnificent way to live. It is within God's will and not our own.

Hope lies above self-consumption. Destiny lies beyond self-directed desire. True joy is found in those who live for a greater purpose than satisfying personal want. We radiate love when we reach toward God's will, which is perfect love. We will never be perfect, and yet we can tap into a viable source of guidance. Our actions are perfected when we seek to understand God's desires for our lives. We grow. We become more fruitful and consequently, more satisfied. And, it is a lasting satisfaction. We are made whole.

How do we begin? The best remedy for reducing selfishness is to place our thoughts on others. When we care for others and their concerns, our own problems shrink. We can show kindness to people as God places them along our path. We can pray for others and ask for their healing and happiness. Lifting our thoughts to heaven for the sake of others frees us from self.

Kindness places us in heaven's realm. We can feel the presence and majesty of God's mighty grace and love. We can step outside of our own little world and join in the great work God intended us to have. We are happier and healthier. Kindness cures our emotional burdens. It frees us from spiritual bondage and brings us nearer to God.

JUNE 16

Courage/Destiny

We need courage to live our journey. Half-measures will not get us anywhere. We cannot be scared of what will happen or of what is to come. Instead, we can trust that God will see us through any and all trials in our future. The road ahead may not be easy, but the sights and treasures we will discover are spectacular. Our lives will be so good.

When we move forward through life with courage, we are able to reach our destiny. Doubt and fear no longer hold us back. We develop the faith to embrace every opportunity God gives. We are confident. We strive to be all that we can be. We experience the best life has to offer.

Courage and destiny go hand in hand. Without one, the other is compromised. Today, let's pledge to move ahead in faith. Let's draw a line and leave fear, insecurity, doubt, and despondency behind. We have the tools we need to succeed. We were born with the talent and gifts to achieve a higher purpose. Let us follow our calling. We will soon encounter many miracles.

JUNE 17

Honesty/Prosperity

Honesty is not always easy. Some of us fear rejection. We think things will be better, or perhaps smoother, if we say what others want to hear. When we live this way, we are sacrificing our beliefs and values. We slowly fall from our created purpose. Self-expression suffocates. Our spirit descends. Our lives become more prosperous when we learn to be honest.

It can be difficult to develop a pattern of living that embraces honesty, especially if we have not made truth a priority in our past. We can pray for God to help us in our efforts. Each day we can ask him for the courage to be honest. This will pave the way for change. Our journey is woven richer and brighter.

Total honesty makes the future more prosperous. None of the ramifications we fear materialize. Instead, we discover a new freedom and a fresh peace of mind. We begin to experience heaven's finest gifts. We see the dawn of hope. Today, let's embrace honesty. It will be a path to future prosperity.

JUNE 18

Resentment/Reconciliation

Some of us are filled with resentment, and we don't even know it. We might be deeply angry with someone or something. We can find no peace. The more we focus on the faults of others or the troubles of our situation, the more uncomfortable we become. Resentment is dangerous. It cuts us off from the spirit of God. When we are full of anger, we cannot experience the light of love. We slowly die.

Instead of letting our minds fill with resentment, we can work toward an attitude of reconciliation. We can make peace with others and in our heart. If a relationship has us frustrated, we can seek to understand why we are feeling the way we are. Could it be time to embrace change? Or perhaps we are not expressing our needs? We cannot expect others to read our minds. Or maybe a situation seems hopeless and out of control. Are we struggling to change the unchangeable, or can we let go and accept it for what it is? These are all hard questions that lead us to the precious gift of self-discovery. When we uncover the source of our resentment, we heal.

Reconciliation is the key to freeing our hearts from bitterness. It is always better to forgive and accept, rather than to blame, judge, and despise. God will help us when it seems too hard. We can ask him to affect our thoughts in a way that allows us to let go of the past and all our disappointments, and embrace the future and the promises yet untold. We are released to live a more abundant life. We are free to live in trust and happiness.

JUNE 19

Against the Grain

Have you ever felt as if you were going against the grain? We become so tired! It is as if we are working against our very being. We are burned out. We are so caught up in doing what everyone expects of us that we have little time for our emotional and spiritual needs. Our soul dries up. It becomes hard and distant. The light of our journey dims.

When we feel like this, we can remove ourselves from whatever is going on in that moment and take some time to replenish. We can take a deep breath and picture the love of God shining upon us in a warm glow. The longer we bask in the warmth and glory we find in his sweet and sacred presence, the better we feel.

Taking the time we need to rest and replenish leads us to the river of hope. Peaceful and tender waters flow across our spirit as if to say, "Welcome home." We feel the fresh breeze of heaven brush across our weary face. There is no need for fear. Faith and love abide in this special place of tranquility. Our spiritual fiber is restored. We are recreated in God's luminous energy. We see the light of destiny and are ready to begin again.

❦

JUNE 20

Burden/Healing

We endure many burdens along the paths of life. We hope and wish they would disappear. We become weak and weary. And yet, we are given challenges to make us stronger. Struggles add substance to our journeys. We are lead to a deeper wisdom and understanding. We develop an utter passion for God upon whom we must depend. We learn to be humble and grateful.

An opportunity for healing comes with each burden we face. We discover that nothing is beyond God's omnipotent love. Tapping into his power and making it our own equips us to overcome. We can go on to share this healing with others. We can mend the brokenhearted, soothe the troubled soul, and help others overcome sadness and despair. We become conduits of God's restoring power. We bring light into the world. We expand God's love.

And in the midst of our burden, we can trust God. This gives us confidence for tomorrow. We know deep down that God is working miracles even in the hard times. Trial and tribulation unveil heaven's finest gifts. Struggle brings us to our knees. This is where healing begins. This is the special place where all pain comes to an end. It is where we connect with God. Today, let us share our discovery with others. Let's share God's love.

❦

JUNE 21

Obligations/Distractions

Obligations can be good and bad. They can help us stay focused, but they can also distract us from our purpose in life. Not all obligations are worthwhile. It takes care and discernment to choose what we really need to be involved in. It takes courage to give up obligations that are not in our best interest. Not everything we do has a place in our heart. We can learn to proactively select activities that are good for us, before engaging in them.

Carefully choosing our responsibilities today lays the foundation for to-morrow's success. We can embrace our most important opportunities, like parenthood, spirituality, love, kindness, sharing, and friendship. We can avoid the distractions that come with the commitments which counteract our deepest desires in life. This keeps us on the narrow path, full of hope. We see our purpose more clearly. God will support us as we begin making better decisions about our future. He makes our path richer and more beautiful.

Today, let's carefully choose our course of action. Let's remember to pull each opportunity through the loom of destiny in order to make sure that it belongs in the tapestry of who we truly want to be. Let us not be dis-tracted by the myriad of opportunities that come our way. We are on the right path. We can embrace faith and watch our lives become a blessing!

JUNE 22

Frantic/Calm

Life is high pressure! Just when we finish one major ordeal, another ur-gent matter arises. Our hearts become divided, our spirits fragmented. It is difficult to keep up, let alone know what it is that we are trying to keep up with. We become frantic. We lose direction and clarity. Unfortunately, we cannot accomplish anything of true value when we are overcome with stress. Instead, we can relax. We can find a place that is calm, deep within our soul. When we do, we are transformed.

We are more effective when we remain calm, despite our circumstances, because we can see better solutions from a peaceful frame of mind. We can take the time to prioritize our work, which helps the day go smoothly. When we tackle our duties in haste, things seem to snowball—our prob-lems get bigger and our solutions drift further away. It is an oxymoron to consider that, sometimes the harder we work, the further away from our goal we end up. It is refreshing to move through the day with grace and ease.

Cultivating a spirit of peace through prayer and meditation helps us re-main calm when everything around us is crying, "Urgent, urgent, urgent!" When we dedicate special moments, each day, to care for our emotional and spiritual well being, we will develop a calmness that helps us deal with anything and everything that comes our way. We will find the peace that passes all understanding. We will discover God's perfect guidance. And in his loving hand, we will experience joy and happiness.

JUNE 23

Guilt/Delusion

Many of us are worn out by guilt. We are under the destructive illusion that we are not good enough. We suffer from the false impression that we are wrong or bad. Guilt pulls against our spirit until we give up. It longs to defeat us. It wants nothing less than to see us stumble and fall.

Thankfully, guilt can be overcome. We can learn to think encouraging thoughts, instead of getting snared in the trap of discouragement. We can practice affirmation rather than sink in self-pity. We can let go of regrets, mistakes, and hopelessness. We can expand our vision to see our past, present, and future in God's miraculous hands. He gave his very life so that we may be free of guilt and shame. We are redeemed!

When we cleanse our soul of guilt, the doors to heaven open wide. We are no longer bound by delusion. We are free to become the beautiful people we are created to be. New energy bursts forth from within. All the time spent on worrying and grasping for forgiveness is now available for us to strive toward our created purposes. Forgiveness is ours. It was given to us long ago. We needn't grasp.

Freedom of spirit is one of the greatest treasures we can experience. We find this when we ask God to wash our hearts and minds of shame and remorse. We move forward, unencumbered toward a new dawn, a brighter day. The light intensifies. It burns like an eternal flame. It leads to joy and happiness. It leads to freedom.

JUNE 24

Worry/Trust

Worry is a wicked trap. It defeats us time and time again, if we let it. It strips the soul of truth and wisdom. It prevents us from living our best life. It removes us from spiritual reality and drops us in the midst of less important, worldly affairs. Worry is our enemy.

The solution to worry is trust. When we reach for God, stress and anxiety disappear. We cannot fully trust God and fret at the same time. Faith and worry cannot co-exist. When we lift our thoughts to heaven, we can feel peace and serenity flow within us. We see a glimpse of God. His glory shines down to reshape our emotions.

Life presents many experiences, both good and bad. Each one gives us the opportunity to grow in trust. God sees the fullness of life's trials, a hidden beauty we cannot comprehend. He knows each and every fiber of every living cell. He understands us with great intimacy and compassion. Trusting him is like believing in our very existence. He is a wondrous Creator. He will never let us down.

Let's say good-bye to worry—right here, right now. No matter where we are along the journey, we can be sure that we will not get much further without embracing faith. It is time. We have waited long enough to let God show us the way. His ways are good. His paths are glorious. They weave together to make us whole.

❦

JUNE 25

Strength/Energy

Life is so busy! It is hard to find the strength to keep up. Numerous obligations press against our spirits. Opportunities and struggles knock at the door of our hearts, creating clamor and confusion. Materialism, poorly defined goals, unrealistic expectations, and imperfect dreams have run us ragged. As our quests pile up, our strength is depleted. We feel exhausted. How can we renew our body, let alone our spirit?

We can maintain our strength, even in the busiest times, when we learn to nurture ourselves with love. Love is the essence of all forms of energy. It is where the world began, where we began. Tapping into its unending source allows us to enter the spiritual realm, where energy is infinite. We can accomplish anything here. It is a place of never-ending endurance and perseverance. We are filled with enduring sustenance. We develop a love for life and work that can carry us through great challenges.

We are renewed each time we connect with God's eternal energy—plugging in to our true source that rejuvenates the mind, body, and spirit. We can open our hearts to receive this power that exists far above the heavens and yet blossoms within. It is the power of love, the power of God.

❦

JUNE 26

Love Yourself, No Matter What

When you are feeling tired, exhausted, worried, and alone—love yourself. When you feel as if life has left you out on the curb—love yourself. When you are afraid, frustrated, angry, or sad—love yourself. Sometimes it is all we have. We may not think it is enough, but it is so much more. Learning to love ourselves brings us nearer to God.

Our lives are more abundant when we learn to love ourselves through life's trials. We are tapping into our source, which is God's love within us, the kingdom of heaven in our hearts, the sacred place in our soul which is the altar of the Holy Spirit. The journey is amazing when we focus our attention on our inner strength and radiance. We are lifted to a higher realm, where everything is electrified in a new and vibrant light. Our world is illuminated, and happiness becomes reality.

As we move into our future and difficult events occur, let us make a commitment to love ourselves no matter what. We will make it with this attitude. We can love ourselves into a future filled with joy and blessing.

JUNE 27

Peace

Peace is all around us. When we lose our sense of peace, we can try some things we haven't been doing—we can forgive, trust, and love ourselves. We can be still, kind, and gentle. We can continue to do these things until peace returns.

We can also seek places of power and healing. We can breathe deeply. We can fill our lungs with the vibrancy of life. With each breath we take, we can release our fears and anxiety. We can relax and trust that our body, soul, and heart are healing. We can release negative energy flow.

We can be gentle with ourselves. A place inside us needs healing from hurt and fear. We feel something miraculous when we begin to heal. Our souls can be at peace.

JUNE 28

Perseverance/Victory

Perseverance is one of the finest qualities we can possess. It helps us keep on going when we feel like giving up. It nudges us to search out the good, no matter how hard the journey. It helps us love, even when we feel like throwing in the towel. Perseverance leads to success. We gain clarity and wisdom. We see grace and mercy.

We all feel like giving up at one time or another. Doubt and disillusionment are common enemies. It is not always easy to keep the faith, especially when the realization of our hopes and dreams is not in sight. But rest assured, uncertainty is not bad. We needn't fear the unknown. Instead, we can embrace the unseen beauty deep within.

Perseverance helps us overcome all obstacles. It leads to victory. Each time we hold on, despite the challenge, we are one step closer to the gifts of tomorrow. Everything we do in love weaves together to make our greatest dreams and desires come true. This is our promise.

JUNE 29

Rejection/Acceptance

We long for acceptance and hate rejection. It hurts when people reject our ideas, feelings, or plans. Somehow this negativity becomes who we are. Thankfully, we can learn that, instead of seeking the approval of others, we need to accept that not everyone will agree with us. People are different and there are many differences in opinion. We do not have to take the reactions of others personally. We are living our own journey, not anyone else's.

Self-confidence helps us deal with rejection. When we believe in ourselves, we can consider the input of others, and yet not be controlled by it. We know with firm resolve that everything that happens to us—good and bad—shows us the way and helps us find ourselves and discover God. Even when we encounter disagreement, we can find peace.

We can redirect our energy. We grow to understand that rejection molds and shapes us. We discover our strengths and limitations. It does not make us wrong, it makes us strong. We gain substance and character.

JUNE 30

Service/Passion

Passion is one of the great wonders of this world. It motivates us to do incredible things! Passion lights a fire within our soul to accomplish great things. It helps us see through the eyes of love. It gives us the strength to continue when our energy is expended. Passion is pure love. It is the foundation of service.

We are most fully alive when we are serving others. Women have many opportunities to express passion. We care for our families, raise children, share our intelligence, creativity and talents at work and at home, and reach out to bless the lives of others. Everything we do with passion brings love into the world. We all have unique opportunities to share God's light. This is why we were born.

It is wonderful to live with passion. It makes the journey miraculous. Having the capacity to see the needs of others is a gift. Having the heart to help God meet these needs is an awesome opportunity with infinite rewards. There is no better way to live than in service of mankind. It may be a friend, a family member, or perhaps even a stranger who needs our help. It is guaranteed that passion will bring grace to our path.

JULY 1

Paralysis/Solutions

Fear and depression seize us at times. We are vulnerable to darkness, no matter how spiritually fit we are. Situations arise that test our faith. Incidents occur and try our patience and trust. Even loved ones can present horrendous challenges that are not easy to overcome. The journey is filled with obstacles and hardships. We become paralyzed with fear and indecision. It seems impossible to find solutions.

Fear steals our ability to see answers. It leads to depression and a state of hopelessness that can be overwhelming. And yet, finding solutions is the key to moving beyond paralysis. Reaching up toward the positive helps us to overcome our troubles. We are lifted into the realms of mercy and grace.

Seeking solutions sets us free. We discover that life is filled with many options, and viewing our choices clearly is a big part of growth. We have been conditioned to view things as black or white. How beautiful it is to see the wide array of colors that really exist. How wonderful to get beyond the pain! How glorious to trust that God will help us through the darkest valley and deliver us safely to the other side. Our solutions are in God's hands.

❧

JULY 2

Risk/Friendship

Friendship may seem risky. When we try to make new friends, we risk rejection. It is uncertain where the relationship will lead. We are apprehensive. We may have been hurt and do not want to be hurt again. Relationships make us vulnerable. And yet, the more vulnerable we become, the richer and truer our friendships can be.

Friendships begin and grow by risk taking. Our best relationships flourish in complete openness, trust, and love. These virtues all require courage. We take risks each time we tell friends what they need to hear—especially when we face resistance. In turn, we must trust in order to accept love and guidance from them.

When we risk getting close enough to express our innermost feelings, the gift of friendship blossoms. We surpass the superficial, extending our hearts in love and compassion. It is here that we truly connect. We are vulnerable. We experience acceptance, support, and unconditional love. We find that our courage has given us wings. We can fly in the arms of those special people with whom we share our lives.

❧

JULY 3

Hardship/Mercy

Life is full of hardships. The journey is not easy. We do not always remember that everything happens for a reason, especially in the midst of pain. We wonder why? How could we be so unfortunate? Why this, why now? The questions spin in our heads until we reach a state of frenzy. Confusion and doubt set in.

We can learn to break the cycle of despair. We needn't fear. We can embrace God's mercy. This is the dawn of faith.

Our deepest struggles make us who we are. When we endure conflict, disappointment, failure, tragedy, and other hardships, we grow. We need challenges to mature spiritually. We do not always understand the reason for the pain, yet we can develop a deep sense of comfort that we are experi-

101

encing this set of trying circumstances for a divine reason. Today's events lead to tomorrow's miracle. We can trust in God's grace.

Life does not give us more than we can handle. God will see us through any hardship. His mercy reigns. His loving kindness and compassion rise with the sun and set in the tender evening horizon to illumine our hearts as he puts all worry and care to rest. He is in control of all things. He will not fail us. We can believe in his faithfulness! His glory is ours, now and forevermore. God has overcome the world. He paved the way for our journey long ago. He will see us through.

<hr>

JULY 4

Conscience/Direction

We all have a conscience. We all have a special place deep within the heart where we can sense if we are on the right path. When something feels wrong, it is wrong. We cannot ignore this secret place. We cannot hide it, bury it, or minimize it. It is where we get direction and guidance. It is where we find truth.

Some of us have disconnected from our conscience. Our emotions have become uncomfortable, and we are unwilling to change our actions. Maybe fear is holding us back, or perhaps we do not dare to make certain decisions because we dread loss. Our lives have been shackled with loss! Instead of experiencing what is deep within, we run and hide from our feelings. We escape to a place where we no longer have to deal with what is real and true. We sink into a cloud of delusion. From this tragic pit, we find no hope.

The good news is we can always turn our face into the light. We can lift our weary eyes to greet the healing love and power of God, who can save us from the darkest pit of denial. He will give us the courage to follow our conscience. He will give us the strength we need to stay connected to all that is good within. He will guide us toward a better way. He will help us make healthy choices.

Today, let's search for the inner voice of our conscience. Let's rebuild the connection we have with our soul, the guiding force that leads us to hope and happiness. We will make a beautiful new beginning.

<hr>

JULY 5

Success Happens Naturally.

Some of us try to force things. We struggle to get ahead at work, in a business venture, with an important project, perhaps even with a special concern at home. We do not realize that success comes naturally. Things work out best when we are doing what is in front of us and leaving the rest up to God. We do not have to swim upstream. Good fortune finds us when we surrender to the eternal flow.

Sometimes the harder we strive to make things happen, the further we drift away. We create strife. We become tired, and yet work against exhaustion. We can stop this unproductive behavior. We can reject desperation and join our hearts with peace. We can trust that God will take care of us when we unite our spirit with his. He will help us reach our goals if they are to be achieved. We can become willing to give him a try first.

And, we will discover that success happens naturally. It is much smoother than we can imagine. When we are working from our heart and participating in our God-given purpose, we are blessed beyond belief. Strife becomes a valuable tool that has brought us closer to our created destiny. Through toil and trouble, we discover those things that we are meant to do, and those that we are not. We find our path. We can live our best journey. We can embrace our destiny!

JULY 6

Belief/Hope

It is hard for some of us to believe. If there is a God, then why are there so many inequities in life? Why are some people blessed and others less fortunate? Why are we let down when we try our hardest? Or why, when we have given it our all, are we inflicted by yet another trial? Our beliefs are challenged as we consider the injustices we have seen. We lose hope.

And yet, we can keep the faith, no matter what. We must believe. Belief gives birth to hope. We can trust that there is a mighty God who lovingly guides the universe, even when all circumstances point toward doubt and disillusionment. Divinity prevails, no matter what seems to exist on the surface. All things happen for our ultimate good. We can trust this truth.

And when we do, hope flows through our spirits like a peaceful river. We are comforted, healed, and inspired. Challenge becomes a tool that builds our strength and character. Iniquities are transformed into blessings and gifts that we can share with others one day. Belief carves an inlet of hope that is endless. Our conviction becomes unfaltering. We are made whole within the love of our Creator.

***

Stress/Play

How many of us are worn down by stress! Situations and events arise that test our patience and push us beyond emotional limits. Some of us are scattered in our pursuits. We accept too many roles, take on too many projects, and dive into anything and everything until we are in over our head. Anxiety builds before we even realize it. In its extreme, stress strips us of our feelings. We become numb. We know there must be a better way to live so we can discover peace and serenity.

A good stress reliever is simple play. How long has it been since we have played? Society reserves fun and games for children. What a blessing to realize that we can play as well. It is therapeutic. We can laugh, run, jump, scream, and be joyful. This brings sweet relief to a tired spirit and rejuvenates the soul.

So grab a friend or go alone. Let go of self-consciousness and reservation. Find a winding road somewhere and just follow it. We can run, jog, skip, or even spin. Nothing can hold us back. We are certain to spice up our lives. Our days will be more pleasant.

***

Walking Through the Miracle

We are sometimes called to journey through tragedy. Our situation might seem impossible. Perhaps a loved one has been hurt, or maybe we are facing financial ruin. We might even be going through tremendous physical or emotional challenges. Whatever the case, there are times in life when the journey leads us through dark valleys. We don't think we will make it through, but we can. We can hold on to the truth that a miracle awaits us on the other side. We are headed toward a new dawn.

In order to reach the miracle, we must continue walking. Step by step, we can make it through anything! It is not easy, and we may want to stop all together. It is good to remember that we do not journey alone. There is one who will carry us through the hard times. He leads us through the dark valleys. We are sojourners of an eternal faith that will help us through this world. God is our friend and trusted guide.

We will be amazed when we reach the other side of tragedy! Our eyes will fill with tears as God's mercy and grace pour out the many blessings he has been gathering for us along the way. We will be enlightened with an understanding that smashes all doubt and fear. We will utterly know the reason for our trial and embrace an appreciation and gratitude that can only be given from heaven above. We can surrender all pain here. It is over.

JULY 9

Highs/Lows

Some of us live on a roller coaster. Our journeys are punctuated with highs and lows. These are the extreme times. We feel either really bad or really good, less than or more than those around us. Eventually there comes a time when we need to examine the roller coaster way of life and decide if it is time to step off. The highs are not always worth the lows.

We may discover that there is no way to exit the roller coaster without change. We have made certain choices in life that led us to our current dilemma. We have made decisions that have molded our family lives, careers, relationships, partnerships, and other facets of our existence. There may be no way to end our emotional extremes without changing our experience. Perhaps we must leave something behind. It may be time to begin anew.

Self-examination leads to the answers. We gain clarity when we take an inventory of our circumstances and decide which ones belong, and let go of those that are causing us grief. New choices may involve our giving up some good times. However, if we look at the complete picture, we will discover that the highs have not been worth the lows. God will help us through this process. It is his desire that we find the good in life. He longs to make happiness a reality for us. He is ever present to give us strength.

JULY 10

Difficulties/Gifts

We all experience difficulties in life. We encounter trying circumstances that test our wisdom and faith. We do not have to become negative in the midst of trials. We do not have to get frustrated. Instead, we can consider that difficulties are blessings in disguise. Instead of viewing tough situations with a "woe is me" attitude, we can ask ourselves what can we learn from our experience. There are lessons in every trial we face.

Each difficulty we encounter in life is a gift. When we walk through the hard times, we discover more about God, ourselves, and our relationships. We develop a strong spiritual fiber. Most importantly, we learn how we interconnect. We gain a keen sensitivity and appreciation for life and those around us.

We can choose our thoughts and actions to build a better world. Experience is based upon attitude. We can view anything positively or negatively; it is up to us. We have the power to mold the rest of our lives. We find this inner strength by using the events along the journey as building blocks. We value each and every occurrence, good and bad, as a necessary part of becoming the person we are meant to be. In time, it will make sense. We will see the beauty of God's full design for our journey. And, we will treasure our difficulties because we will see they have added a richer hue to the work of art that has now become our life. We will not wish we could have done without hardship. Through it, we have grown.

JULY 11

Temptation/Salvation

Life is filled with temptation. We fell away long ago. God knew before the beginning of time that our destiny would be marred. That is why he wrote our story to include a Savior.

We will slip. We will fall. We won't always make the right decisions nor do the right thing. The good news is we can turn our faces into the light, no matter what we have done, or how far we have fallen. This is a promise. We can hold onto the hope of forgiveness.

No matter what we are going through, God is there. It doesn't matter how bad we feel or how wrong we are. The key is surrender. We can lay our temptations and shortcomings at the foot of the throne of forevermore. We can turn from the dark and embrace the promise of a bright tomorrow. We do not have to continue in our weakness. We are no longer victims.

We can also remember to ask for God's care and protection regularly as we journey along life's challenging paths. The Lord's prayer is a very simple prayer that asks, "Deliver us from evil." We cannot do this alone. We cannot be successful unless we are willing to ask God to help us along the journey. He will carry us when our wings are bent and broken. He will give us the strength to fly again. It is certain he will see us to heaven.

JULY 12

Responsibility/Self Respect

Self-respect radiates joy in our lives. It fortifies the journey. As we grow, we develop self-respect. We learn to take care of ourselves and make decisions that compliment our path. We make positive choices, which affect our relationships, family, career, finances, and personal lives. We build a brighter future, day by day.

One sign of self-respect is care. How much care are we giving to those that are most important in our lives? Some of us have not dedicated much time to showing our loved ones true affection. We have not cared for our families and spouses the best we can. Others have let things slide like career and finances. Perhaps we have not dedicated any energy toward having a career we can call our own. We are all born to be successful in a unique field in life. Or maybe we have let our finances slip and have acquired debt that is not being repaid, and we cannot see any way out.

Developing a deep respect for who we are and for what we stand for can help us with these problems. When we value our inner being, we will not let precious relationships go by the wayside. We will understand our innate need for love and affection. We will want to share this with our families and friends. Day by day we will take the steps necessary to manage our budgets and responsibilities when we value the importance of financial security. We might also explore a career or field that will add value to our lives.

JULY 13

Don't Beat Around the Bush.

This common expression has positive implications when we apply it to our lives. It deals with the way we communicate. Many of us are scared to express our ideas and feelings. Perhaps we have been shamed in the past and learned at a young age that self-expression can lead to disaster, especially when our opinions are not in agreement with those around us. We retract into a shell in fear and lose our ability to communicate.

But we no longer live in yesterday. We have our own lives, a special journey, and it may be that we have carried some of our survival skills from the past into the present without even realizing it. We can develop the confidence and courage we need to express ourselves clearly now. We can learn to be precise and direct in the things we say and do. We have come far along the journey and have reached the point where our thoughts and ideas are not only good, they are inspired. It is time to let our light shine!

We may face resistance, at first, especially if we are still in a dysfunctional family system. The good news is that we will succeed in becoming more effective communicators if we continue to express ourselves openly, honestly, and directly. The best part is that we will discover how much easier life becomes. The energy we have spent beating around the bush in an effort to be loved and accepted can now be redirected toward God's path for us. We can be our best selves. We can work out our destiny!

<hr />

JULY 14

Worship

Who and what are we worshiping? What is worship? Is it going to a temple to bow down before God? Is it singing from hymnals and listening to a sermon? Is it even on Sunday?

True worship is where we spend our time. It is found in the day to day activities we perform. And it is also found in "how" we perform—in love or in haste. When we look at our days, where are we putting our time and attention? Are we chasing material things? Are we wrapped up in a career? Are we enmeshed in a relationship or romance? These are all examples of the things we worship. If we are not careful, they can steal our peace and devotion. We lose sight of the beautifully divine.

Each moment is created in order for us to worship—not the material but the eternal. We can lift our hearts and embrace that which is found above all worldly concerns. We can praise the divine king, the maker of the heavens and earth, our hope and redeemer. God is real. He is worthy of our praise. He will not let us down when we put our trust in him. Our souls will be delighted when we learn the precious gift of praising in the moment. Gratitude will wash over our spirit. We will be filled with the river of hope.

<hr>

JULY 15

Past/Future

All we truly have is today. Some of us go to great lengths reminiscing about the past. How we wish we could recreate our journey! Those mistakes we made, opportunities passed, and dreams we didn't dare follow—oh, if we could only relive those precious years!

Stop! The past is dust. It has blown away in the wind and left us on our present trail. The gifts we are left with are in the present.

There are others who wonder where the path leads. What will we find at the end of our road? Will we receive new opportunities to replace the old; be given new chances to turn around our past mistakes? Our thoughts often race into the future. We expect to find more happiness there. Again, stop! We are here. Our future begins with now. It is time to embrace the moment.

The present is a gift to be lived fully. The moments directly before us are full of rich experiences, chances that we will miss if we are caught up in the past and future. We will miss the miracle of today. And the future is only an illusion. Until it is here, it does not even exist. It is created, step by step, by living each moment as if it were our last. All good things are found in the time and space we see, feel, and experience in the present. This is where our dreams truly lie.

Just for today, I will remember that the past is dust, and the future is an illusion. This will free my mind to embrace the moments at hand. I will accept the many gifts of the present. I will find peace and satisfaction here.

<hr>

JULY 16

Thoughts/Energy

Thoughts are a funnel through which energy flows. They are the gateway to action. Our thoughts precipitate the things we do, good and bad. They also guide our feelings. What we think becomes what we do and how we feel. It all interconnects.

Choosing our thoughts wisely becomes important as we seek to live a better life. When we hold onto negative emotions, worry and fear are overwhelming. If we do not consciously break this cycle, it will get worse. We spiral downward to a sea of darkness and despair. Everything seems confusing. It is hard to find direction and solutions.

Instead, we can turn our face into the light. God will illumine our thoughts if we ask him to. We do not have to remain in despair. When we focus on the radiance of the gifts that surround the situation, we are elevated to a higher plane of consciousness. We are given a glimpse of all that really matters. We discover and experience God's love for us and know deep down that it will see us through.

In this light, our energy flows. We are more effective. We no longer spin our wheels in anxiety and doubt. God has laid opportunities and responsibilities before us to be handled with love and trust. We can embrace them. He knows what is going on. He controls all events with divine authority. Letting go and accepting this truth provide a smooth path within—one where the most precious energy can flow. We radiate the energy of love, grace, and wisdom in all that we do.

JULY 17

Let It Be...

Many of us expend much time and energy over-analyzing the things that occur in our lives. We must know our future and understand our past. There has to be a reason all this is happening! We add certain events together and hope the sequence leads us to our next step. Should we be here or there? Are we on the right or wrong track? We seldom just let go. We cannot "just be."

An easier, healthier way of living is to relax and just let things happen. This frees up our precious time and energy. We can participate more fully in life as it unfolds just the way it is meant to be. We begin to experience the utter magnificence of God's divine timing. We discover that God's plans are truly remarkable—far better than any design we could have created on our own. We can learn to trust this truth. We can just be.

Today, I will step back and just let things be. I will watch with gratitude and splendor as God's destiny is revealed in the moments of the day ahead. I will not become so busy with my own goals and plans that I miss the miracle. God, help me. I am yours.

JULY 18

Confession/Freedom

We are far from perfect. No matter how far along we are, we still get caught in old behavior patterns. We say and do things that we are not proud of. We become disconnected. Although we may not be able to identify our feelings, somewhere we are adrift. We have lost our rudder. We have slipped away from the Spirit that leads us.

Confession is the beautiful pathway that brings our soul home, time and time again. When we experience guilt, frustration, impatience, discontentment, or fear, we can reflect on the root causes of our emotions. Have we said something that was inappropriate? Have we done something to cause someone harm, either intentionally or by accident? Many times, we are the source of our own troubles. We are not victims. We possess all we need to be happy, joyous, and free.

Let's confess our sins. We can surrender the roadblocks that are preventing us from living our journey to the fullest. We can ask God to give us the courage, strength, and wisdom not to repeat the same destructive behaviors. We hurt others and ourselves when we are unwilling to change. God can, and will, change our hearts if we ask him in willingness and faith. This is the great truth of his love.

The more we surrender, the more freedom we discover. We create our feelings. There is no limit to the gifts of confession and communion. God does not forgive a particular number or quota of defects. His love and forgiveness are endless. His grace and mercy are beyond measure.

JULY 19

Battles/Growth

There are hard places in life. There are points along the journey when we are challenged beyond the strength of our emotions. Tragedy occurs. Bad things happen, and we do not understand why. We are lost in disappointment and disillusionment. It becomes difficult to see beyond the chains that have bound us. We succumb to fear and indifference. We continue to struggle, but forget what we are even fighting for. Let us turn our hearts to the light, right now, in this very moment.

Instead of putting all our efforts into trying to overcome the obstacles along the journey, let us try something new. Let's pause and recognize that the events we are going through are difficult, and we deserve to care for ourselves well during this time. It may be we do not hold the answers to solve our problems anyway. It could be that the things that are happening in our lives right now are meant to occur exactly as they are. We could be learning. We may be growing. One thing is for sure. Our spirits are evolving.

It is not easy to step back and trust that the solutions will present themselves when the time is right. We want so badly to control the situations we encounter. And yet, it is like giving a gift to simply let go. We can redirect our precious energy inward, caring for and nurturing ourselves with love and compassion. There is no need to fight. The battles are already won. We will discover this, the longer we journey in faith. It is our destiny.

JULY 20

Letting the Past Go

There are times throughout the journey when we are placed in situations that bring back memories. We are fond of some. Others, we would rather not recall. We may be captured in reminiscence. We might slip backwards for a moment and remember who we once were. Or, we might not want to experience our past. We shut the door. Whatever our reaction, we can learn to feel the past, and then, gently let go. It is behind us now. We are embarking upon a beautiful new journey.

Life is full of discovery. We pass through many portals. Each one is designed to help us grow and mature in our created image. There are bright and dark seasons. There are times we face severe challenge and times of happiness and prosperity. We can savor each segment of our past (the good and the bad) as it has helped us become who we are. Then, we can let our memories go, to embrace tomorrow. We can open our hands to the freedom of a new day.

I will learn to feel the situations that arise in my life that stir past emotion. I will be still and brave. Instead of running, I will stay for a while and experience the moment. Then, I will gently let go.

JULY 21

Powerlessness/Power

How we wish we could control others, especially our loved ones! If only they would do as we say, everything would be so much better. Or, so we think. We funnel great efforts toward trying to change the people we love. We want what's best. We forget that we are powerless over others, and we do not always know what's best. There is only one who can truly affect those we care for. The realms of change are divine. We can leave our relationships in God's hands.

Healing begins when we redirect our energy from our relentless efforts to try to make our loved ones understand, to understanding ourselves and our own limitations and strengths. Only God can bless and inspire our loved ones. He wants what is best for them, and for us.

And, as we believe and lift our hearts in prayer, wondrous miracles occur. Problems we thought could never be solved suddenly diminish. Situations that seemed hopeless are solved. Differences that appear irreconcilable are healed and renewed. That is true power. It is God's.

JULY 22

Challenging Perfectionism

We set such high standards! It is not always easy to live up to our own expectations. Some of us have set the mark very high. We are not easily satisfied with others or ourselves. It is time to challenge our perfectionism. We must consider how it has been working in our lives and in our relationships. Have we passed our unrealistic standards on to those we love? It is time to loosen our grip.

New life fills us when we lower our expectations. We no longer struggle. We are set free. When we are easier on ourselves, we can be easier on others. We no longer expect them to do everything perfectly. We create room for mistakes and forgiveness.

Relationships flourish when given the time and space to grow. We mature as we learn to accept the reality that we are all human. Part of our individuality includes our weaknesses as well as strengths. When we focus less on our downfalls and the defects of others, our strengths come forward to shine. We present compassion and forgiveness rather then resentment and bitterness. People will love to be around us. We will be a beacon of light in a world of hurt and pain. Love will grow in the places we have been—most importantly, our homes.

Owning the Journey

Our journeys are our own. We might have people in our lives that try to control our thoughts, emotions, and decisions. But ultimately, we are on a personal journey, one given to us by God. And through his guidance, we will make it through. We may face opposition along the way. Not everyone will agree with our choices, including our loved ones. We can kindly assure them that we have not begun the path we are on without prayer and reflection. We are strong, intelligent, and gifted.

We may find that we are shamed, especially when we have people around us that are stuck in unhealthy patterns of thinking and behaving. When we resist the control of others, their first reaction is usually to try even harder to make us do what they want. They are not trying to be harmful. They may even love us very much—therefore, wanting us to experience the very best. However, what is best for them may not be best for us. God has instilled a deep inner sense of what is best in each and every one. We can trust this instinct, even if it goes against the grain of others. We are almost there. We cannot give up now!

Our journeys were given to us alone, not to our friends, nor our family, nor even the ones we love the most. When we sharpen our vision to see that which God has inspired, our road becomes easier. We can quit feeling torn, guilty, ashamed, and confused. We begin to see the eternal beauty of why we were created. And shining through this illuminating truth will be the guidance we need to move forward in faith. It is time to begin anew.

Juggling/Focus

We are a generation on the move! Few of us have the luxury of dedicating our time to a single task. We juggle numerous responsibilities. It is challenging to keep our focus on the task at hand. Some of us have never had focus to begin with.

We can grow to develop focus in our lives. We can search our souls to discover what we are created to be and do—our destiny. It is the most important responsibility we have. It is what our heart cries loudest to accomplish. Then we can learn to direct our attention to what really matters. We can develop and nurture our life purpose. This leads to joy.

There are times along the journey when maintaining our focus can be difficult, and yet it is critical to our spiritual well being. Dashing in too many directions can deplete our energy, stealing precious gifts from our destiny. Juggling multiple tasks diverts us from our greatest goal. Holding that which is most important to us in the forefront of our mind keeps us on track. We learn to prioritize and to say "No!"

There is no better way to live than by honoring our destiny. Keeping our focus helps us to reach this wonderful place. In this place, we feel safe and content. We experience God's favor here.

JULY 25

The Miracle of Love

Love is powerful. It affects each of us in a personal and spiritual way. It penetrates and heals the deepest wounds. It illumines the darkest path. It forgives the worst of sins. It changes human hearts and lives.

There are times in our lives when love seems distant because we put up walls. We cannot feel the tender mercy of God. We shut out kindness and compassion. Thankfully, love does not give up. It remains ever-present until that precious day when we are again ready and willing to receive God's mighty gifts.

Love can turn the darkest trials into pure heavenly light. It is the miracle of the universe. No matter the condition, despite all obstacles, and apart from how we think or feel—God's love can turn things around. It transforms resentment into understanding. It bridges the gap of indifference. It is the answer we are looking for. It is the archway of hope.

JULY 26

A New Path

We all find ourselves in situations that are not of our own choosing. It is part of the journey. Our paths lead us up winding peaks and mountains and then back down through valleys of challenge and confusion. Just when we think we have acquired faith and stability, life throws us circumstances that send us back into doubt and chaos. But there is hope. We do not have to stay down in the valley. We can keep moving upward.

Sometimes we feel stuck. We lose sight of the many choices and options we have. We fail to embrace the constant opportunity God gives us to overcome our troubles. Perhaps we are scared. Maybe we are used to feeling victimized and defeated. It may feel comfortable, in an illusive way. And yet, we can move forward. We can leave the place where we are, the situation in our life that is causing us grief, and open our hearts and minds to welcome a brighter, calmer future. It is our choice.

And when we move, things begin getting better. Perhaps not right away, but surely our lives become more spectacular moment by moment. We discover that we are not victims. The only one who holds us down is self. We can quit diverting blame and turn to God for solutions. Our new path is known deep within our spirit. We can seek it now.

⁕

JULY 27

Questions/Faith

Life is full of unanswered questions. We seldom know the outcomes of our actions, especially when others are involved. We encounter many situations with no reasonable explanations. Logic slips through our fingertips, and we are left with faith alone. And yet, as we mature spiritually, we discover that faith is sufficient. It is all we need!

We need faith to embark upon new beginnings. Life is full of change. We are led to multiple points of new beginnings along the journey. Each time we step in a new direction, every time we travel an unfamiliar road or head down a different path, we cannot help but question what lies ahead. We may fear the future. What will we find in the distance? It may be hard to step forward.

We can cleave to faith. Faith is the answer. Holding on to faith helps us live our journey in confidence. We discover happiness and peace. We accept that many of our questions will remain unanswered. Even the answers we find often lead us into yet deeper perplexities, larger problems to be solved. We accept this as well. Faith is true wisdom. It is the fiber of our existence. It is what leads us to destiny.

⁕

JULY 28

Responsibility/Self

Women have many responsibilities. We are talented, creative, intelligent, and compassionate. We are well suited for many assignments. Our biggest challenge becomes accepting and embracing responsibility for "self." We can learn to understand that we are more important than the things we do. Our work becomes a reflection of our inner strengths and values. We are defined within. We radiate our being as we express ourselves in all we do.

We all have special needs. We have deeply rooted desires for love, affection, understanding, support, encouragement, and affirmation. When we learn to care for ourselves, we nurture these needs and give them priority. We are cautious not to give up the things that are most important to us. We know that caring for ourselves enhances all other relationships. Our lives are enriched.

So many things beckon our time and attention each day! Remembering to take care of our inner being will continue to be a challenge, but we can do it. We can let go of trying to please everyone. We can pay attention to our dreams, desires, and inspiration. We find balance. Hope is set in motion. Our lives begin to heal and change. We discover a better way.

JULY 29

Expectations/Rewards

Expectations are dangerous because life seldom hands us what we hope for. This leads to disappointment. But our wishes are not always realistic, and our hopes are not always part of the destiny we were created to experience. We unknowingly set ourselves up for failure. As our expectations rise, our serenity disappears. Our spirit becomes weak.

When we let go of expectations, we find hope and happiness. We discover that life is full of rewards if we quit trying to control situations and people. When we surrender our ideas of "what should be" and embrace "what is," our lives begin to improve. We can open our hearts to God's beautiful, purely spontaneous gifts.

And, God's rewards far exceed our greatest expectations. His love surpasses our highest hopes. His gifts unveil our wildest dreams and satisfy our deepest needs. When we place our limited understanding aside, we can be enlightened by heavenly wisdom. Our lives are filled with beauty and grace. We become one with God.

Transitions

Life contains many transitions. The seasons of our journey change, time and time again. Some of us do not cope well with change. We fall captive to fear. It is hard to trust that God has a perfect plan for us that is unfolding daily. His love and guidance help us climb high mountains, but also carry us through deep valleys.

There are no guarantees, other than that God will see us through anything. Unfortunately, we do not know what "anything" is. We long to see the way each season will unravel. Instead, we can rest in God. He is faithful to help us through our trials. He protects and guides us in the midst of transition. He will lead us to the end. And each ending is followed by a beautiful new beginning.

Let's prepare our hearts for transition. We can be sure another one will come. We can be ready to enter the next new beginning with hope and trust.

Depression/Action

It is hard to function when we're depressed. We feel like giving up. Precious energy seeps away, revealing an empty void. Our spirit is depleted. Our heart is subdued. Our mind is clouded. Depression has no place in a healthy lifestyle. It erodes faith and undermines love.

Clinical depression is not our fault. It is caused by a chemical imbalance. There are physiological causes at its root. It also arises through environmental causes, many of which are also beyond our control. Some of us feel shame and guilt when we are depressed. These feelings magnify an already negative frame of mind. It is healing to begin focusing on love and forgiveness. Loving thoughts can save us from the severe throes of depression because they lead to the positive, which sets us free.

Instead of wallowing in our sorrows or wishing that our lives were better, we can make a conscious effort to act upon love instead of sadness.

We can smile at a stranger, fix a nice meal for our family, or call a friend to say hello. Action brings relief. Our focus shifts from negativity to finding solutions and happiness. We leave destructive thinking behind and place our future in the realm of light. Here we find hope.

AUGUST 1

The Inner Garden

There is a garden deep within, a place where we can go to be with God and our innermost self. It is a tranquil place of peace and joy. We can rest and replenish here. We are renewed. But sometimes it is hard to find the garden. Although it does not move, we do. We are diverted with the many concerns of life. We erect walls without even realizing it. We become detached when the rhythm of our journey is disrupted. Sometimes we are going in too many directions.

Thankfully, we can slow down and ask God to give rest to our spirits. He will lead us beside the quiet stream and restore our soul. When we let go of all that is blocking us, and follow his stream, we find the garden again. Our walls gently crumble. We are reborn.

AUGUST 2

Sticking to Decisions

Some of us have a hard time sticking to the decisions we make. We reach a point where we draw the line. We know what is best for us. We discover that we cannot continue the way we have done because the cost is too high. When we lose precious peace and happiness, it is time to change.

So we make a decision to change certain aspects of our lives. We adopt new attitudes and behaviors. And yet, sometimes it doesn't work. Our best intentions are muddled by the situations we encounter later. The ideas and opinions of others cloud our plans. If we're not careful, our original goals fade. We forget our decision all together and return to square one.

We need to hold tight to the decisions we make, especially when they are critical to our well being. People and situations will challenge us, but in place of giving in, we can use these experiences to reinforce the changes we have made. We are building a new character, and we can trust this process. The choices we have made are leading us to fulfill our greatest dreams.

AUGUST 3

Vision/Belief

Many of us look toward the future and envision what we would like to see. God plants hopes and dreams in the heart of each and every one. Some of us wish we could accomplish certain goals. We might have a career or lifelong dream in mind. Or, perhaps there is a family situation that we pray will be resolved, or financial issues we hope will be rectified.

Belief is the beginning of many things, including the accomplishment of our goals. We create our future. Our hopes and dreams become reality if we have the faith to trust they can happen and they are part of God's destiny for us. We don't have to be discouraged. Good things take time. There is hope on the horizon.

So let's dare to envision the best for our future. Let's not hold anything back! We have caught a glimpse of what could be. Let's not give up.

AUGUST 4

Self-Pity/Kindness

Self-pity is tragic. It works against the soul, making us feel unworthy. It convinces us we are no good. It destroys the destiny of many of us, and prevents us from living a full life.

A healthy alternative to self-pity is kindness. Instead of feeling sorry for ourselves, we can reach out and help someone in need. No matter how bad we believe our circumstances are, it is guaranteed there are those who are worse off than we are. If we compare our troubles with theirs, we will find we are truly blessed. We just need a reminder of how bad things really could be.

Kind deeds replace selfishness, which is at the root of self-pity. Our hearts are changed. Fear is replaced by love when we take part in activities like feeding the poor, visiting the lonely and abandoned, consoling the broken hearted, even spending quality time with our families.

Kindness leads to joy and opens the door to the light of change. It radiates the dawn of a better way. It reveals the path to freedom and happiness.

AUGUST 5

Nothing Is Perfect

We try so hard! We want everything to be perfect—our families, careers, relationships, plans, even our homes. We painstakingly work so that our environment will meet our expectations. We do not give up until we're satisfied. The problem is that we seldom are.

What a relief it is to embrace the idea that nothing is perfect! What freedom we find in accepting the fact that no matter how hard we try, certain things will remain the same. Everything is in God's hands, including us. Even though this may be difficult to accept, it is true. Thankfully, it is the best place anything could be!

We can rest in the certainty that we cannot make anything or anybody perfect. One of the most beautiful aspects of creation is its uniqueness. Diversity cannot exist without flaws. The delicate balance of nature and personality hinges on this awesome wonder. It is time to let go.

AUGUST 6

Accomplishment/Perspective

We all like to feel good about ourselves. We like to be noticed. It is especially nice when people acknowledge the things we do. We set goals and work hard. Achieving helps us to feel worthy.

Accomplishment is an asset when we keep it in balance. It's when we lose perspective that accomplishment becomes dangerous. We cannot let the things we do become more important than who we are. We must know deep down that *we* are worthy, apart from our achievements.

We all struggle with self-worth. Some of us feel empty. We do not have a strong sense of inner value. Some of us try to fill the void by external means—jobs, relationships, degrees, or awards. These temporary things make us feel good, or so we think. How about feeling good about ourselves just for being who we are?

Acquiring a solid sense of inner value is a liberating freedom. What we do can radiate from the beautiful people we are. We can be proactive as we move forward. We can select work that matches our values. Some accomplishments only get in the way. They pull us further away from who we really want to be. And we cannot lose our way. We are on the track of a remarkable destiny.

AUGUST 7

Stress/Exercise

Our world is plagued by anxiety. Pharmaceutical companies earn billions of dollars creating, perfecting, and distributing consumable remedies to help alleviate the symptoms of stress. We search for answers everywhere: in calming stones, new age literature, yoga, aroma therapy—anything we can get our hands on. We must find the answers! We sometimes forget that God is the ultimate source of our rest and replenishment.

And God provides us natural, healthy remedies for stress. One of the best is exercise. It not only releases anxiety; it allows us to have fun. It stimulates our emotional and spiritual health. When we make it a regular part of our day, we will be amazed. Our personalities will be renewed.

It is amazing how interrelated the physiological and emotional parts of our being really are. People with chronic pain are often diagnosed with depression. On the opposite end of the spectrum, people who exercise regularly are clinically proven to suffer lower rates of depression, anxiety, and disease. It really works!

Let's make a commitment to our health today. We can lay down our troubles and get up and go for a walk. We can release our worries and pick up a monthly pass to the gym. We can let go of stress and grab the hand of a friend and take her with us. We can do it; it just requires a little motivation!

AUGUST 8

Frustration/Balance

We get frustrated when things don't turn out as planned. Some of us get lost in discouragement. We find it difficult to turn bad situations around. We don't see the good that can come from unfortunate circumstances. And yet, we do not have to be overcome by frustration.

Balance helps us deal with frustration. When we have a balanced outlook on life, we know that God's hand is in everything, leading us, guiding us toward better days ahead. Everything happens for a significant reason, including the events that cause us grief. Balance is a virtue. When we view life as a spiritual experience, designed to strengthen us and help us grow, we can turn frustration into acceptance and learn from it.

No one ever said that life would be easy. Our journeys will not be without trouble. Times will arise that try our patience. Dreams will be dashed, desires unsatisfied, and hope thwarted. This is the dark reality of life, but with darkness comes light. In fact, without darkness, the light would not appear so brilliant. We catch a glimpse of the eternal picture. We see that all things work together for good. All we need to do is trust.

AUGUST 9

Fear/Trust

Fear is miserable. It holds us in a dungeon where we lose faith and hope. If we remain in these chains, we slowly die. Fear poisons the soul. How do we escape fear? How do we break free from darkness when there is not enough light to see our way out? Trust is our light when we cannot see. It guides us to freedom. It brings us closer to God. God is love, and there can be no fear where perfect love exists.

Some women refuse to trust. It is not easy to rely on something we cannot see. It is even harder to have faith in something we do not understand. And yet if we can learn to trust, fear disappears and so does confusion. Our vision clears, and we see the way out.

Trust is developed over time with practice and patience. Each time we feel overwhelmed, or are frightened by life's tragedies, we can trust God to see us through. He takes care of each and every detail. His love is strong enough to turn the worst situations around for the better.

Placing our lives in God's flawless care frees us from the painful grip of fear. Focusing our thoughts on love brings us comfort and peace. We do not have to remain in the dungeon unless we want to. We hold the key. We can let trust lead us to the light.

AUGUST 10

Neglect/Responsibility

We never want to neglect anyone, especially those we love. Unfortunately, our goals sometimes interfere with caring for those who are most important to us. This can result in neglect. We do not plan this; it just happens. It creeps up on us when we least expect it. Hopefully, we recognize it before it is too late. We can change our attitudes and behaviors today.

We can accept responsibility to thoughtfully care for those we love. We can set aside less important tasks and pay full attention to family members and friends. God has entrusted us with these lives. We can either ignore or enrich them. Spending time with our children, nurturing our marriage, visiting grandparents, and taking a walk with a friend—these are all relationship building activities. We need to create strong bonds with others.

We can also learn to cherish those we love. We can hold each relationship we have as if it is a valuable treasure. God has given us friends and family. Each one is a gift. Every life we share becomes a part of who we are. We, in turn, help those around us to become who they are meant to be. Our destinies are linked; we depend upon each other. This is the synergy of love. It is the beauty of God.

AUGUST 11

Helplessness/Baby Steps

We all feel helpless from time to time. We want to change a situation that is beyond our control. It hurts. We try and pray, and then try some more. When it doesn't seem to get better, we become angry and resentful.

Instead of succumbing to bitterness and anger, we can take baby steps to deal with the situation that is causing the grief. We may not be able to change it, but we can at least change our attitude toward it. We can shift our minds and hearts away from resentment and toward acceptance. We can take small actions that will help us feel better. They will eventually lead to a solution.

We can also discover gratitude. No situation is absolutely hopeless. The light of hope shines down to illuminate the deepest, darkest valley. Even the worst situations offer learning experiences and insight. They make us strong. They add fiber to our spirits. Each challenge we encounter helps us evolve. Instead of freezing in feelings of defeat, we can faithfully move forward. Even the smallest steps eventually lead us away from the darkness and into the light. Praise God that the hope of the universe rests right in our hearts.

AUGUST 12

Perfectionism/Insecurity

Perfectionism is a cunning enemy. It tells us that if we are perfect, our lives will be perfect. It convinces us there is such a thing as perfection, but it is an illusion. The world was created with many imperfections and and so are we. The hope lies in the reality that with our imperfections we possess unique and diverse beauty. It is not all bad.

But insecurity fuels our need to be perfect. Many of us have grown up in broken homes. We labored long and hard trying to restore our families to normalcy. We tried so hard to make our loved ones happy. Some of us have forgotten what it is like to just relax and be ourselves. We began to fear peace and quiet. We developed deep insecurities that remain with us today. We try to disguise our fears by trying to be perfect. Our lives lack reality and maturity. Praise God, there is another way!

We can begin healing from perfectionism. We can make a commitment to change. We can spend as much energy "just being" as we have spent pretending we are perfect by hiding who we really are. We can embrace our quirks and weaknesses. We can laugh at the mistakes we make. Instead of disguising them, we can acknowledge them. We can deal with our problems instead of brushing them under the rug. This is the dawn of a better life.

We will feel a new strength and security within. It takes the place of fear and avoidance. We find that mistakes do not ruin our journey; they simply show us the direction in which we can begin again.

❧

AUGUST 13

Self-Discipline

Self-discipline is a valuable trait. Let's face it, we don't always feel like doing the right thing. We encounter many alluring opportunities that steal us away from our purpose. It is difficult to resist the attractions of this world, even when we know they are wrong. Self-discipline helps us avoid temptation. It keeps us on the path of hope.

Our journeys are weakened in the absence of discipline. We are born to discover our purpose. Our journeys are made for us to practice this discovery. We learn about love, and we share it with others. This is our ultimate purpose. It takes discipline and commitment to be faithful to this calling.

Each day is a series of choices, large and small. Some of our actions help us grow, while others set us back. Disciplining ourselves is an act of love. It prevents us from falling off course. The more we make good decisions, the better our lives become. Each day is a gift, and we can spend it as we wish. We will find our way and see the many blessings that are in store for us.

AUGUST 14

Amends/Maturity

We sometimes unintentionally hurt people with our actions. After all, we are all entitled to make mistakes, right? We find the answer to this question by searching the soul. Even though our actions might have been unintentional, there are times when amends are in order. And we are seldom emotionally released until they are made.

Amends are not easy to make. They test our character. Apologizing takes humility and maturity. It can be hard to even realize we have done something wrong, let alone admit it to another person. It might seem easier to turn the other way and pretend like it never happened. But the past festers within us. It is better to offer sincere amends when situations arise.

We grow and mature in this way. The willingness to admit our weaknesses and mistakes makes us stronger. The person whom we have hurt may or may not forgive us. At least we have wholeheartedly tried to make things right. No matter the result, there is One who always forgives us.

AUGUST 15

Bottled Emotion

People today learn to bottle their emotions at a young age. "Be polite. Use your manners. Don't cry. Be quiet." These are the rules we grew up with. Some of us have trouble expressing emotion as a result. We do not dare vocalize our anger. We hold our sadness in. We don't cry. When someone hurts our feelings, we hear those words, "Be polite." We try to mind our manners at any cost. And so, we bottle emotion. We feel like screaming, but nothing comes out. It is all trapped inside. We slowly die.

Life is about learning and relearning. Thankfully, we can let go of past behavioral patterns. We reach a point along the journey when we discover that our responses are no longer working for us. The pain is not going away, so life is also about transformation and change. We cannot carry the same set of attitudes and reactions across the entire journey. We come to the place where our emotions long to break free. We can feel them well up inside. We need to express ourselves if we want to continue growing.

It is refreshing and healing to express our emotions instead of keeping them bottled up inside. We're preparing our heart to feel love and joy. We are clearing away all the negative rubbish that has blocked us from freedom.

We can cry when we are sad or call someone when we are lonely. We are breaking free from the chains of depression when we behave in new ways. We are no longer held down by suppressed feelings. We embrace a new light and discover eternal happiness.

AUGUST 16

Frustration/Trust

Some things are just the way they are. No matter how hard we try, we cannot change them. This can be frustrating. We get discouraged. We wish we could do something, but we can't. We find no peace until we accept that the situation is exactly the way it is supposed to be. We don't know God's plans, nor do we understand how he is using each occurrence to benefit us in the long run. We need to trust God with what is happening.

Trust is not easy. It is acquired over time and with much perseverance. At first, the thought might seem foreign. Some of us have never trusted anything or anybody because we were hurt when we were young. We are accustomed to doing things ourselves if we want them done right. It is safe. It is understood. It is comfortable. And yet, there are things beyond our control. In fact, the best things in life are beyond our influence. They occur, it seems, at random. We cannot predict or even conceive the magnitude of each and every occurrence in life. This is where trust comes in. It is the key to surrender and peace.

We can let go of our frustrations today. We can turn them over to God and know that everything happens for a reason. We are in this place for a great purpose—one we will soon discover if we diligently follow our path. We have entered this season of our life to learn something new. All we need to do is stay open. We can quit trying so hard. We can surrender our control and release our discomfort. It is time to trust.

AUGUST 17

Cornerstones/Miracles

There are days when we feel out of sorts. We may not be able to put a finger on it. Perhaps we're tired, nervous, confused, or feel defeated. Although we cannot define the source of our discouragement, we can continue moving forward in faith. God is working something out in us. He is transforming some part of our life and transcending our inner landscape. He is in the process of affecting the fibers of our personality. He is leading us to another cornerstone in life. Do not be afraid.

Life is a process in which our souls evolve. With each segment of the journey, through the good times and bad, we experience a different set of challenges and blessings. They all work together to change us. Our characters deepen, our vision clears, and our hearts become strong. We may be uncomfortable or hate certain times in our lives, and yet, we can remember that God is changing us. We are beginning to fulfill our created destiny.

So the next time we feel out of sorts, let's be grateful. Let's pause and thank God for the great work that is underway in our hearts and lives. He gives us exactly what we need to find our way. We are blessed with His guidance and direction. And, we are headed toward a miracle.

AUGUST 18

Miracles

Life consists of many miraculous events. For example, it is no accident we are held safely and securely by the gravity of a planet that is rich in minerals and other substances like water and oxygen. We are blessed with a climate that fosters human life. Earth contains abundant riches.

And then we find an even higher realm of miracles. We discover these by tuning our minds to the tiny blessings that surround us. We learn to recognize God's work in the universe and in our lives. Even the smallest elements in this world are perfectly balanced. God orchestrates each molecule to perform a valuable function. We do not always see the value in everything, but it is there.

We are all created for a reason and have special assignments. Miracles lead and guide us. They affirm our position. They help us learn whether or not the decisions we have made are leading us in the right direction.

The goal is to some day share our gifts with others. We can radiate God's love and power to the people we encounter along our path. There is nothing better than a smile between strangers, forgiveness among enemies, love where there was once hate—these are all mighty miracles. God depends on us to help make his miracles shine!

AUGUST 19

Envy/Contentment

All we need is within. We are distracted by the external. We think things, or even people, will make us happy. But the key to true contentment is in our heart. We can unlock it now.

It is time to stop idolizing other people. We can shut the door on envy. We no longer have to wish we were as enlightened, or as inspired, or as pretty as another. We all possess a unique inner beauty. We discover this when we reach deep within the soul.

Then, we can act upon what we find there. This takes courage. We will sometimes fail. There are no guarantees in life. But we will learn as we go. We can fine-tune our talents and abilities as we move forward. We discover that all we ever really needed was with us all along. What a relief!

AUGUST 20

Gratitude/Blessings

Some of us focus more on what we don't have than on what we do have. We spend so much time thinking about what's missing that we miss the many gifts before us. Instead of thanking God for the good in our lives, we close our minds to his love and grace.

But now we are embarking upon a new era: a time for gratitude and peace. We can be thankful for all we have. We can count our blessings rather than our disappointments. In doing this, we will grow. We will build a character that surpasses the many obstacles we face in life.

Today, I will be grateful. I will thank God for the many gifts as they unfold along my path. I will not hide in selfishness. I will not miss the blessings. I will embrace God's love for me.

AUGUST 21

Second Chances

One of life's gifts is second chances. Let's face it, we all make mistakes. We have multiple interests, not all of them good. We try to do the right thing, but we are set back by selfishness, insecurity, doubt, and fear. God gives us many opportunities to rebuild our spiritual fiber. He always provides second chances. It's up to us to recognize them when they come our way. We can make the best of them and learn from our mistakes.

Some of us do not feel as though we deserve any opportunities after going through a major setback. We feel as though our chances are gone. We might have hurt others or even ourselves in the past. Opening our hearts to future possibilities requires the courage to believe in forgiveness. We can come to terms with our past and learn to forgive ourselves. God already has.

We can be kind to ourselves, despite our mistakes. This allows us to embrace second chances. When we are kind, we are also patient. Just because we didn't get it right the first time, it doesn't mean we should give up. The best works in world history were written and practiced many times. God is not done working in us. He will not abandon the work he has begun. He will continue creating us until our souls leave this earth. He will help us reach fuller potential every time we begin again. All we need is to do our best.

AUGUST 22

Ordinary Moments/Extraordinary Life

How many of us would love to have an extraordinary life? We wait for that big moment. We look for a major breakthrough. We are sure good things must be in store! We set our hopes high. Unfortunately, we are sometimes disappointed.

Take heart. Life is composed of many ordinary moments. We do not realize that simple portals of time, if well lived, can lead to the extraordinary. We can make the most of our time, even the mundane. When we embrace our present circumstances, our journey becomes all we ever wanted it to be. This happens step by step.

So let's make the most of each ordinary moment. Let's believe that each step we take is leading us somewhere better. We will be fascinated before we are through. We will have created an extraordinary life.

AUGUST 23

Lessons/Reality

Life contains many lessons. Each one helps us progress along the journey. They show us what does and does not work. Hopefully, we grow from our experience. We are forever moving upward. Our souls are reaching for something more.

There is no particular time frame for learning. We learn our lessons when we are ready. They are not always easy. Learning involves facing reality. This can be hard, especially when we do not like what we see. And yet, we cannot move forward on certain issues until we are willing to face reality. There is no going around it—we must go through it.

Our journeys are enriched when we step into what is real. We may be frightened and yet we gain security by embracing the fact that God is with us. He will help us through. He will be right by our side until our lessons are learned. We can be patient and persevere. We are almost there. Let's not give up now. We are approaching the beautiful dawn of something wonderful. We are on the edge of a miracle.

AUGUST 24

Illusions/Safety

Illusions are safe. Illusions are comfortable. We understand them. They feel good. They protect us from feeling vulnerable and afraid. Unfortunately, they are false. When we build our lives on them, it is like building our future on a sandcastle. When the tide rushes in, all is swept away.

It is not easy to let go of our illusions, especially if we have nurtured them for a long time. We may not even be able to separate illusion from reality. We need to take steps to change our perceptions. We can begin by viewing what really is, rather than what we hope might be, someday. This applies to our work, relationships, home life, even our goals and plans. We can restructure our thinking to make room for reality.

This leads to lasting safety and security. In looking back we see how vulnerable our illusions themselves have been. They set us up for continual pain and disappointment. How refreshing it is to live a different kind of life—a life rich with reality and truth. Soon, many of our problems slip away along with our distortions of what we wished was there. What remains are the gifts that have been with us all along. We will find that life is good. In fact, it is better than we could even imagine!

AUGUST 25

Meeting Challenges With Grace

Life is full of zingers. Unexpected challenges arise out of nowhere. When we encounter a huge obstacle, we panic and shrink in fear. But there is another way. We can meet our challenges with grace.

God shines his mercy upon our journeys. He excludes no one. He gives us the strength and wisdom we need to face each and every trial. He gives us peace. Even when we are going through a tough time, we can rest in our knowledge that God will see us to the other side. His grace will sustain us. He carries us until we can walk again on our own.

God's grace is truly amazing. It is a never-ending source of energy and guidance. Its power sustains us through anything. It lifts us from the deepest pit. It sets us upon the highest mountain and brings us comfort and peace.

AUGUST 26

Reaching Goals/Reinforcement

We work hard to reach our goals. We maintain the household, care for those around us, establish good careers, and try to do what God calls us to accomplish in life. We are multi talented and goal-oriented. Reaching our goals helps us feel valuable. It assures us that we are okay.

It is important to take some time out to reinforce ourselves when we reach a goal. It takes work and dedication to accomplish anything of value. We deserve to rest for a while. Some women race from one goal to another without rewarding themselves in between. This leads to fatigue. We eventually lose our stamina and even our heart.

Periodic reinforcement is not only necessary; it is life sustaining. We can learn to care for ourselves in a special way, which involves pausing to appreciate each milestone along the way. We can gratefully recognize that our works are in God's hand. All we do is a miracle of his love. We need not plunge forward to the next event. We can take some time for refreshment.

Our work is the most beautiful when we have loved ourselves enough to rest in between accomplishments. When we are not pushing so hard, our minds can be more intelligent and creative. We find space for our greatest thoughts and ideas and express them clearly. And, we find a place in the heart to be inspired by love. This is our highest goal. It is our destiny.

AUGUST 27

Destiny

Destiny has a way of finding each and every one of us. We are busy living our lives and minding our own business, and then something happens. We are moved. We feel a nudge in the recesses of our being. An inner voice speaks to us. Our soul is awakened.

Some of us dare to listen and have the courage to respond. We make room in our lives to embrace the warmth we are feeling. This may involve change. We may have to give up certain things in our lives to follow our calling. For some, this is too risky. But for others, it is the dawn of a bright and beautiful future.

Destiny knocks on the door of our hearts when we are ready. It does not ask us to do anything we are not capable of accomplishing. We can let it move us. We can be willing to let go and follow. We can trust that it is our time. We are on the brink of eternity. We are approaching the outskirts of heaven. We are stepping onto the path of hope.

AUGUST 28

Finite Perspective/Infinite Hope

We tend to view life from a finite perspective. We look upon our relationships, careers, and families through a limited scope. We expect things to work out the way we want and in our time. We hope to get that promotion by the end of the year. We pray that our kids will begin to cooperate better. We long to have a relationship work out. We are restricted by our finite views.

When we realign our thoughts with the infinite force that blesses all things, we realize that we have an entire lifetime to watch things unfold. We may find we don't even want that promotion. Perhaps it would result in more work and less time for family. And who knows? Maybe our kids are behaving the best that they can. Then, there is that relationship. True love always happens at the perfect time.

We can turn all our worries and fears over to the infinite plan and let it carry us along the river of hope.

AUGUST 29

Fear/Exertion

Sometimes it feels as though we are trying to break through a brick wall. We try, and try, and try, and we can't get through. The situation does not change. We try to control people and events, and yet, they don't get it. No one understands that we know what's best. No one is listening! Can't they tell life would be better if they would do as we say? Doesn't God know we can't handle this right now? Sound familiar?

Fear is a funny emotion. It is virtually invisible, and yet it can destroy us in a heartbeat. It tries to run our lives and never takes them in a good direction. It makes us run the wrong way. It fuels our need to work too hard. It makes us want to control others. Anything we can get ahold of might help—or so we think. If we can change the people around us or the situations we face, then maybe our feelings will change. Life would be easier. We are just scared and don't even know it. It is time surrender to a new way of life.

Instead of overexerting ourselves when we are fearful, let's try to face our emotions. Instead of overworking, let's stop and take a look at what has led us to feel the way we do. This allows us to consciously deal with what is really happening. Our troubles dissipate. Peace seeps into our days. We are released from anxiety, worry, and fear. We find new energy. We are better equipped to continue the journey in faith.

AUGUST 30

Without Condition

How often we put conditions on the things we do. "If I help you, then you should help me." "If I work overtime at the office, I will get that raise." We expect "x" to result in "y," and that's all there is to it. How sad! We are restricting our experience. We are denying ourselves the many gifts that accompany a life without conditions.

When we let go of our expectations and learn to give unconditionally, our lives begin to change. We encounter another dimension, a realm of this world that far exceeds our wildest dreams. We are at peace. We can work out of love and compassion. We can let others be the way they are and leave the outcome to God.

And we will see that these results are far better than we could have ever imagined. Our journeys become rich, and genuine expressions of our Creator, the maker of all things. We are free to live abundantly.

~~~~~

AUGUST 31

Communication/Openness

How we long to communicate how we really feel! We dance around important issues like we are waltzing in a social ball. There are issues that need to be addressed, and things that must be said. We cannot circle around them any longer. We can face the truth and express its reality. This is necessary for us to become all that we truly want to be.

Many of us have grown up in closed environments. We have experienced hiding, secrets, and a false sort of living. We have grown accustomed to going along with whatever is happening. It is the path of least resistance, or so we think. We live in an illusion of false security.

We can break this negative cycle by being open. This takes courage. Thankfully, God provides us with exactly what we need. His grace never leaves our side. When we willfully and honestly express what is on our minds, great freedom is born. Relationship barriers disappear. We overcome the worst of problems. Peace begins to unfold in, and through, our lives.

Our lives become more beautiful with the openness and courage to communicate. We catch a glimpse of our destiny. We discover that the best way to live is in complete openness with our Creator. We come to understand and feel his love for us. This lays the foundation for a bright future.

~~~~~

SEPTEMBER 1

Resistance/Peace

Have you ever wondered what it is that you're fighting? Is it hard to relax? What harm would come if we just sat for the afternoon and read a good book? Will our lives fall apart if we rest for a day? Some of us fear relaxation. We resist it like a plague. We view it as the first step in losing control of our lives. A good question is, who is in control? Are we? Or, is there a larger force out there, a higher power that holds us in the palm of his hand?

We find peace when we give up resistance. We discover there is no need to fight. We can let calm waters rush through our spirit. We can be brave and still. We experience peaceful bliss. We deserve peace. We are worth having good feelings. We have traveled far in our journey, and each challenging road has led us where we are today. We can rest in this place.

We find grace and mercy when we quiet our hearts in trust. We find these gifts when we let go of self-will and strife. We surrender to the depths of God's loving plan. We are embraced and held above all the troubles that seemed so big. We are protected from the storms of life. God's love and protection are always with us. He is our deepest need. His love breaks through the barriers of resistance. When we tap into this energy, the walls tumble down. We are carried along the river of hope where we find great beauty and comfort. It brings us to the garden of joy.

SEPTEMBER 2

Persistence/Self-Confidence

Persistence is a fine quality. It enhances life. Nothing comes easily, especially things of great value, including our hopes and dreams. Persistence leads us along the path of destiny. It helps us climb over the stumbling blocks that get in the way. It gives us the strength to keep trying. It sees us through to the end.

Some of us lack persistence. If something doesn't go our way, we give up. If things do not happen along our timeline, we decide that maybe they are not meant to be. We lack the confidence to keep on trying. We do not have the energy to hold on. We are afraid that we may encounter another dead end. We lack determination. We need confidence.

When we are confident in ourselves and our abilities, just because something does not turn out right away, we know that it doesn't mean it never will. Everything has a time and place. We can keep trying and not give up. We can maintain hope. Positive thinking leads to positive outcomes. When we evoke miracles and wonder in our lives, we succeed in our destiny.

SEPTEMBER 3

Defeat/Rebirth

No one likes to admit defeat. It might mean the end of the road. Perhaps we have just seen our hopes and dreams come crashing down. We might have to start over.

It is even harder to handle defeat when we have worked hard to attain a goal, whether it is a relationship, a career, or our journey of personal discovery. And yet acceptance is the dawn of a new day. It helps us move beyond disappointment and despair into the realms of rebirth.

We are all moving toward a greater understanding of God, the universe, and ourselves. Everything works together to help us grow—especially failure. We are learning about living in a spiritual way—loving, caring, and trusting that God is at work in our lives. He is right beside us, even when we feel hopeless. He helps us take necessary steps toward change. At the end of each road, we can consider a new direction. Defeat adds fiber to our spirits. We move into a more effective future. Our character is reborn.

And for some of us, it takes a series of rebirths to discover who we really are and what our purpose in life truly is. We do not always comprehend the master plan. Some of our decisions will be good, others bad. We will encounter relationships that will flourish and others that bring us down. We rise up and then wither and fade. We are like a flower in the field. We are refined in the process of weathering. We gain strength with each heavy rain. We dry out in the sun. We are growing toward our created destiny.

<hr>

SEPTEMBER 4

Encouragement/Energy

There is a little bad in the best of us and a little good in the worst of us. Nothing in God's world is black and white. Everywhere we look, we see an eternal array of colors that diversify and highlight creation. We can learn to appreciate the variations of humanity as well. Everyone possesses some positive traits. We can seek the good in people and be encouragers.

There is tremendous power in encouragement. Each time we compliment someone, we are adding more love to the world. Kind words are uplifting. They cheer us up when we are feeling down. It is not only important to encourage our friends and loved ones, we can also compliment strangers. We can show them care and compassion.

When we encourage others, we release the energy of love. It fills the space around us. It radiates to bless the lives of others. Love cannot be contained. Its energy flows from one to another. It is contagious. Encouragement fills this energy with great strength. When we help others feel good, they, in turn, are kind and compassionate to others. They are inspired to carry this along. The ripples go on and on and on. They become an endless chain of hope.

SEPTEMBER 5

People-Pleasing/Assertiveness

We want to be liked by others. Affirmation feels good. We sometimes go overboard trying to fit in. Some of us will do almost anything to please others. We hate conflict. We put up with a lot to avoid rejection and abandonment. We have grown up this way. It is comfortable. It is hard to picture any other way of life. And yet when we live to make others happy because we want to make them like us, we are not truly living. We are slowly dying.

Assertiveness helps break the barriers of people-pleasing. We learn to take care of ourselves. We quit trying to control the feelings and emotions of others. We needn't live anyone's values but our own. When we don't agree with someone or if our ideas differ from those of the crowd, we can voice our thoughts in confidence. We do not have to fear the reactions of others. We can focus on our inner wisdom. We can trust our instincts.

Assertiveness is remaining true to the heart in the face of adversity. We may be tempted to quickly resolve an uncomfortable matter by sacrificing our own beliefs, but we do not have to. Each small sacrifice adds together to deplete our spirit. It does not take long to disassociate from our feelings and emotions. We lose sight of our goals and give up on destiny.

So let's be assertive! Let's stand for what we know is real and true. Let's not be afraid. We will not bend just because the pressure is too great. We know our boundaries. We have them for a reason. We are protecting our deepest values. We are following a great journey.

SEPTEMBER 6

Silence/Connection

We talk too much at work, at home, and in between on the cellular phone. Some of us spend most of our waking hours talking. We think we are getting somewhere with constant conversation, even if it is trivial. We are deathly afraid of silence. We listen to the radio, television, talk shows. What would happen if we became silent for any length of time? Would our plans fall apart? Would the world come crashing down? Of course not.

We can learn to be quiet and still. We can shut off the television, radio, even the phone. When we become silent in space and time, we encounter the sacred and profound. We experience a peace that passes all understanding, a wisdom that goes far beyond the knowledge we attain through conversation. We are fully connected to God. Our minds and hearts are cleared so that we can feel a divine presence. A new energy flows in and through us.

We are renewed and inspired in this connected state of mind, body, and spirit. There is nothing better than resting in peace and quiet so that we can spend time with our Creator. God loves us so much. He waits patiently for us to relax and meditate. When we are connected to our Source, we experience this love and gain strength and vision. We are prepared to move into the future with grace and ease. We face the dawn of a new destiny. A fresh breeze sweeps across our cheeks. We feel heaven's embrace.

❧❧❧

SEPTEMBER 7

Helping/Enabling

There is a big difference between *helping* and *enabling*. Helping is offering unconditional love to others. It is assisting them with handling things that are temporarily beyond their control, whether due to tragedy, loss, or misfortune. It is something we can do to help them get back on their feet, overcome their circumstances, and rebuild. Unfortunately there are people who might take advantage of this.

Enabling is detrimental to everyone involved. It arises out of fear and insecurity, rather than love and true commitment. It is something we do to gain something, whether we are looking for care, attention, or just positive reinforcement. The person we are enabling only gets in deeper trouble because they do not have the chance to learn. Unfortunately, we go deeper together with them. We are not facing reality. We are spiraling away from truth.

There are many people who take advantage of others. We are all at different places along the journey. Some people do not care for anyone but themselves. The good news is we can love without enabling. We can offer help in a way that does not advance negligence. We can let others know we are there for them, but we will not participate in their destruction. This is the most courageous form of love. It is brave and supportive. We are giving our very best. We are facing rejection to really help. They will begin to learn their own lessons, and we will be set free. Our lives will change for the better as a result. Our journeys will become brighter. And the road is made clearer.

❧❧❧

SEPTEMBER 8

Dipping Into Peace

We get so caught up in worry, problem solving, doubts, and fears. We spin our wheels. Our brains churn and stir up information, expectations, and experiences in an attempt to make life better. We are exhausted. We do not get anything accomplished, and yet we feel as though we have run a marathon. Anxiety slowly destroys our serenity.

Thankfully, peace is always at hand. It is within the very fiber of our being. We can dip into this ever-present force of comfort and protection whenever we choose. We can silence the mind and let go of the problems we are trying to solve. We can surrender doubt, worry, and fear. We set our anxiety aside, in a place it cannot be touched, and rest in the depths of faith and trust. We enter the eternal realm and experience divine reprieve.

Let's dip into peace today. Pause and clear the mind. Listen to the chirping birds, the cackling squirrels, the soft breeze rustling through the trees. It is our privilege to enjoy life. Peace is a precious gift, and we can embrace it whenever we choose, wherever we are. Feel all the tension drain from your body. Let go. Imagine. Dream. Be inspired. Relax. Enjoy.

SEPTEMBER 9

Feelings/Joy

We need to experience our feelings to move forward. But, some of us repress emotion, especially the unpleasant. We mask sadness, shame, guilt, remorse, and anger. We hide under layers of superficial clamor. We act as if we do not feel the way we do. Feelings creep up, and we shut them off. We divert our attention elsewhere. We escape that which is happening within.

Yet, there comes a time when we must experience our feelings. They have built up long enough. It becomes increasingly difficult to ignore them. Our lives are now affected, and our hearts ache.

We need to pause and go back to the place where our hurt began. It takes courage, but we can remain there long enough to experience and sort through past emotion. We are preparing to release these feelings once and for all. It is time to let go.

The process of feeling past hurt is an important part of spiritual growth. We remain stagnant until we dare to experience certain life events, especially those that are tragic. It is not easy. In fact, it is one of the most difficult things we must do to live healthy, productive lives. And yet, once we are through this process, we are born to a new freedom and happiness. We are released from pain. We find true and lasting joy.

SEPTEMBER 10

Standing Still/Dealing

Some of us are runners. Trouble comes our way, and we want to head for the hills. It is hard to deal with problems. We dread conflict. We hate rejection and fear abandonment. The last thing we want is to lose any more. Unfortunately nothing is solved this way. Our lives become worse. We fall short of God's greatest desire for us.

Instead of running or hiding, we can learn to stand still and deal with the situations that we are faced with. We can surrender our fear of failure and communicate. We may need to tell someone we love how we feel. We may have to humbly ask God to help us along our journey. Perhaps it involves change. In any case, we can remain still until our work is done. We can continue dealing until we reach the other side of the problem.

The rewards will be spectacular! It is amazing to see our difficulties disappear. We resolve our problems so they will no longer hinder our path. We feel much better and so do the people around us. Even if we do not share our problems, our loved ones know they exist. It is time to deal with them.

SEPTEMBER 11

Gratitude

We can say we are grateful until we become grateful. It is as easy as that. It works like magic. We can rise up from the pit of despair by simply saying "out loud" all the things we have to be grateful for. We can include family, loved ones, friendships, the warmth of our home, reliable vehicles—all the things we are blessed with. We can start with the small things in life. These are often the most precious gifts we have.

Before we know it, our hearts change from frustration to peace. Our troubles disappear in the presence of our many gifts. We can count our blessings anywhere—at home, at work, in the car between activities. We can also count them anytime. When we get up from the wrong side of the bed and feel out of sorts, we can start verbalizing what we are grateful for even on the way to the coffeepot. If work isn't going very smoothly, we can take a short break and list the things we are grateful for. Perhaps we can take time in the evening while preparing dinner for the family. Gratitude always brings comfort to our spirit.

<hr>

SEPTEMBER 12

Belief/Inspiration

When we believe, we are inspired. When we really believe, great things happen in our lives. When we know in our hearts there is good in the universe and that we are an intricate part of unveiling this good, we embark on the beginning of the spiritual journey. When we decide to embrace destiny, we move even further along the path. We are created to contribute to the good in this world. It all begins with belief. We are created to believe.

When we fully believe in the power of God in the universe and open our hearts to feel this power at work in our own lives, we can be inspired to great levels. We become conduits through which amazing miracles flow. There is no limit to what God can do through us. It all begins with belief in God's goodness and love, belief in the potential of others, and belief in our own strengths.

Inspiration is God's magic. He graces us with thoughts and ideas at unexpected times, and yet his timing is perfect. His love and providence are incredible. When we believe in this, our future is boundless. We can do anything with God's help. His guidance is unfailing and wonderful. He designed a unique journey for us long ago, before the stars, before there was light. He loved us even then. How much stronger is his love for us when we choose to walk within this design! He will never let us down. When we follow Him, we cannot fail. We can simply believe!

<hr>

SEPTEMBER 13

Wounds/Healing

Psychological wounds run deep. They infect the crevices of our soul, stealing joy from our lives. We work hard to overcome them. Unfortunately, events occur that trigger old emotions. Some thought and behavioral patterns are so deeply ingrained that they will always be part of who we are. Our burdens resurface, and we discover our need for healing again.

Thank God, healing is of infinite proportions. God's grace has no limits. His love reaches down to fill our every need. It soothes every raw emotion. It runs far deeper than our wounds and stretches wider than the most difficult problem we could ever encounter. It is higher than the highest mountain we must climb. There is no place apart from God's love. It is boundless.

God will restore us time and time again. He carries us along the spiritual journey. He puts us in a position where we can reach out and help others with the lessons we have learned. Healing moves like ripples in a stream—the circles broaden until they eventually disappear in the smooth, calm water. We can help God calm the storm in others. We can move through their lives by listening and caring. We can offer kind words, share experiences, even reach out with a helping hand. We are all extensions of God's grace and kindness. We are the energy he uses to show the world a better way.

SEPTEMBER 14

Understanding/Compassion

It is not always easy to understand others, especially our loved ones. Sometimes the harder we try, the further away they seem. We long to know how they are feeling, and what is going on inside. We wish we knew why they behave one way or another. And yet, the thoughts and emotions of others are beyond our grasp. We do not know the source of their words or actions. Most importantly, we are not responsible for them. Life becomes a bit easier when we realize this.

Compassion helps us to understand others by giving us new eyes. We begin to see more clearly how our loved ones truly feel. Instead of becoming frustrated by their behavior or even lashing out in anger or retaliation, we are able to communicate in a way that strengthens friendship and peace. Our love grows. We encourage those around us, which enriches our path.

Compassion and understanding are key notes in the composition of love. They are the roots that support and nourish happy, harmonious relationships. We gain the wisdom and insight to view others the way God sees them. We focus on their positive attributes, as opposed to being critical of their negative ones. Our whole world becomes more beautiful. We strengthen the journey of our loved ones. We give them the gift of letting them be who they are.

SEPTEMBER 15

Assessment/Change

Assessment is a valuable tool along the road of personal discovery. It helps us gain introspection. We can look at our thoughts, behavior patterns, and actions to determine if we are living our "best life." When we don't take the time to stop and evaluate, the heart goes astray. We are fragile and easily swayed. We can lose sight of our purpose and direction. Love slips away.

Self-assessment opens the door to change. We do not always like who we see when we look in the mirror. We might see mistakes, poor choices, bad judgment calls, or even wasted opportunities. We may cringe, wishing we could run and hide, or at least take it all back. And yet, somewhere in the recesses of our soul, we know we can change. Each moment holds the possibility to begin anew. Life is filled with the gifts of rebirth.

Change is the backbone of emotional growth and wellness. Time and time again, it leads us to peace and happiness. No matter how impossible it may seem, we all have the ability to improve. Each one of us has the inner strength to turn away from negative behaviors and past mistakes to embrace a hopeful future. But, change takes courage. It is difficult to let go of characteristics that are ingrained in our personalities. The good news is, it is possible. With God, all things are possible. We can let go of fear and welcome this new beginning. It will be so good. We will see.

✦

SEPTEMBER 16

Alternatives/Serenity

Some of us are set in our ways. We have inflexible mental images of how things should be, how situations should turn out, or perhaps how those around us should behave. The problem with each of these thoughts is the word "should." Life is filled with surprises. That is what makes our journey so delightful. The only thing we can really expect is the unexpected.

We can become willing to accept alternatives when life does not unfold the way we plan. This heightens serenity. Black and white thinking strips us of peace of mind. When we restrict our vision to see only one way, we are setting ourselves up for disappointment and failure. When we welcome alternatives, it adds variety and spice to our lives. It helps us enjoy our many blessings.

Serenity makes the journey sweeter. It is the conduit of God's energy, manifested in and through us. Serenity brings us to a quiet state of mind and body, where questions leave and answers appear in their place. This is where we discover purpose and meaning. God guides us here. When we dare accept the unexpected, we reach this beautiful state of peace and usefulness. We are electrified to see that all we ever wanted is right here, right now. Need we ask for anything more?

SEPTEMBER 17

Caring/Joy

We involve ourselves in so many activities. It becomes impossible to dedicate our full attention and energy to any one. We skim the surface of life. We do not explore the reason for our actions. We lack depth. Perhaps we are avoiding something. Maybe we are avoiding ourselves.

Our lives begin to change when we learn to operate on a deeper level, engaging in activities because we truly care. We can slow down, look within our soul, and see what is truly important. We can eliminate the things that do not compliment our highest values. We can dedicate more time to enhancing our spiritual well being. This is easier as we become more comfortable with who we are. We learn to care for ourselves and others.

Caring is the taproot of life. It is wonderful when we love something or someone with all our heart, and act out of that love. We can fully attune our minds to the preciously small, and from there, grow into a fuller existence. We notice the fine details of the journey. We appreciate the way God embroiders the world with magnificent sights and sounds. We hear the charming melody of springtime robins. We listen to the crickets as they share an evening melody. We sit and enjoy the smiling giggles of our children. This leads us to a world filled with joy and peace.

SEPTEMBER 18

The Soul

There are many things we value: family, friends, homes, careers, financial stability, and our physical well being. Our attention often lies with the external. We seldom look within to discover the greatest gift of all—the soul. This is where our most precious blessings are held. It is here that we appreciate life on a deeper level. The soul enhances and enriches the journey. The soul contains our finest virtues. It is the truest part of our being. It is gentle, yet profound. It holds all we want to be. It connects us to God.

The soul is not always easy to find and so we must search it out. Not many of us are accustomed to connecting at such a deep level. But, we all have an inner eye. Through this delicate looking glass, we see who we really are. We see our true worth, which adds new meaning to everything around us. All of our relationships are enriched when we are living out of the depths of our being. We are living with God here.

When we find our soul, it is like entering the garden of paradise where our worries and troubles seep away. We embrace a peace that passes all understanding. We do not need to change anything. Everything is perfect here. The soul provides everything we long for. It satisfies us like only God can. It lifts us to a higher realm. It leads us to a beautiful tomorrow.

SEPTEMBER 19

Loyalty/Moving On

Women have such fine qualities! We are loyal. We have spent our lives dedicated to worthy causes like raising families, maintaining successful careers, building relationships, and to community affairs. It is somewhat odd to imagine that some of our purposes in life are now behind us. We may continue doing some things purely out of habit. Are we ready to move on?

There is a time and place for everything in life. There is a season for each endeavor. Loyalty is a virtue that requires balance. There comes a time when hanging on to past obligations can deplete the journey. It can inhibit us from experiencing the gifts of moving forward. Sometimes the very thing we hold onto is the obstacle holding us back. A careful search within will show us the answers. We will find our way to the future.

We can pray for the courage to change the things we can in life. We can develop the willingness to explore unfamiliar avenues. We catch a glimpse of destiny. This is the beginning of a lifelong journey of finding, day by day, the many blessings God places along our path. As we let go and move forward, our goals intensify. We encounter our purpose and pursue it with great vigor. We are no longer held back, not even by loyalty to the past. It is a new day. We will greet it with confidence. We will embrace its beautiful horizon. We will meet God here.

SEPTEMBER 20

Shame/Grace

Some of us cannot move beyond regret. We die beneath the burden of shame. We are unable to see past the choices we have made and the things we have done wrong. We wish we could change the past, but we cannot. It is millions of heartbeats away. It is time to let go. The present is here, and its gifts are about to unfold before our eyes.

The hand of grace extends to cover us all, no matter what we have done in the past. There is nowhere we can go where grace is not abundant. It is the constant miracle that frees us from shame. It erases all transgressions. It heals the worst sin. No burden is beyond its reach. It is the hope of each and every one of us. It is the love in all things. It is the essence of pure beauty.

We can choose grace today, just like we once chose to hold onto the past. We can allow God's love to work within us, releasing guilt and shame, and preparing us to make better decisions in the future. God extends his mercy to comfort us, no matter our circumstances. He sheds his light into a world of darkness, reaching to illuminate the dark.

SEPTEMBER 21

Confusion/Patience

Life can be so confusing. Where should we go next? What should we do? Are we on the right track? There are times when we are overwhelmed with confusion. Perhaps we are faced with a huge decision and are not sure which way to go next. There may be many paths or opportunities before us. We flounder. We dare not move, or maybe we move too fast. Unfortunately, nothing of true value can be accomplished in the midst of confusion. But we can pause and wait for clear direction.

We can seek patience. Patience helps us remain calm and still as confusion dissipates. There is no need to act right away. We do not have to choose one path or another right now. Opportunities will remain.

Surrender the sense of urgency. There is no need to panic. Life happens in perfect time. We will eventually arrive at our final destination. We cannot rush the process, no matter how hard we try. It is time to let go.

Patience leads to answers. It creates a clearer picture where we escape confusion and madness. We find a guiding force that leads us to the next step, and the next, and the next. We discover an order for living that makes better sense. This is not hard. We do not have to force our way through.

SEPTEMBER 22

Guilt/Powerlessness

Some of us feel guilty about everything. We take on responsibility for the actions of others. No matter who is really at fault, somehow it must be our fault. Sound familiar? This is the negative, broken record we play in our mind. It is the rhythm of our past that brings us down repeatedly. The time has come for us to change our patterns of thinking. We are not responsible for everything that happens to, and around us. We are actually powerless.

Our journeys are renewed when we truly accept the idea that we are powerless over other people, events in life, and the situations we face. We are freed from the bondage of guilt and shame. These are the chains of our past. They are the remnants of our broken homes and families. Many of us grew up trying to make sense of chaos. We tried to justify the perverse. We had no real control then, and we cannot control others now, either. The only thing we can truly influence is our own personality. We can affect our own reactions to what happens around us. But we cannot change our environment. When we admit our powerlessness, we embrace freedom.

We can let go and let the river of life take us peacefully down the stream. We can surrender our illusion of power and control. We can loosen our tight grip, open our hands, and become willing to let God give us his many gifts. This is the way of peace and happiness. It is the cornerstone for a new way of life.

SEPTEMBER 23

Assertiveness/Wellness

Some of us have spent years being taken advantage of. We would rather not say anything than risk rocking the boat. We like our waters calm and comfortable. We fear the storm. But sometimes we must brave the storm to reach our destination. There are times to stand up for our families, friends, and especially ourselves. We must uphold our beliefs and values. If we don't, no one will.

Assertiveness generates a positive flow of energy through our lives and into the lives of others. We do not have to feel bad for expressing ourselves. Some of us are too passive. We have learned to avoid conflict and preserve peace, no matter the cost. But what if the cost is too high? Are we losing our emotional, physical, and spiritual health? If the answer is yes, we must stand up. It is time to draw the line. We can learn to care for ourselves.

This requires courage. We overcome our fears by facing them. We learn to be assertive through practice. It does not come naturally, and that's okay. The more we stand for what we believe, the easier it becomes. We gain self-respect. We have no idea how good our lives will be. We can believe in our future! New energy will blossom to help us achieve goals we only dreamed could be. It will happen. We will see.

SEPTEMBER 24

Words/Encouragement

The gift of speech is powerful. We can use our words to encourage or discourage others. There is little room in between. What we say has a positive or negative impact. We can learn to be silent if the outcome of what we say will hurt someone. We can pause and formulate the words to make a situation better, and not worse. We can speak with care.

It is difficult to hold silence, especially when we are angry. We become defensive. After all, we are not to blame! And yet it is sure that our words will be more effective when delivered with kindness and patience. This will go further toward solving our problems. It leads to restitution and healing.

Like anything, this requires balance. Choosing our words well does not mean we should let others abuse us. This has its own dangerous array of consequences. But even the best relationships are not immune from conflict. This is part of human nature. We can reduce tension in our relationships by not participating in the battle. Instead of rebelling, we can offer love and support. Love is a healer and friend. It is the giver of happiness. It is the foundation of hope.

SEPTEMBER 25

Hope/Believe

How often we settle for less. We have hopes and dreams, but we bury them so deep that even we cannot find them. We continue doing what we are doing, working where we are working, going where we are going. We are trapped in routine. It is familiar. We develop a false comfort. We live in illusion. We are afraid to change. What would happen if we did?

There comes a time along the journey when our hearts scream for more. We may not feel it right away, but it is there. A small inner voice, the most precious part of who we are, begins to speak. We listen, but sometimes we shut it off, in fear.

Instead, we can pray to be open to our inner voice. We can dare to hope again. We can find the dreams we left in the dust of yesterday and believe that they can come true. We are headed for the best that life has to offer. Our inner voice is God speaking to us. He cares beyond human conception. He will give us the very best if we will only listen and follow. This is a fact of life. It is the foundation of human destiny.

So let's hope for the best and believe it can be ours. No matter what mistakes we have made in the past, and despite our many poor decisions, God has a plan for us. The time has come for us to search it out and to embrace the many treasures we will find along the way. We will not be sorry. God will not let us down. We can trust and believe.

SEPTEMBER 26

Forgiveness/Healing

The wounds of pain run deep. When people harm us, we become resentful and defensive. It is not easy to forgive. It is usually the last thing on our minds or in our hearts. We build and maintain thick walls to protect us against future disappointment. If only we knew how much better we would feel if we let forgiveness enter our heart. It opens the door to healing. It frees us to experience spiritual delight.

The world is filled with wrongs. It reeks of retaliation. But we can live above fighting and hatred. We can reach toward love and treat others with compassion—even those who have caused us pain. This is the way of heaven. It is the will of God.

When we replace hate with love, we are not only healing ourselves, we are healing the world. We are offering others a bit of the grace that we have been so freely given. Our lives become beautiful journeys as we travel in peace. Resentment no longer weighs heavy on our spirits. We will lose the chains that bind our hearts and spirits. We exit the darkness and embrace the light of a new day.

SEPTEMBER 27

Catastrophes/Acceptance

How we despise catastrophes! If only they did not occur. We look back. We rethink our actions and wish we could reverse time. We want to change what happened, but we cannot. The only thing to do is accept what is and move forward. This is the beginning of dealing with reality. It is necessary so that we may heal and grow.

Acceptance is the key to many problems. We can embrace the powerful truth that everything happens in God's world for a reason. What seems like a catastrophe might be an intricate part of a miracle. We do not always see the eternal picture. We do not see how all things are sewn together perfectly in heaven to form a radiant tapestry. Our journeys are created with love and care. The tragedies we experience become some of the richest, most brilliant threads in the tapestry.

When we accept tragedy as part of the growing process, we are made anew. When we welcome hard times as tests that are being used to mold and shape us, we bloom as individuals. Some of the hardest challenges we face become our greatest blessings in time. We can trust this process. It is the process of discipline and God loves us so much. He teaches those he loves. Each lesson makes us stronger, and together, they help us become all we are meant to be. We become happy. We rest in the security that we are children of God.

<hr>

SEPTEMBER 28

Messages/Lessons

Life is filled with messages. They are tucked in the nooks and crannies of our days. Small things happen to help us see the way of our future. They are much more than coincidences or accidents. So small they might go by unnoticed, they are still present. We do not always fit them together in our minds, nor do we realize they may have a greater purpose. They are tiny miracles, unfolding the work of something far greater and revealing our path.

God speaks through each and every situation we face, especially the small things. He arranges the events around us to mold and shape our personalities and characters. The more aware we are of his messages, the more effective they become. We learn more about our purpose in life, as well as our own strengths and limitations. We discover who we are created to be, and we grow to fulfill our God-given purpose for our future.

We are all called to fulfill a higher purpose. God will provide exactly what is needed for us to reach his goals. When we remain attuned to the lessons he teaches us, it broadens our channel of understanding. We see success that we only dreamed could be possible. We step out of God's way. We join him in his will for our lives. This is the road to true happiness. God's love washes over us like a peaceful bath. There is no strife and little pain. We are on the path that leads to hope.

SEPTEMBER 29

Change/Willingness

We are not easily moved. We have grown accustomed to our lives the way they are, and the thought of change is disturbing. We refuse to envision the future any other way. We cleave to the past. We fear anything other than that which we are used to. We are unwilling to move beyond our preconceived notions. There must be a better way!

Instead of remaining inflexible, we can develop a willingness to change. Life is ever unfolding. Nothing stays the same for any length of time, including us. As we grow, our needs change. What used to work may not work any longer. Old habits can be exchanged for new tools of living. It is the only way to continue growing along the spiritual journey.

Willingness brings about inner freedom. The chains that have prevented us from adapting and maturing no longer hold us down. We accept that there are better ways to move into the future, even though they are different. We release the past. We can take our experience and apply it in creative ways. Everything we have gone through—all the suffering and the joy—fit together to make us who we are today. We can let go and trust God to guide us into the future. We find hope here.

SEPTEMBER 30

Knowledge/Confidence

The time has come for us to bravely know what we know. Some of us have spent many years questioning our opinions and ideas. When others say we are wrong, we believe them without hesitation. But what if they are wrong, and we are right? Would we ever know it? Consider for a minute that our thoughts and actions are not only right, they are beautiful expressions for others to enjoy. And, we are valuable. We are fearlessly and wondrously made to bring love into the world. We are God's hands.

It takes confidence to know what we know. If we are to quit second-guessing our judgment, we must develop faith in ourselves. We can rediscover our deepest feelings and truest values. When we base our actions and decisions on these, we cannot go wrong. We can show others what we are all about. We can live out our destiny.

Knowledge yields nothing without confidence. It remains dormant, unexpressed. When we reveal what is in our hearts so that others can see, we add beauty to life. We bring others to God.

OCTOBER 1

Trust/Decisions

Trust does not come easy for some of us, especially when we have been hurt in the past. We may have loved ones that we can rely on, but we do not know where to begin when it comes to trust. It is a frightening thought. If we trust, we may lose control and then what? Our world may fall apart!

And yet, trust begins with a simple decision. If we are in a caring and safe environment and the only thing getting in the way is our own self-will, then perhaps it is time to make this choice. Nothing will change unless we let go of fear and insecurity. We can lower our guard and let the ones we love in. We can lean on others. We are created to depend upon each other.

Making a decision to trust requires courage. We are forced to rely on someone other than ourselves. We surrender independence. This is easier if we adapt an attitude of humility. We begin to see that life is not as difficult when we let our walls down. Our paths are much easier when we let others help. We accept and appreciate God's grace.

Today, let's make the decision to let our loved ones in. It is time to trust. We can let them care for us, nurture us, love us, and hold us as long as we need to be held. It has been so long. It has been so hard. The tide has changed. It now rushes across the hope of a beautiful, new horizon. Our lives are beginning. We are finding freedom.

OCTOBER 2

Evolution/Growth

Everything evolves. The universe has been changing since before the beginning of time. We develop as well. Life is a series of experiences and learning; and through our many lessons and seasons in life, we transform. We change. We achieve higher levels of existence and understanding. We move closer to love and our Creator.

We grow as we evolve. We acquire a deeper connection with our soul, and we long to journey closer to its presence. We gain the ability to assert our thoughts, ideas, and values in the world. We see that we can impact the lives of others. We receive the power to heal, and within our source, we can help usher in a new dawn. We can embrace eternity.

Transformation is a movement that forever lifts our spirits. When we live the spiritual life, we reach higher and higher ground. We eventually become who God ultimately wants us to be. We find joy and happiness.

This process takes time. We can learn to be patient. Each stage of transformation is necessary. We are being prepared to live within the journey of God's heart, one he prepared for us long ago. This is the path that will lead us to our ultimate hope. It will satisfy our every need. It is our destiny.

OCTOBER 3

Selfishness/Self-Love

Some of us confuse self-love with selfishness. We are unsure whether we should take the time to care for ourselves. We do not regard our spiritual, emotional, or physical needs with much importance. There are so many other things on our agendas. We do not realize that we count, too!

As we grow along the journey, we learn we must love ourselves. This is not selfish, but it is necessary to our spiritual well being. If we do not take care of our inner needs, we cannot be of true value to anyone or anything else. We are ill-equipped to deal with all the other items on our agenda. We are unable to reach out. We miss out on the best part of life. We miss out on love.

Love begins within. It grows when we care for ourselves and the needs of those around us. It is the most unselfish expression in the universe. We can dare to embrace it. We can find the courage to let it blossom within us. We can befriend this delicate emotion.

Self-love leads to positive change. We find new energy that can be shared with others. People will want to be near us. They will feel love's energy radiating around us. It is magnetic. Caring for our inner needs creates the magic that makes this happen. It opens the door to experiencing the beauty of rich and meaningful relationships. We are enriched.

<hr />

OCTOBER 4

Surrender/Joy

How long and hard we have worked to see our dreams come true! How often we have hoped that today might be the day. How many times we have prayed for the right break or the missing piece of the puzzle. If only we knew that surrender is the key to turning our lives around and leads to joy and satisfaction.

We live in a world where surrender and defeat are synonymous terms. The thought of giving up on anything seems premature and weak. Little do we realize that surrender paves the way for great strength to wash over and fill us. It places us on the path to a new and better way. It holds us near God.

When we turn the details of our lives over to our Creator, we make room for miracles. God knows what is best for us. His omniscience unfolds time and space together in perfect rhythm. His love raptures the universe, and we can be part of this eternal flow.

Surrender is the beginning of experiencing true and lasting joy. It enables us to make a difference in this world. We give our strengths and weaknesses to God so that he can use us for a greater purpose. This is what hope is all about. It is the way of heaven.

<hr />

OCTOBER 5

Frustration/Boundaries

We sometimes feel helpless. We know deep down what is right, but we struggle to express ourselves. We are not familiar with boundaries. We have always tried hard to avoid tension. We fear conflict because it leads to frustration. It brings our spirit down and inhibits spiritual well being.

Boundaries are the answer to many of our troubles. We can develop guidelines to help us preserve our strength and values. We can have the courage to enforce our boundaries in our relationships. There are many people who will challenge truth and question our knowledge. We need not be ashamed, or even diplomatic. We know that we stand in God's grace and wisdom. We cannot be hurt there. We stand protected.

Sometimes attack makes us foggy. Those who are causing us hardship will try to convince us that they are really not doing anything wrong. Boundaries help us break through the cloud of confusion. They reinforce the truth we know. They help us implement solutions. They show others we value ourselves including our serenity, needs, values, time, space, and freedom. We especially value our relationship with God. It is our lifeline.

OCTOBER 6

Presence/Divinity

We can learn to be still and feel the awesome presence of divinity. We can listen to silence and serenity. It is tempting to do other things. We might be frightened by calmness. Rest assured, we are safe in solitude. It is the key that opens the door to freedom.

We waste precious moments chasing around, trying to conquer the hours that are already our own. Our lives belong to us. It is time we realize our significance and purpose. We are created in the divine image. Our souls are in the process of travelling back to heaven. This is the journey of life. Deep down, we want nothing more than to fulfill our destiny. We long to be in the presence of God.

Divinity graces the heart that is pure. It gifts the trustworthy and diligent. It rejoices in good and despises evil. When we seek the divine, we enter God's presence. We are given new eyes with which we can view the world in a different light. Sadness becomes joy, discouragement encouragement, and fear is cast into an endless sea of faith. Regrets disappear and hope surfaces to become our only reality. Divinity is love. It is God's expression here on earth.

OCTOBER 7

Love/Understanding

Love does not come easily sometimes. There are times in life when we strain to love. Not everyone is lovable, and yet we know it is our highest calling. We want to honor it. We long to embrace it. Our soul cries out to feel it. Could there be some sort of magic remedy to help us love more fully? Is there any way it can come more naturally? After all, love is free.

Understanding is the magic that helps love flourish. When we take the time to understand the position of others and to see things from their perspective, we draw nearer to love. We see the situation from their eyes, which can bring restitution. We can let go of how we think things should be and open our hearts and minds to how they are. Our relationships are so important. They bring us closer to God and others.

Understanding builds bridges on the road to a brighter tomorrow. It enhances our experience and enriches the journey. It can help us befriend strangers, make peace with enemies, and bring healing to the broken-hearted. It equips us to reach above insecure and selfish motives. We enter a higher realm, one where we can dance in the beauty of all we are created to be. We become all God wants us to be here. We are strengthened to live out our destiny.

❦

OCTOBER 8

Accidents/God's Will

Accidents are not always bad. Sometimes what happens unexpectedly can turn into the best thing that could ever be. We can learn to be patient and see what God has planned. We can remain open to his will.

Some of us meticulously organize every little detail. We take pains to lay everything out—our schedules, the day ahead, even our future. Then, we experience a change or disruption that comes out of nowhere, and we are thrown off base. We panic. We scramble to get back on track. After all, this does not fit our idea of how things are supposed to be!

But many times what seems like an accident is really part of God's will for us. Life is filled with divine interventions—unexpected occurrences leading us along the course of destiny. Without them, we would miss the many miracles that God has in store for our future. We might not like what is happening at the time, but we can be patient and accept that everything is part of God's will, especially the surprises. We may not understand, and yet we can trust that God is caring for us in a way that is enduring and sustaining. He does this in ways we do not expect. This is the magic of his grace. It affirms his mighty love.

❦

OCTOBER 9

Isolation/Reaching Out

Isolation is deadly. It suffocates the spirit. Some of us feel unworthy. We hide our faces from God's heavenly light. We think we are less than. Maybe it's because of the things we have done in our past. Perhaps those we love have hurt us deeply. We withdraw, little by little, and sink into the illusion that nothing matters, nothing will ever work out. We lose heart. We lose life.

It is during these times of severe depression that it is imperative to reach out. We are all worthy, no matter what we have done or experienced. Nothing removes us from God's love. There is no situation that is truly hopeless. All we need to do is open the door, if only a little. If we can only tell one other person our hurts, fears, and shame. They will listen. We will be amazed.

When we dare to reach out and share our pain, our burdens are lifted. The weight of the world is removed from our shoulders. We are free to heal and hope again. Darkness is transformed into light. We develop the courage to face it. We know that we deserve the best, and this will not come about without friendship and fellowship. God has given us many people to lean on. We are reborn in our new relationships. We can dance again!

OCTOBER 10

Action/Motives

Women do so much! We balance homes, careers, budgets, and raise families. Our lives are not lacking in action. The question is "Are our actions lacking?" We need to look closely at everything we do. What are our motives? Are they pure? Are we sincere? Are our hearts in the right place? And, is love involved? This is the driving force of a rich and meaningful journey.

We are defined by our motives. They show others who we are. They direct our actions and our future. When we are humble, kind, patient, and understanding, we become mirrors of eternity. We radiate God's love. We reflect his heart. People are drawn to our presence. They catch a glimpse of the Creator.

Purifying our motives and introspectively evaluating the reasons behind our actions enriches our lives. We can gauge our activities and prioritize our concerns. We might discover that some of the things we are doing are for the wrong reasons. We may find some things are more important than we thought. In any case, we can honestly decide which commitments are healthy, soul-building endeavors. We can become willing to let go of those that are not.

We gain freedom in this way. We will feel a new and vibrant energy flow through our spirit. This produces ecstatic joy. It releases the explosion of love within our hearts. It rockets us into a new dimension, one where sadness disappears and happiness reigns. We enter the gates of peace.

OCTOBER 11

Forgiveness/Freedom

Resentment binds the heart. It plagues us with discontent and despair. It hurts. But how freeing it is to become willing to forgive those who have caused us harm! We can find kindness for those who do not seemingly deserve it. This is the beauty of forgiveness. It opens our hearts to experience love, peace, and happiness. It is the road map to abundant living.

Freedom is the foundation of spiritual living. We cannot truly enjoy life when we are held down by the bondage of hate. We can let go of grudges. This cultivates our personalities with the rich fibers of a good nature. It liberates our spirit. We are filled with the confidence and energy that we need to lead successful lives. We develop lasting, nourishing relationships.

Forgiving our friends and enemies opens the door for freedom to flow. We spend less time fixating on the bad, and we plant our perspective in the good. We are blessed with so many gifts, including the ability to forgive those who have wounded us deeply. We shine in the love of God when we let go of our resentment and frustration. Our actions are a piece of God's great heart. He loves all of creation incessantly. We are conduits of his infinite grace and mercy. It is ours. Pass it on!

OCTOBER 12

Troubles/Helping Others

Sometimes our troubles seem so large. We may be faced with circumstances that seem irreparable. The longer we focus our attention on the magnitude of our misfortune, the more hideous it becomes. We are consumed by our problems. We are trapped in despair.

It is refreshing to consider there are problems beyond our own. We do not need to look far to find someone else in greater need. We are indeed blessed in many ways. Trials and loss can help us find the wisdom we need to move forward again. We can trust God to care for us and turn our attention to the needs of others. As we reach out, we discover that our lives can be restored.

God's grace is truly amazing, and his love assures that all is well when we trust in him. We are not promised a life without trial, but we know God will walk with us through every dark valley. Life is enriched when we share our experience with others. Instead of wondering if God will see us through, we can help another find God in the midst of their pain. We can offer comfort and support. In turn, we find the answer to all our problems. We discover faith.

OCTOBER 13

Self-Esteem/Hope

One of the finest qualities we can develop in life is self-esteem. Self-esteem begins with affirming that we are lovable. It grows when we strengthen our connection to God and his love for us. It flourishes when we begin to see ourselves as God sees us. We are all his precious children, born with an incredible and unique destiny that only we can fulfill.

Self-esteem helps us discover our many gifts and abilities. It also helps us choose relationships that enhance our spiritual being. Friendships can be channels of hope. Like all of creation, people radiate energy. It can be positive or negative. Our environment affects our attitudes. When we value ourselves, we chose to build our future around those who vibrate with truth and kindness. This is the way we grow.

Life hands us many questions and challenges. At times, situations become hazy and the lines seem unclear. We may lose conviction and become discouraged. Rejuvenating our self-esteem can be the key to regaining clarity. When we restore our vision to see all we are in God's eyes, we regain perspective. We see promises in each moment. We are renewed in hope.

OCTOBER 14

Self-Confidence/Growth

Self-confidence is a window of inner peace. It lets us be who we are, no matter what our circumstances. We can stand our ground in the midst of conflict. It creates a path for self-definition. We dare to express our gifts, ideas, and abilities. We display our values and live out our destiny. This fills our hearts and lives with serenity and peace.

When we are confident, we learn to set boundaries. Boundaries help us live within our destiny. They represent our character, morals, and purpose. They prevent us from being used or abused. They also inhibit diversion, which is a primary cause of failure. They protect us from physical and emotional harm and help us achieve our goals.

We can be patient with ourselves as we develop and mature along life's paths. Peace and confidence will grow if we continue to work toward our spiritual goals. Each step we take, however small, adds beauty and detail to our creation. We are becoming. Self-confidence refines this process. It adds fiber to our existence. It helps us follow God's will.

❦

OCTOBER 15

Relationships/Values

Friendships enhance the journey. They bring out the best of who we are. But we must be careful. We cannot compromise our values in a relationship, even if it is dear to us.

We are all born with values. They are the foundation of our psyche. They develop as we grow, emotionally and spiritually. Our values complete us. They show others who we are and what we believe. They highlight our personality. It hurts deeply when we compromise them.

We can sense when relationships begin to cost too much. Perhaps we hear the inner voice that protects us from harm. We might feel the nudge of wisdom pressing against our heart. We can listen and remain attuned to our inner landscape. So many times it is too late when we realize we have been hurt deeply.

We possess the inner strength to end sorrow before it begins. We can spare those we love, and ourselves, the pain caused by poor relationship choices. We are free to engage in meaningful, healthy relationships. We can choose friends and even partners who have values and characteristics similar to our own. We can support each other and share love and guidance. Hand in hand, we can face the world together, without resistance, and with little commotion and turmoil. This path is easy. It is the way of love. It leads to a brighter future.

Problems/Solutions

Problems exist to be solved. Unfortunately, we become paralyzed. We let our problems get the best of us. "How terrible!" we think. "Why is this happening to me?" "Why now?" "Life is so unfair." We fall into the victim trap. From there, we are unable to see solutions. We are defeated.

But the good news is that there is a solution for every problem. Sometimes the answers are quick. Other times, we need to be patient as solutions unfold in their own time. There are some problems which we are meant to solve and others that we need to turn over to God. There is no problem in the universe above his power. We can learn to trust God for the solutions that we cannot find on our own.

So many times problems work out for our good, anyway. What we fear will destroy us might make us stronger or even point us in a new direction. We may discover a path we would not have chosen any other way. We may be pushed into trying something we have always wanted to try. If it were up to us, we would have stayed in the comfort zone and missed the delightful beauty along our newfound trail. Problems nudge us to change direction and discover better ways.

Solutions will always come if we remain positive. And problems are inevitable. They will continue to occur. Thankfully, we are learning to overcome them more quickly. Instead of freezing in self-pity, we can maneuver through life with grace and ease. We conquer each hurdle with confidence and faith. We believe in our abilities. Troubles do not bring us down. They only make us stronger!

Healing/Energy

Healing is an ever-present source of energy. It surrounds each and every moment we live. It protects us. We can tap into the depths of healing whenever we choose. We can let this energy flow through us. We can open our hearts to grace and peace. This helps us become one with God and others.

Some of us might fear that our burdens are too great. We've gone too far. Our time is past, and so we give up hope. We think healing is for others. We are not good enough. And yet light shines most brilliantly in the darkest of corridors. The deeper our wounds, the further we can rise again someday. Healing is for all of us. We can believe in this infinite source of energy. It does not discriminate. It embraces each and every one. We can turn our faces into the light.

We will feel our burdens lifted one by one. Our lives are illumined by the golden sun of a new day. We will feel the cool, soft rain, smell the flowers that perfume the air, and hear the soothing sounds of nature. Life is reborn. Our journeys come alive. We are no longer hurt.

Healing is one of God's great wonders. It is an endless gift. Its energy runs freely through the universe. It surrounds us. It holds us. It is within us. It is time to accept it and let it be. It will move us toward a brighter tomorrow. It will lead us home.

OCTOBER 18

Blessings/Acceptance

The journey is filled with many hardships and blessings. Some of us learn to expect hardship. We focus on our troubles until they become all that we see. Our vision is restricted. It is as if someone has placed a telescope before us, and each time we look through the lens, we see worry and sorrow. The lens becomes our future. We cannot see beyond the scope.

And yet our lives are filled with just as many blessings, if not more. Unfortunately, we miss them. We are afraid to accept that the very best can yet be. We are accustomed to heartache.

Acceptance can turn our journey around. It is the key that opens the door to happiness. When we broaden our vision to recognize the many blessings around us, we realize that God is taking care of us. He does for us what we cannot do for ourselves. He provides the way. He is guiding us, slowly but surely, into a miraculous future.

Some of us might say, "Wait a minute. I don't deserve this." "I have sunk too low for good things to happen now!"

Rest assured, God's gifts are for everyone. They shine on the darkest parts of creation. His destiny was completed long ago, and through an undying love, our journeys were born. We can now accept the abundance that God sprinkles upon our lives. It is ours to hold. It is ours to embrace. We can build our lives upon it.

OCTOBER 19

Releasing the Mind to Heaven

We get so preoccupied. Our minds become cluttered and confused. We are filled with negative emotion—worry, remorse, doubt, and fear. It runs through our veins like poison and clouds our vision. We can wind up completely consumed in negative thinking if we are not careful. Hope begins to fade. Our outlook darkens.

Thankfully, we can be healed. All it takes is a little faith and the willingness to open the door. We can make a conscious effort to close our minds to anxiety and fear, and open our hearts to all the gifts that lie before us. We can be still and listen. They are all around. They are within. We can hear the faint rustle of the leaves, the tender sound of crickets, or the soft laughter of a friend or loved one. These are the greatest gifts of all. When we close the door to frantic thought patterns and begin enjoying the treasures around us, we heal. We are releasing our minds to heaven.

This is where the magic begins. God can change our complete psyche if we will only let him. It does not happen overnight. It requires practice. And yet, the more often we release our minds to heaven, the easier it is to turn things over. We can let go of all our worries and fear. Doubt is turned into a faith that endures. We develop a stronger personality and character—one that will outlast the fickle changes in life. We find peace here. We discover sweet release.

I will pause today if I am worried or fearful. I will clear my mind and rest until I can feel and hear and taste and smell God's wonderful world. I will release my mind to heaven.

OCTOBER 20

Sacrifice /Sin

Some of us feel hopeless. We have sunk so low. There seems to be no way for us to be redeemed. We cannot fathom our healing or change. We are unable to forgive ourselves, let alone believe there is anyone in the universe that will forgive us. We give in to despair.

And yet we can lift our minds to discover that special place where sacrifice meets sin. Nothing is truly hopeless. This includes our lives and the challenges we face. The very God of the universe sacrificed his life long ago so that no situation would be without hope. Nothing is beyond repair. We find hope and healing in this great fact.

We can learn to embrace forgiveness and integrate God's grace and mercy within our daily lives. This is the way toward freedom and happiness. Our deepest, darkest sins are not even remembered by the creator of the universe. We can all journey with confidence and faith. Nothing can cut us off from our spiritual source except our own doubt and despondency. We cannot let this happen. We are created to live fruitful lives. We need to find that special place where sacrifice meets sin and rest there.

OCTOBER 21

Gratitude in the Present

Gratitude is found in the present. It is not in the past or the future. We find God in the moment. Many of us are busy searching. We are looking for ways to make our lives better. We focus on our past, trying to uncover where we went wrong. We think that if we can learn from our mistakes, perhaps we can make the future better. Or our thoughts plunge toward what lies ahead. We are wrapped up in what we can do tomorrow.

Unfortunately, we are missing today, where we discover and experience the gifts of the journey. It is in the present where we find true peace and happiness. When we relax our minds in the moment at hand, gratitude pours in. It is like fresh water rushing into an empty well.

The manic efforts to make our lives better dry us out. Let's suppose for a minute that everything is fine just as it is. There is no need to panic; no need for strife. We are where we are supposed to be. Our lives are working themselves out. We can sit in silence and count our many blessings.

Gratitude rejuvenates the soul. It lifts us to a higher realm of living where the journey becomes lighter. Our paths are illumined with hope and happiness. We are set free.

OCTOBER 22

Priorities/Spirituality

Life is so busy! We rush from here to there. We juggle children, appointments, goals, commitments, obligations, and numerous schedules. We have struggled for so long. We do not know any other way. We lose ourselves in the shuffle. We have lost balance.

Establishing priorities is a way to regain balance and lead healthier, happier lives. We can search our souls to discover just what means the most to us in life—children, family, relationships, friendships. We can consider how much time we have dedicated to the very things that are the foremost in our hearts. We may discover that we need to restructure our days. Change may be upon us. We cannot forget our families and friends, and we shouldn't forget ourselves either.

Prioritizing our time enriches our spiritual lives. We are letting love in. The journey is not complete without the light of love. The smiles of our children, the touch of a loved one, the hug of a friend—these are all things that we need to help us along life's path. They lead us closer to becoming who we need to be. They bring us closer to the spirit of God.

OCTOBER 23

Solitude/Awareness

Solitude is a priceless gift. It reaches down to a secret place within. It brings us to a spiritual level where nothing else can reach. We are filled with peace here. It is during the tender times when we are alone—with no pressures or distractions—that we experience the depths of our inner being. We become aware of God and all the power he contains. We feel all that is within us. We gain inner strength and clarity. Rays of hope illumine our hearts and minds. We encounter God's unseen treasures.

Solitude prepares the heart to journey in love and peace. We enter a plane of infinite energy. We are renewed in stillness and silence. We can shut off thoughts of fear and frustration, doubt and discouragement. We cultivate healthier emotions, virtues like patience and trust. All things happen for good in our lives. We can believe in this process. We gain faith in ourselves. We are being led surely and steadily along the course of destiny. We are almost there, and at the same time, we are still so far away. We can accept this. God's timing is perfect.

We are born to a new awareness when we embrace the gifts of solitude. Feelings of rest and replenishment flow through our veins. We are recreated. We are changed. Instead of worrying or obsessing over things we cannot predict or control, we give our lives to heaven. We place our future in the hands of divinity. We don't look back, only ahead. We find a new life here. We discover a peace that passes all understanding. We have found a piece of heaven on earth. We are finally one with God.

OCTOBER 24

Thoughts Create Our Future.

So many times our minds are filled with fear and regret. "If only I had_____" or "I should have_____." We can fill these blanks with many things: missed opportunities, poor choices, bad decisions, and broken relationships. Negative thoughts are lethal. They are poisonous to our spirits. We cannot change the past. It is what it is. We can accept reality and move on.

This frees the mind to entertain the light of a new way of thinking. It is on the horizon. Instead of muddling in shame and remorse, we can embrace the great truth that each one of us is given an infinite number of chances to succeed. There is no limit to what God can do through us. His love knows no bounds. We possess a power that is beyond understanding. We can lift our minds to heaven in praise.

Our thoughts create our future. As we focus on God's love and all he has in store for us, we see a brighter tomorrow. We can trust the flow of life. We take new steps that lead to better places. We learn to make different choices: decisions that support who we really are. We recognize opportunities when they come our way and seize the moments that mean the most. We will even see relationships renewed.

The power of thought is phenomenal. It can change lives. We can all tap into this source of new energy and strength. Our spirits will be rejuvenated, our lives restored. We will be healed.

OCTOBER 25

Second-Guessing

Some of us are held back by second-guessing. We are so insecure. We lack a deep sense of inner faith. We do not realize that we are worthy, intelligent women, created to succeed, born to make a difference in this world. Second-guessing slows us down. It prevents progress. It interferes with the natural process of intuition. God speaks through our conscience to guide and protect us.

When we give up second-guessing, we gain new strength and energy. The time spent thinking and considering whether or not we have made the right move or correct decision can be redirected toward the many more choices and opportunities that lie before us. Life moves at a fast pace.

Although there are brief periods of calm between the storms, life is forever challenging us to grow and develop. This is especially true when we are living the spiritual journey. We can turn all the energy that we have wasted, trying to decide if we have chosen the correct path or made the right turns, into solidly and securely completing what is in front of us. Everything will work out in the end. We will see.

And God is directing our journey. When we turn our lives over to his care and protection, we can believe without doubt that he will see us through all the challenges we face. He will carry us through the worst of storms. He will be our shelter, the lasting calm, our safety. No matter what, God is here for us. If we go the wrong way, he will bring us back. We can count on this. He will never let us go too far. We are his sheep. We can rest in his green pasture of peace.

OCTOBER 26

Obsession/Freedom

It is easy to be obsessed with worry. We let our troubles become so big. They swell in our minds until we are confused and filled with fear. We are trapped. We spiral down the wrong path. Frustration and panic lead us into making the wrong choices. We make decisions in haste, almost out of sure desperation. We are in the danger zone. We must break free.

Thankfully, there is a way out. There is a power greater than the negative emotions we are experiencing. There is a trusted leader of the universe who will show us the way to freedom if we will lift up our hearts and ask. We can let go. We can give our troubles and concerns to God. We are cared for perfectly in this way. We will begin to see the dawn of a new way of living and coping. We will feel the tender caress of freedom.

How we have longed for the day when we can release all fear and worry. Our spirits have craved rest, relaxation, trust, and love. When we lift our hearts and minds to heaven, the door is opened. Obsessive thoughts and questions leave one by one. We can shut the door behind them. Our lives are changed. There is no more room for fear. Faith has come now. It is here. It is ours.

OCTOBER 27

Waiting/Power

Waiting is an art. When we quiet our spirits and learn patience, we usher in the power of God. Sometimes we can achieve things through waiting that we could have struggled for years to accomplish if we would not have yielded. We can surrender to time. We can let go of self-will and embrace God's world. Everything is exactly as it is supposed to be—right here, right now. We can trust in the freedom and comfort of turning our thoughts and fears over to a greater source of strength than our own.

We cannot always have what we want when we want it. There are many reasons for this, many of which we may never know. Perhaps something is being worked out—in us or in someone else. God has a plan for each and every one of us. He sees the tapestry of who we are created to be and what we are to become. We needn't make ourselves crazy trying to be someone who we are not, or accomplishing goals that are outside the realm of our destiny. We can relax and breathe. The right choices will come to us. We will learn to make good decisions with ease.

We do not have to put our lives on hold while we wait, either. We can practice gratitude and acceptance to enjoy the many gifts in the moment at hand. We may wish we were ahead of where we are. We may long for the gifts of yesterday and yet our truest source of happiness and peace is in the here-and-now. Patience provides a bridge so we can experience this awesome revelation. We are renewed as we accept what is. Let us learn the art of patience and embrace the power of waiting.

<hr />

OCTOBER 28

Grace/Gratitude

When we consider God's grace, when we fully recognize it for what it is and what it does, our lives are transformed. We are made new.

Some of us get caught in our troubles. We let gloom and disillusionment rule our lives. We have lost our conscious contact with God. Our channel of faith has been dismantled by life's crises. We experience a serious blow and give up hope. This is the pattern of depression. Thankfully, it is not who we are. It is only a symptom of an old coping system. The time has come for us to find new strategies for living. We can enter the kingdom of heaven here on earth. We can begin by fully appreciating the magnitude of

God's grace in our lives. He is holding us close to his heart each and every moment of the journey. Through trial and tribulation, peaks and dark valleys, God is here as our friend, companion, helper, and Savior. There are tears in heaven when we hurt. God knows there is a better way. He will show us if we can only surrender our pain and fear and listen and watch. Healing is in the distance and yet very close. God's grace is upon us.

We can see it in the stars. It sits upon the horizon. It rises with the sun and sets in majestic painted colors in the evening sky. We can feel it in the soft breeze. Grace surrounds our every move, protecting us, loving us, holding us near. It washes over our spirit to refresh and renew us. It sweeps the depths of our soul when we let down our walls of defense and lift our faces into the light. It is beauty. It is love. It is divine. It is ours. When we fully recognize its bountiful presence, we are transformed. We have found gratitude.

<hr />

OCTOBER 29

Fear/Faith

How many of us are held down by fear? Fear is like poison to the soul. It infects every aspect of our personality and character. It suffocates our spirit, causing us to live on the defensive. We put up walls to shelter our hearts from impending doom. We enter the illusion that nothing will ever work for us. We feel defeated and hopeless. We are scared to do what needs to be done. Sometimes, we cannot even see beyond the delusion to truly know what is before us. We are confused. Our vision is blurred. Fear has moved us far from reality.

There is an antidote for fear. It is faith. This is our way out. It is the light that colors the horrible darkness we have been stuck within. If we can find the courage to open our hearts (even just a little bit) to the idea that God has a better plan for us, we will enter the realms of faith. We are lifted into a new dimension. Our thoughts and attitudes are enlightened, and we begin to see that God can do anything in our lives. He can bring about healing and restoration. He can invoke change and give us new strength. With him, all things are possible. This is the great fact of humanity.

The journey becomes wondrous when we firmly root our inner landscape in faith rather than fear. Decisions that we have been fretting over become clear choices that we can make with ease and comfort. Worry turns to trust. We will know that all things happen for our ultimate good. We are exactly where we are supposed to be in this moment in time. We are learning and growing. Soon, we will reach a destination that is beyond our wildest dreams. Faith will bring us there. We can count on it!

❧

OCTOBER 30

Love/Relationships

Some of us suffer from a void deep within. We do not see much to live for. We survive for our families, friends, and loved ones. It is as though our lives are on automatic pilot. We do what we think we should be doing, go were we think we must go, and yet we are unconcerned, unaffected by the things that happen around us. We are in a bubble, shut off from the stream of life. Our hearts are empty. We must be filled.

And so we seek to fill the void. We reach for things like relationships, material items, drugs, alcohol, sex—anything we can get our hands on that might soothe our broken hearts, anything to dull the pain inside, anything to help us forget how we really feel or how things really are. The truth is we are dying. We need help. We need to open our hearts toward the tender dawn of hope and healing. This begins by opening the door to self-love. It has been a long time since we have loved ourselves. Perhaps we never have.

Love is the unfailing remedy that returns us to the stream of life. It reconnects us to those around in ways that are healthy and mature. We can really care about those we are in contact with. Our relationships grow and flourish. This is all possible if we can learn to love ourselves. We can develop a deep conviction to nurture ourselves with the same kindness and consideration, which we show others. We can care for our inner being and do the things in life that support who we most want to be. It is not easy, but it is beautiful. We are becoming.

Loving ourselves equips us to live a better life. It helps us share ourselves with others in ways that are more gratifying and rewarding. It is truly awesome when we take the time to nurture and care for who we are.

❧

OCTOBER 31

Learning To Have Fun

For some of us, it is hard to be happy. We have not spent much of our lives smiling, let alone laughing. We may feel like there have been far more tricks than treats. The good news is it is never too late to learn how to have fun. The time is here.

Having fun begins with letting down our guard. Some of us have become defensive. We were raised in tough environments. Our lives were filled with hurt and fear. We had to be in control to survive. We had to stay on top of things so that our world would not fall apart. We have brought these coping skills into our present life. We have not stopped to consider if they are really necessary anymore. After all, haven't we come a long way?

Today, let's release stress and worry, and let our hearts be light and free. It will not hurt to just relax and have fun. The world will not fall apart. We will not lose control. Everything will be just fine. We will see. And if it works for today, how about having fun tomorrow, and the next day, and the next? We are embarking upon the road to happiness and freedom! It is time to celebrate our lives. The journey is a gift!

⸙

NOVEMBER I

Pausing/Planning

Some of us are very busy. We get on a roll. We can't slow down. There is so much to do. The thought of pausing seems absurd. There are not enough hours in the day, let alone days in the week. We think faster is better. We work harder to get somewhere. But where are we going and what do we really want out of life? These are important questions to consider.

Pausing allows us room for consideration. Instead of just thrusting forward without a solid goal, we can plan the day ahead. This helps us use our time more efficiently. Our work becomes more fruitful. We discover we do not necessarily have to work hard to see results. Sometimes letting go creates the space needed for good ideas and solutions to flow in. If we slow down and relax, our minds can be illumined and inspired by the many gifts of wisdom that are waiting to unfold. We are led to better ideas and, therefore, realize greater results. Pausing paves the way of success.

Pausing also helps us open our hearts to God's plan for our lives. Sometimes we get so busy trying that we miss all that He is doing in and through us. We focus and obsess on our little plans, all the while missing the big picture. We are created to accomplish great things. We all have a purpose. We are given a destiny. Taking the time to contemplate the higher realm of our existence leads us to discover and follow our mission. This is where we truly want to be. It is where our work is the most enriching. It is

172

the special place that fulfills our every need and desire. Let us pause and plan how we can embrace God's will for our lives.

⚜

Be Optimistic!

Many of us are pessimists. We fear the worst in all cases. When the boss calls us into his or her office, we think we must have done something wrong, and perhaps we will be fired. We do not consider that we may be in store for a promotion or an increase in salary. When a child is late getting home from school, we fear he or she may have been hurt or lost. The thought that he might have been held late after school does not dawn on us.

We believe that we are bound to fail at the onset of any project. We are reluctant to begin new endeavors due to self-doubt and poor self-esteem. Fortunately, we can change the way we think, just as we have already changed many of the other aspects of our lives. We can enter the hope and light of optimism.

We learn to be optimistic by practice. We can literally train our minds to be hopeful rather than doubtful. We can taper our overreactions and consider alternative views toward the circumstances we face. When we are called to a meeting at work, we can assume the best. We can be self-confident and know that our ideas and contributions are valuable and substantial. Instead of assuming the worst when a loved one is late, we can patiently wait with objectivity and reason. We can transform our feelings of failure into the sure knowledge that we are intelligent, successful people who can accomplish anything we set our hearts to. We can conquer any endeavor. Our destiny depends on it.

So let's say good bye to doubt and fear one last time, and commit to changing our thought patterns. Each time we think, "No, I can't" we will replace these words with "Yes, I can and will."

⚜

Doing What's Right/Satisfaction

Many seek satisfaction. We are empty and do not even realize it. We work hard and keep ourselves busy in an effort to reach a level of comfort and security. We may think work is the answer. Perhaps earning more money or acquiring more things will make a difference. People chase many roads to happiness. And yet, there is only one true way to reach a state of satisfaction that endures. Happiness is a by-product of doing what's right. Lasting peace arises out of taking the time to do what we know God would have us do. When we turn our lives over to his guidance and direction, great things happen. Our journeys' are blessed.

It is not always easy to do the right thing, especially when we are influenced by selfish motives. We usually think that we know what is best, not only for us, but also for those around us. We attempt to run the show. We try to control our lives and the actions of those we love. The longer we live in this manner, the more frustrating life becomes. We cannot be satisfied until we let go of self-seeking motives. We need to care for others in the same way God cares for us. We can love our neighbors as we do ourselves.

We are rocketed into a new dimension of living when we begin focusing on what is right rather than what we want. We gain a deep and sure sense that life is good. The struggle ends. Instead of worrying about what is in store for us, we trust that God will show us the very best in our future. His gifts will unfold when we are ready to receive them. Everything is happening in perfect time. Our journeys are flowing to a place of hope, where we will soon be reborn. It is time to find peace. It is time to embrace the light.

⚜

NOVEMBER 4

Grief/Healing

It is hard to pass through times of grief. A place within us is hurt so bad that we could scream. How unfair! We hate life and what has happened! We do not understand how a loving God could allow such misfortune. Is there anyone up there? Does anybody hear our cry, feel our pain? Or are we alone in a cold world of hardship and despair? We sink deeper and deeper. We have fallen.

Or, we play the shut-off game. We go on like nothing has happened. We pick up where we left off and move forward, seemingly unaffected. We shut off our feelings. We put on armor and erect walls of protection. The pain is just too much to bear. We vacillate between denial, anger, and sadness. We bounce back and forth like we are a ping-pong ball. We are stuck. Our wounds will not heal.

The only way to experience hope, and freedom from grief, is to allow it to move in and through us. We can experience it long enough to thoroughly feel it. We must process our emotions. We cannot run and hide any longer. We are only postponing the light on the other side of the tunnel. We will not travel in darkness forever. God does love us, and he wants only the best for our futures. He does not cause us pain. He carries us through.

We are free at last when we open the door to experience and deal with our grief. It loses power over us. We find forgiveness and renewal. No matter how far down we have fallen, no matter how deep our wounds, no matter our circumstances, we begin to see the other side of pain. We are embarking on a new freedom and a new happiness. We are discovering the love that heals all wounds.

NOVEMBER 5

To Thy Own Self, Be True.

Sometimes we get caught up in the storm of the needs and feelings of others. We let other people dictate how we should act and think. We want to please our friends and loved ones. We crave acceptance. We are dependent on their approval. It is time to become who we are.

We can learn to listen to ourselves. What do we need? Are our needs being met? How do we feel and what are our feelings telling us about ourselves and the direction we need to go? These are important questions. We can pause and listen to our conscience. It is trying to lead us to a better life.

But instead, we get caught up in confusion. We let the demands of others control us. We are led by their expectations rather than following our heart. Our lives become a complicated mess. We lose the inner self. We forget who we are. We live for the external rather than embracing our precious soul. We may think we are living wisely, but we are being untrue. We are denying our true selves.

We need to simplify our lives and return to the basics. We can let go of confusion and honor and respect ourselves. We can lift up our dreams and desires and follow our hearts. This may mean disappointing friends and family. Not everyone will agree with the choices we make or the places we chose to go. And yet we are on our way to a richer life, one that we can call our own. We are following a destiny that we can see and feel and taste and touch. We do not need third-party affirmation. It is between God and us. He provides all the direction we truly need. He brings us to the miracle.

NOVEMBER 6

Freedom From Isolation

Some of us do not feel safe sharing our thoughts and experiences with others. Fear holds us captive. It shelters us from the joy that's found in allowing other people into our lives. We hold them at arm's length. We keep our friends and family at a comfortable distance so that we do not feel exposed or vulnerable. We slowly die in this way. Our soul is longing to let others in. It longs for companionship.

It is hard to consider changing our ways, opening the door, and letting people in. Where do we even begin? And what will happen to us? Will we be ridiculed, rejected, or worse yet, put to shame? Many of us have experienced harsh criticism when we expressed ourselves in the past. We have come from dysfunctional homes. But it is different now. We no longer need to isolate ourselves.

And so we step outside of our shell, one moment at a time. Change is never easy, but it is always beautiful. We begin by letting just one person in. A friend, relative, loved one—someone we trust and can be totally honest with. This opens the door to our hearts, which has been shut for so long. The light shines in. It warms the darkness that has haunted our emotions. Our spirits are illumined. We are not alone.

We will become more comfortable letting others in as time goes on. We will experience the freedom of living in peace and harmony with the world. Finally, we become connected. We enter the stream of life. We are set free from the bondage of loneliness. Praise God for His creation! What a blessing to become part of it now.

NOVEMBER 7

Tension/Release

Many of us are tense. We can feel the side-effects. Our blood pressure is high, and perhaps, we have headaches. We are crabby and short with our children. We may even snap at our co-workers. The longer we ignore it, the higher the tension builds. We are consumed in frustration and anxiety. We need release.

Thankfully, there are many simple methods for relieving tension. One of the best is exercise. This releases positive chemicals in the bloodstream such as endorphins, which elevate the mood. Sometimes all we need is a good workout or a run through the park. We feel much better when we are done. All we needed was physical exertion.

There are other times we can turn to spiritual cures like prayer and meditation. We can become silent and turn our frustrations over to God. We can breathe deeply and focus on our trust in him. God is loving and kind. When we surrender our problems to his care, they leave, one by one. We find release.

What a gift it is to release tension. What a joy to calm our spirit in the hope and freedom of knowing that we can deal with our worries and anxiety in constructive ways.

Let's release our tension in healthy and spiritual ways and trust the Lord to take our problems and handle them well.

NOVEMBER 8

Relationships/Balance

Many of us have worked very hard to make relationships work. Some of these relationships did not even stand a chance from the beginning. The other person may have been unavailable or unable to fully care for us. Their heart was not in it. Not everyone is capable of love. And love is what we all deserve.

To compensate for the other person's lack of affection, we may do all or most of the work. We get very tired, becoming resentful and angry. This tires us further. We notice that our actions are not being reciprocated. We feel victimized. We fall captive to delusion. We think we are traveling a two-way street when actually, we are on a dead-end road. We are wearing blinders.

There is a lack of balance when we are doing all of the work in a relationship. An alternative is to step back and just allow things to happen. They either will or they won't. We can relinquish control and let go of the outcome. If the relationship is meant to be, it will be. We do not have to hold on so tightly. We can breathe. We can let others breathe. Good things cannot be forced. They come naturally. We can learn to relax and simply let things go. We can stop worrying and obsessing. We cannot make things happen by willing them so.

This leads to balance. The significant others in our lives will appreciate the space we are giving them. Our friendships will be enriched. Our marriages will gain strength and intimacy. We will no longer cling. We become content with who we are, where we are, and our relationship with God. This is a beautiful place to be. It feels like home.

NOVEMBER 9

Discipline/Waiting

Discipline is not fun, but it brings about security. Children need discipline. We do too.

When we are disciplined, we understand there are logical consequences to our behavior. We act responsibly and make good, healthy choices. We also adopt new behaviors. We become willing to work for, and toward, what we want, instead of wanting things right now.

Discipline also involves patience. We can be willing to wait. We can develop understanding and accept that we are where we need to be, right here, right now. We can cast our feelings of frustration aside and wholeheartedly tend to the schedule before us. We can perform our tasks day by day. We can trust that our goals will be reached, even though we cannot see the end in sight.

Discipline can be a grueling process. We may feel afraid. At times, we are confused and uncertain. And yet if we are patient and wait, we will see a purpose for all that we have been through. We generally do not gain this clarity until after we have passed through our moments of trial and tribulation.

We may not believe we are moving forward, but we are. We will reach the other side of the rainbow through trusting that God is surely leading us to a place where everything will make sense someday. We can surrender to his discipline. It is through his great love that he cares to lead us, guide us, and show us a better way.

God, help us know that, as a result of discipline and learning, something valuable will have been worked out in us.

NOVEMBER 10

Hope

When we have hope, we are happy, optimistic, positive, and therefore, effective. Hope is a disposition of the mind that completely transforms our personality. It is the antidote of depression and despair. When we have hope, we are happy. We look at our lives with gratitude and appreciation. We count our blessings and cherish our moments. We are filled with peace. We are content in mind, body, and spirit. Hope is the light of the journey.

When we have hope, we are also optimistic. Instead of looking at the negative and diving into self-consuming thought, we can view our lives with new glasses. We can focus on the good aspects of every event we face. There is some good, even in the worst of situations. We can embrace opportunities and develop the confidence to join in God's wonderful plans for us.

Hope gives us a positive frame of mind. Instead of giving into self-defeating thoughts and behaviors like avoidance, doubt, and impending doom, we seize the moment before us. Each event that comes our way is a gift from God. We can make the best of it, or fear the worst. The choice is ours. Hope brings about positive reactions. When faced with new situations, we can look for our chance to make a difference in this world. It can be as simple as smiling at a lonely beggar on the street, or as incredible as beginning an outreach that will one day touch many lives. We will see how all things work for good when we trust our God.

Lastly, hope is effective. It equips us to reach out to others. It illumines the journey with joy. It enriches our lives and the lives of those we meet. Let's embrace it today!

NOVEMBER 11

Being Who We Are

Some of us have no idea who we are. We are quick to rattle off our status, such as where we work or live, but when it comes to who we are at a deeper level, we are puzzled. We haven't spent the precious time we need to explore our inner landscape, search our soul, and discover the depth and fiber of our spiritual being. We have not yet developed the rich and electrifying relationship with God that will carry us through all of life's challenges and troubles. We discover our most precious selves in this connection. We are all beautiful creations of the loving God of the universe. We can find him now.

We can discover who we are by leaving the daily grind behind and taking a retreat. It is not a waste of time. We needn't fear. Everything will still be there when we return. We can lift our hearts and minds to God. Then, we can open our spirits. We have been closed off for too long. It is time to feel the tender wings of freedom and healing brush across our tired and confused minds. We can reach above the scattered plans, broken promises, and shattered dreams we have encountered throughout our lives. There is a place of healing, a special space within each of us, where we find reprieve and renewal. We discover nothing matters as much as our connection to God and others. We find our heart here.

We discover who we are in this sacred place. We can begin our journey anew, prepared to make time for the things that matter the most. God will meet our needs along the way. He will provide exactly what is needed to help us reach the great destiny He has prepared for us. Being who we are makes it possible for us to walk this path. We are no longer diverted. The journey becomes amazing. We can celebrate.

⁂

NOVEMBER 12

Boredom/Blessings

We cannot stand boredom. We run from it as if avoiding a plague. When things are boring, we like to stir things up. We are fidgety. We are used to chaos. It is hard to be still for any length of time. We reach for things to occupy our minds: television, radio, video games, or Internet-surfing. It is so hard to be silent. What makes us this way? Perhaps we are avoiding something. Could we be avoiding ourselves?

Our lives are illumined when we learn to be still in boredom. We can accept that chaos is a thing of the past. We were used to our broken homes and volatile families, but things are different now. Our journeys are changing course. We are reshaping and renewing. Things do not always have to be happening. Our security is not dependent on how much we get done, or what occurs around us. We do not have to fear the silence. It is healing. God speaks to us here.

Learning to be comfortable in boredom is a skill that takes time. Thoughts and behaviors do not change overnight. We can be patient with ourselves. We can develop this ability in small steps. Each day, we can accept a little bit more. We can allow moments of stillness and rest in these precious times. We can resist our urge for distraction.

The good news is that, each time it becomes too much, we can ask God for help. Every time we panic, each time we feel we could scream, or we are going to lose control, we can ask God to help us lie down in his green pasture. He has created a garden here on earth where we can go and rest in his love. We find this special place in silence. It is the blessing of boredom.

NOVEMBER 13

Irritability/Tools

Something or someone is bothering us. We can feel it. We are unsettled. We are discontent, annoyed—even angry. It is festering. We may not acknowledge it, but we are irritable. We are frustrated. We are far from peace.

People can make us irritable. Perhaps they do not understand us. Maybe they are doing things that make us angry or sad. Situations can also cause discomfort. There are many times when things do not go our way. We work hard and never achieve the desired outcome. We do not reach our goals. Dreams are dashed. Life deals us a short hand.

Patience and faith can help us to diffuse irritability. Instead of getting furious or allowing the agitation to fester, we can pause and ask God to direct our thoughts and actions. We can take some time apart from the person or situation that is making us angry. Sometimes it is better to leave a particular event, before things get worse.

Other times, we need to be more direct. Some of our anger stems from our inability to express ourselves. We may be scared. We might fear that if we tell those around us how we really feel, they will leave or abandon us. Thankfully, we are discovering that we can survive in our love for God and ourselves. We do not need the approval or affection of others. Although it is nice, it is not our lifeline. And if we allow anger to build, eventually we will explode. We will cut ourselves off from those we love.

Irritability is a sign that we could be doing things differently. Something or someone needs to be dealt with more constructively, whether it is by practicing patience, love, tolerance, or directness. We have many tools. Let's use them today.

NOVEMBER 14

Inner Growth

We travel through segments of learning and experiences that challenge and stretch our character. Our spirits are extended beyond a point we had ever imagined. We have faltered and returned to faith. We have doubted and been restored. We may feel as if we have arrived. We have reached our destination at last. We are now prepared to live. And yet, the journey continues.

Life is a journey of inner growth, from beginning to end. The lessons do not cease until the day our souls are lifted to heaven. We may reach a plateau and decide we are done growing. We may not make this decision consciously, but somewhere in our subconscious, we feel as if we have had enough—enough learning, enough growing, enough hardship, and enough pain. And yet we know through our experience that we have changed the most through periods of sadness. God uses challenge to mold and shape us. Change has helped us become the beautiful people we are today.

The road to inner growth is not easy, but it is the most miraculous path we will ever travel. There are plateaus, but we can learn to recognize them for what they are. We can celebrate each one, knowing we have passed through another set of obstacles. We can take some time to reward ourselves for the things we have learned and accomplished. Then, we can move forward once more. There will be plenty more lessons ahead and each one will bring us nearer to our final destiny. They will bring us nearer to God.

NOVEMBER 15

Doing the Best We Can

We are so hard on ourselves. We carry high expectations. We set goals and make plans. We are upset when we do not achieve them. "Why couldn't I do that?" "If only I had thought of that!" "Perhaps if I had gone here or there, things would have been different." Broken records play in our heads. They tell us we are worthless. We set ourselves up for failure. It is time for change.

It is good to realize that we do the best we can. Everyone makes mistakes. We all fall short of our ambitions. We try and fail. We go the wrong way. It happens. We are imperfect. That is what makes us so beautiful. We are just doing the best we can. We can accept this and move forward.

We are empowered when we find contentment in the realization that we are doing the best we can. We have wasted needless energy in the past. We have wished that too many things could have been different. The time is here to embrace the imperfections of our personality. We are right on course. We are learning. We are growing. We are human. This makes us all the more beautiful. Let's relax and know that we are doing the best we can. This is enough for us.

NOVEMBER 16

Stability/Serenity

Some of us have been through many changes over the course of our lives. We have experienced the painful breakdown of family. We have lost our hearts in relationships and love. We have endured death, divorce, forced relocations, job change, and other tragedies. We have lost homes and friends. We have experienced periods of time when more things changed than remained the same. These segments of the journey challenge our strength and beliefs. They test our faith. We need to be careful, for our reactions can make or break us.

Some changes are necessary. They bring us to a better place. Unfortunately, we can become addicted to the negative feelings that come with the unexpected. We unwittingly carry a need for constant change into the future. We become addicted to the chaos it brings. A part of us remains numb from the constant distraction. And yet, our hearts crave stability. We can learn to find comfort in our present circumstances and accept our lives as they are, in this moment. This brings about serenity.

Stability provides the space needed for our souls to breathe. When we are on the run, we leave our spirits behind. We do not have the time or energy to nurture our inner being. Our lives become more enriching and rewarding when we seep into our current environment and surrender our need for chaos. We don't have to run. We don't have to hide. All we need to do is relax and be who we are. This is enough. It is God's design for us. We are on the course of destiny. Let's continue our search for stability and peace.

NOVEMBER 17

Illumination/Surrender

An illumination surrounds us, a depth of life that we can only see through the eyes of faith. Our vision intensifies when we are quiet and still. God's light reflects around us and permeates our spirit. It magnifies the beauty in our midst. It sparkles within us. Heaven is not as far away as we might think. It's healing rays of light stretch across the atmosphere. They brush across our soul. They grace each of our moments—those of happiness and those of despair. This illumination can heal and change us when we surrender to it.

Some of us have never seen the light of heaven. We have been preoccupied. We are busy trying to solve our problems and fix our pain. We reach for all the material solutions we can find. But it's not working. Thankfully, we have reached a point along the journey where we have no choice but to surrender. We have had enough. Our solutions are getting us nowhere. Our best efforts are leading us astray. It is time to let the light of heaven into our lives. It is here. It is waiting. It is patient and loving. God wants to come in and be Lord of our lives.

Let's pause today, wherever we are, whatever we are doing. Let's relax in silence and expand our vision to encompass the tender illumination that surrounds us. We can open our hearts and minds to embrace this light. It is a feeling more beautiful than any we will ever experience. We enter a heavenly realm here on earth, and in this moment we are strengthened and renewed. There is no need for fear. We can trust in this power that washes over us. God is guiding us to a place where the journey is joyful and enriching. He is marking us with grace and love. It is time to surrender.

NOVEMBER 18

Space

Some of us do not know ourselves very well. We do not spend much time alone. We are continually occupied with work, people, events, appointments, and other diversions.

We are surrounded by distractions, consumed with obligations. The list of things to do grows longer while our lives become shorter. We are living in haste. What a blessing to say, "Stop!" It is time we get to know ourselves better.

The only way we can know ourselves better is by spending time alone in peace and solitude. We can escape from the busy life for a while. We can let everything go—family, friends, coworkers, projects, goals, and agendas. It will be okay. The world will continue revolving. It does not need us.

We can take the time to search our soul. It may have been many years since we have reflected on our deepest, most sacred inner needs. Perhaps we never have. We learn who we really are in these moments, and what we truly want and need. It may be that we are spinning our wheels in life. We may discover that we are going nowhere. Perhaps we will even realize that we are headed down a path of destruction. We may have never taken time out for reflection. Quiet time is well spent.

We will come to understand ourselves during this time. We develop self-intimacy. We learn to love ourselves by nurturing and caring for our most precious needs. One of these is our need for space. We are one with our Creator when we are quiet and still. He touches our soul in these sacred moments. He brings peace to us here.

❦

NOVEMBER 19

Telling God How We Feel

It is not always easy to express our feelings. We keep them bottled up inside. We hold them in. Fear holds us captive. We are scared to express our emotions. What will happen? Will we lose control? How will others react? Will we be accepted? Will we be loved?

And so we go on, ignoring the cry of our heart. We long to express our feelings. We can only hold them in for so long before we explode. It may not be an outward explosion, more often than not we will feel like we are suffocating within. We are far from the happiness and freedom that accompanies self-expression. We are dying on the inside.

We begin healing when we tell God how we feel. We can turn to prayer anytime any place. We can open our hearts to heaven and tell God what is going on with us, whether we are worried, scared, frustrated, discouraged, sad, disappointed, or angry.

He already knows of our despair. He sees our confusion and doubt. He feels our pain and turmoil. He cries before we even shed a tear. He is our Savior and friend. His heart hurts when we do.

We can share all our feelings with God. We can literally spill our guts. We can pour out every emotion, each worry, all of our fears. God is faithful. He will see us through. We gain strength as we pour out our heart and soul. God fills us with the power of renewal. Our journeys are reborn. We find freedom and peace.

God loves each one of us so very much. He longs to have an intimate relationship with us. This begins by telling him how we really feel. It is no secret. He understands. And yet, through this process, we gain an understanding of ourselves and are transformed.

❦

NOVEMBER 20

Gratitude

As Thanksgiving approaches, we can prepare our hearts to celebrate in gratitude. We have been through so much. God has carried us across many mountains. He has held our hand through many dark valleys. He has brought us to the other side of pain, that sacred place where we can begin to see all the good that has come to pass along the way. The light is shining in to warm our torn and tired spirits. We are returning to peace.

And now, we celebrate. We praise God for the countless blessings he has freely given along the way. We can reflect upon the good that has come through our years of challenge and growth.

Gratitude leads to hope. It is a frame of mind that prepares us to live happy and victorious lives. When we are praising God for his many gifts, we are not as likely to succumb to negative thinking. Our perspective is positive. As we focus on the good in our lives, we magnify that portion of the journey. Failures and disappointments disappear. Happiness and joy fill us.

The longer we practice gratitude, the more rewarding our lives become. Each time we bow our spirits in utter appreciation of all that God has given—families, homes, careers, friends, good health—our gifts increase abundantly. Our thought patterns are completely transformed. We cleave to the peace and comfort found in the reality of God's love for us. It is endless. It knows no bounds. We can simply look around and we will see.

NOVEMBER 21

Emotional Freedom

Some of us hide our feelings, even from ourselves. We only go so far when it comes to exploring our emotions. We feel a bit of anger, a little sadness, a hint of failure or disappointment, and we shut down. We run from the depths of life. We jump forward and forget. This is how we cope.

And yet healing begins when we are willing to reclaim the part of us that is broken down and hurting. We can avoid our emotions for only so long. Our hurt and pain do not go away. Sadness only festers. We cannot pursue our dreams when we are weighed down by negative emotion. The only way to truly move forward is to feel the hurt. We can stay in the pain as long as it takes to move through it once and for all. Then, we can let go. This leads to hope and release.

If we are not living our dreams, it's because of emotions we are not willing to feel. This is a powerful reality. When we avoid our feelings, we mute the best part of our inner being. We may be numbing the discomfort, but we are also numbing the joy, hope, and inspiration of our future. When we miss the bad, we also miss the good. Life presents the two, hand in hand. They balance our journey.

Staying in our feelings, even in times of heartache, puts us on the path to emotional freedom. We will even discover that our worst fears are only an illusion. We can feel what we feel. We will not be abandoned. We will not be harmed. Our spirits will be cleansed so we can build a future that includes our greatest hopes and dreams. We are now in a position where we value them all. We deserve the best!

NOVEMBER 22

Comfort/Peace

Parts of the journey are very hard. We enter seasons where the trials and tribulations seem like more than we can bear. We may question why we are experiencing such grief. We may even question God. After all if he cares for us, then why the pain? Why the sorrow? Or, maybe we question ourselves? Perhaps we do not deserve a good life. We give up. We cave into despair.

And yet, these are precious times that can lead to glory. Pain carves us more deeply into the image God has designed for us. Each time we move through a period of challenge, we become stronger and more beautiful. We move closer to our destiny.

God does not wish hardship upon us. He cares deeply about our well being. He loves us incessantly, especially during times of challenge. He will return us to comfort and peace. We can trust and hold on. He will not let us down. He never has.

We will see all the glory the journey has to offer when we reach the other side of hardship. We will experience a new peace. All of the things that did not make sense suddenly fall into place. Even the worst things have an important purpose. God is working things out in us. He is weaving his love through the universe. He is moving us to a place where we can receive perfect love and care. We can turn our lives over to love and know that all is good when we trust in him. This is our ultimate destiny. We fall in love with our Creator. Here, nothing else matters. We are at peace.

NOVEMBER 23

We Are Survivors!

Life has presented many challenges, and today we can celebrate the fact that we are survivors. We have overcome many obstacles. We have surpassed great challenge. We have been strong and resilient. We have been patient and persevered. The time to celebrate is here. We have come a long way!

Looking back, we could not see the light at the end of the tunnel when we were in the midst of our pain. We seldom knew which way to turn, let alone how our tough situations would be resolved. And yet, we held on. Faith continued to flicker in the corridor of our hearts. We knew that things would get better. We knew we would survive.

This provides hope for the future. We have seen and experienced great challenge. We have moved beyond what has seemed like insurmountable obstacles. We have climbed jagged mountains and journeyed through dark valleys. Each path has led us to a better place. We have found that there is nothing we cannot deal with. We have the power to survive anything. The kingdom of God is within us.

We can live differently today. Instead of falling victim to the obstacles life presents, we can remember we are survivors! There is nothing greater than the kingdom within us. We have the power to overcome. We have seen this time and time again. We are strong. We are intelligent. We are genuine. We are pure. We are created to discover these things. We are born to hope and dream the best. It can be ours!

NOVEMBER 24

Relationships/Attention

Strong relationships require attention. It is too easy to take people for granted, especially our loved ones. We can count on them. They are always there no matter what. They love us unconditionally. We become accustomed to their support and affection. We figure it will always be there and although we are probably right, there must be more we can give. We can learn to love others the way that we would like to be loved.

Relationships need time and space. This means time together and time apart. During our times together, we can share ourselves completely. Instead of being distracted by the many thoughts that have crowded our day, we can dedicate our full attention to listen and understand. We can have a true interest in sharing hopes, dreams, fears, concerns, ideas... We can let go of our own little world and take part in the concerns of others. It is truly a gift to share in the life of another human being.

We also need time away. Everyone needs space. We all need special time, away from people, removed from the hustle and commotion of life. We get refreshed during these times. We discover new things about the universe and ourselves. We gain a deeper understanding of God and his love for us. As we strengthen our connection to God, we gain an ability to love others more completely. We also learn to love ourselves, which is the foundation for more fully loving others. We can give them what they need—our full attention.

Let's step on the path that leads to stronger, healthier relationships and watch as our world gets brighter.

NOVEMBER 25

Life/Balance

Life is a delicate balance. It is precious. We never know exactly where it will take us. Sometimes we wonder where we are going. We may feel lost and confused. And yet we know that if we take care of ourselves during the process, through each interval, we will reach our destiny. We are only as far away as we imagine.

We have not always had balance. Many of us have spent years trying too hard, wishing too much, or relying on false hope. It is a gift that our spirits have now joined in the harmony of God's world. We have discovered that we can leave our hopes and dreams in God's loving hands, the place where all is good and safe. This has brought us peace of mind. It has given us wings. It has shown us true balance. We are no longer fighting. We have learned to relax and take it easy. Most importantly, we trust that God is directing the universe and our lives in the way that they should go.

God's guidance is omnipotent. He is the Creator of balance and has orchestrated every detail of life, down to the finest molecule. He will never abandon or disappoint us. He is the great protector, the one who moves the world and our hearts in perfect rhythm. What a miracle to feel the wonder of balance in life. What a blessing to feel eternity move within us. What joy there is in giving ourselves to God's order! Let's surrender to the delicate balance of life and trust that he is guiding and protecting us.

NOVEMBER 26

Self-Sabotage

Some of us put forth half-measures. We dive into one project after another, failing to bring any one to completion. This is the story of our lives. It is self-sabotage. We do not realize we are doing it, but we are. We are afraid to succeed. Deep down, we do not feel like we deserve the best. We dance around solutions that are right in front of us. We have the tools to win and yet we lose time and time again. The beat goes on. We are merely surviving.

We are living in delusion. We are operating inefficiently by choice. We subconsciously complicate everything we get our hands on. There could be a straight road in front of us, and we would meander on the crooked path. We do this to fulfill a need. It helps us continue to feel discomfort and pain. We are used to these feelings. We have known them since childhood, and therefore, we feel at home here. And yet, this is so wrong! These feelings no longer belong in our lives.

We can learn to change our thoughts and behaviors to overcome the negative consequences of self-sabotage. This begins by catching ourselves when we first start setting ourselves up for failure. There are subtle clues that help us become aware of what we are doing. Perhaps there are critical steps that must be taken in the initial phase of a project or relationship for it to be successful. We can take these steps early on. And instead of complicating simple tasks, we can take them for what they are. We can learn to do what is in front of us and keep moving forward. Our lives will be transformed when we quit sabotaging our success. We will be set free!

NOVEMBER 27

Tiredness/Guilt

Tiredness spells guilt for some women. We go and go and go. We think we should be able to handle everything. We carry on like we are superheroes. We live as if we are immortal. And still, we are only human and with our humanity we have limitations. We can only do so much. When we push ourselves, we become tired. We may not want to give in to the feeling, but physically and emotionally, we can only go so far. Some of us have trouble drawing the line.

We do not have to feel guilty when we are tired. We have worked hard. Our minds, bodies, and spirits become physiologically beat. We reach a point where we cannot continue at the same pace without rest and replenishment. This is natural. It is the normal process of human transition. We were not created with an endless supply of energy. We are finite, by design. We are dependent on an infinite source of strength. We can learn to rest and nourish ourselves in God.

Our lives change when we accept our moments of weakness. A door is opened, through which we begin to love ourselves in a deep and enriching way. We are set free from the bondage of guilt and shame. There is nothing wrong. We all reach the end of the road sometimes. Thankfully, it is here, in this special place of surrender, where we can ask for help. We can go to God. We can reach out to another. We have many options. This helps us see the world in a new light.

Releasing guilt and surrendering to our inner needs is a process that takes time and practice. Let's begin on the journey of healing today.

NOVEMBER 28

We Count!

We take such good care of everyone except ourselves. We go to great lengths to raise our children well. We bend over backwards for our spouses. We work hard to be valuable employees, reliable coworkers, and supportive friends. We are kind and compassionate. But we must remember that we count, too. In the midst of caring for everyone else, we mustn't forget about ourselves. We are precious and valuable just for being who we are.

It is time to turn our attention inward. We have neglected our needs for many years. We can learn to treat ourselves as well as we treat others. We can celebrate and congratulate ourselves for a job well done. We can encourage ourselves during times of struggle. If we fall short of our goals, we can gently motivate ourselves to try again, in a new way. We can forgive ourselves when we go wrong. We can view mistakes in a new light, one that helps us learn and grow. We give these gifts of understanding and support to others. It is time we forgive and encourage on a personal level.

The journey becomes more beautiful when we begin caring for ourselves. We make different choices, ones that nurture our needs. We are beginning to see that we have value. We are an intricate part of God's creation. We are precious. We are special. We are worthy of care and attention.

True love blossoms from our ability to love ourselves. Let's start today.

NOVEMBER 29

Patience/Tolerance

It is not always easy to be patient and tolerant. People irritate us sometimes. They get in our way. They slow us down. Sometimes they make things hard, or so it seems. Situations can also frustrate us. Things happen that are beyond our control. Obstacles arise to challenge us. The harder we try to change things, the further we fall behind. We get resentful.

We can try being patient and tolerant when things are not going our way and people are bringing us down. This is better than being bitter and frustrated. Life is too short to harbor resentment. This moves us away from the spirit of light. It prevents us from living joyous and free lives.

Patience and tolerance illumine the journey with forgiveness and understanding. They free the heart to breathe eternal life. Instead of forcing a situation our way, we can release our energy and trust that God will work things out in good time. He orchestrates the universe in perfect rhythm. He does not miss a beat. He will not neglect our needs either. We will see this as we trust in him.

We can learn to be more tolerant of others. We are only human and so is everyone else. We all make mistakes. We can show others the same compassion that we experience daily by the grace of God. We are continually forgiven for our downfalls. We can do the same for others.

Patience and tolerance flow in the river of hope. They light up our lives with rays of acceptance and peace. It is time to embrace these fine qualities.

NOVEMBER 30

Courage/Fear

Courage is doing something, even though we are scared to death. We do it anyway because we know it is right. We have no doubt. The inner voice has spoken, and we have heard. We may try to pretend like we didn't, but we did. We heard the answer. We know which way to go. We know what must be done.

But we are scared, scared to death! We can hardly breathe. We cannot sleep. If only the nudge would disappear, but it won't. It is there for a reason. It beckons a response.

Courage moves us through these difficult times. It helps us do what needs to be done despite our reluctance. It is not easy. It is never easy. But the most treacherous roads are also the most beautiful. Visualize the most beautiful mountains and valleys of the earth, majestic, mighty, rich, and glorious. The paths through these lands are steep, but they lead us to the top of God's beautiful creation. And the view from here is incredible!

It takes courage to continue climbing, especially when we are tired and afraid. We are strong women. We are intelligent and incredible. We can do it! We can put one foot in front of the other—step by step, day by day. We will reach the point where we are no longer afraid. We will experience the mighty gifts that await our arrival on the other side of challenge. They are only a heartbeat away.

⌁⌁⌁

DECEMBER 1

Strengths/Weaknesses

Some of our greatest strengths are also our biggest weaknesses. Many of us are compassionate, and yet there are those who take advantage of our kindness. We bend over backwards to make sure we do not disappoint the people we love. We try to make everyone happy. Unfortunately, we are lost in this external focus. We show understanding, yet there are times when our empathy takes us too far. We are patient and miss those crucial times when action is in order.

It is good to keep our strengths in check. Balance is the key. Even our greatest assets can turn against us when we neglect to keep them in proper perspective. We can be loving and kind and still express our values and convictions. We can be understanding and maintain wisdom and integrity. We can be patient without putting our lives on hold—hoping that something will happen that never will. These are all gifts we can learn. The journey is not over.

Our strengths make up the best of our personality and character. We should not be ashamed of them, or of our weaknesses, for that matter. We are all on our way to living a more successful, productive life. We are merely at the beginning of self-discovery. The more we learn about who we are and our psychological makeup, the better equipped we will be to deal with the problems that come our way.

Life is full of challenges. We are continuously tested so that we may fine-tune our strengths and weaknesses. Our reactions will improve as we journey forward in faith. So will our lives.

⌁⌁⌁

DECEMBER 2

Holiday Blues

Not all of us are full of cheer during the holidays. Some of us have lost loved ones. Others have separated from friends and family. This can be a lonely time, especially when we are dealing with sorrow and loss. Thankfully, we do not have to do it alone. There is someone in our heart just waiting to comfort and sooth our emptiness. May we find him this holiday season!

Depression can be worse this time of year. We look around and see families celebrating joy and love. We watch commercials reflecting the many hopes and dreams fulfilled at Christmas time. We wonder about our hope. Do we have any left? We think about our dreams. How long it has been since we have dreamed. This is the time to reach up. We cannot stay down any longer. Our souls are suffocating. We are dying inside.

Let's make the best of our circumstances this holiday season, no matter how bad they seem. Let's close our eyes and open our hearts, and embrace the One who is waiting to help us through. We have a mighty companion who is ready and willing to restore our hope and make all our dreams come true. He is the light of the season, the reason for joy and love. May we find his comfort and peace this holiday!

DECEMBER 3

Rage/Poison

Rage is poisonous to our system. It eats away at our soul. It removes us from the spirit of God. Nothing good comes from rage. It only ties us up inside. We develop tunnel vision. We lose our creativity and inspiration. We become consumed with the object of our anger, and in the midst of frustration, it is impossible to feel any serenity. We cannot live this way.

The best way to combat anger is to release it. We can express it and let it go. We cannot continue bottling it up inside. We can allow ourselves to feel the way we do and then release our negative emotions so that love can fill our hearts once again. Love and hate cannot exist together. We must purge our spirits of resentment to feel the river of hope flow through our lives. We are blessed when we do this. Our journeys are illumined in heavenly light.

The longer we allow rage to eat our spirit, the harder it is to turn our hearts back to God. And yet, we can turn to him anytime. Our emotions soften when we cry out for help. God experiences our feelings with us, including rage. He sympathizes with our ignorance. He knows we are only human and waits patiently with the gifts to help us reenter the garden. We can surrender our hatred and return to this perfect place of peace. We are the ones who are holding back. It's time to let go.

⚜

Refuge/Strength

Some of us are tired. We have worked hard to get where we are. We have overcome insurmountable obstacles and journeyed through great hardship. We have become weak and afraid. But there is hope. God is our refuge and our strength. He is the infinite power of all we possess. He gives us many gifts and tools for living including strength. We find this when we take refuge in him.

It is not always easy to remember that our greatest strength comes tin times when we feel the weakest. We experience this when we take refuge. We retreat. We take time out and go somewhere peaceful and quiet, all alone. We meet God and spend time with him in this place. He awaits our attention and affection. We can open our hearts and minds so that he can fill us with his wisdom, courage, and love. We find new energy here. We tap into the eternal energy source, a flow of positive energy that is inextinguishable. We are made strong and new.

When we feel tired and fearful in the future, let's remember the strength we find in refuge. We needn't feel defeated or useless. Everyone needs to recharge. Human strength is finite and, therefore expires, especially when we have been stretched beyond the limit.

We can leave life behind, if only for a moment, and meet with God who will regenerate our entire being. Every fiber, each molecule of our creation will vibrate with profound peace and love. It is truly a miracle. May we discover it now!

⚜

Giving

There is a difference between healthy giving and care taking. Some of us give out of feelings of guilt and shame. We try to make up for past wounds through lavishing others with more than they need. Or, we give because we think we have to, which leaves us feeling victimized. Neither of these are healthy forms of giving. They leave us feeling resentful and used.

Healthy giving makes us feel good about ourselves and others. We do not give out of feelings of obligation or inadequacy; rather, we give out of love and charity. This leads to high self-esteem for the giver and receiver. We do not feel like victims. We do not feel slighted or trapped. We are able to experience the fullness and beauty in giving unconditionally with genuine motives. We expect nothing in return. This leads our hearts to freedom and happiness.

Giving is one of the finest gifts of the journey. It illumines the path along which we can affect the hearts and lives of others. We can share a piece of God with everyone we meet. We can give our loved one's our very best, not because we have to but because we want to. What better time of year to tap into the power of giving in our lives! Merry Christmas!

⬤━⊱⊱⊰⊰━⬤

DECEMBER 6

Hope/Freedom

It is horrible to live in the bondage of fear. We know. We have been there. It's a living nightmare. Granted, things happened that put us there. Perhaps our families were torn. Some of us were even hurt and abused. Others have been neglected and abandoned. We did not experience love and safety. This is how fear develops. It has infected our hearts. It has ruined our lives.

As a result, we have spent the majority of our days scared. We have worried about things that never came true. Our deepest fears never happened. Thankfully, we have found a new way to live. We have discovered hope and freedom.

Faith has led us to this special place along the journey. We have traveled long and hard. We have worked on our inner landscape, replacing the negative with positive energy. We have changed our thoughts and behaviors. It has not been easy, but it has been well worth the while. We now see the dawn of a beautiful new horizon. A new life awaits us, one where we can finally leave worry and fear behind. The time has come to find our destiny.

There is no better way to live than within the realm of hope. We are free from our past and trust that our lives will be good. We cooperate with God in creating our future. Our thoughts lead us in the direction we will go. We now keep our minds on God and his magnificent love and guidance. We will follow this to the end. This is where life truly begins. It is where our souls are reborn.

DECEMBER 7

Healthy Tolerance

Many of us have years of practice at discounting what hurts us or makes us angry. We may endure an unbearable situation, telling ourselves it's really not that bad. We think we shouldn't be so demanding. We put the needs of others before our own. We convince ourselves that the actions of others do not hurt, after all. Maybe it's just us. We are hiding behind the walls of confusion.

We fight and argue with ourselves about the validity of our pain. We question whether we have the right to feel it, let alone do something about it. Often we tolerate too much. We discount our inner needs and emotions. We tell ourselves we do not count. We play second fiddle. Destiny dies when we sell ourselves short. We miss the great purpose of the journey.

We can learn to develop healthy tolerance. We do this by setting boundaries. We can accept our feelings and validate them. When we are hurt or angry, it is real. It is true. This is how we feel, and we cannot change anything until we quit punishing ourselves. We needn't feel guilty. Our feelings are there for a reason. It is not our fault. This helps us place boundaries so that we are no longer hurt or taken advantage of. We are teaching other people how to treat us. We are laying the groundwork for a brighter future.

We do not have to apologize or defend ourselves for the boundaries we set. We can learn to accept the discomfort and awkwardness that will follow. We have the right to have limits. This does not make us selfish or bad. We are caring for ourselves at last. We are growing and becoming. We are discovering the heart of happiness.

DECEMBER 8

Serenity

Serenity in life is our connection to God. When we lose our serenity, we are quickly disconnected. We become miserable and confused. It is hard to focus or make good decisions. We waver. We stumble. We fall. We cannot see the light of the spirit. There are so many things that disrupt our serenity. Thankfully, we can learn to stop the negative cycle early on. When troubles arise, we can maintain peace of mind by asking ourselves a few simple questions like, "How important is it, really?" We can question whether the situation that disturbs us is worth giving up our serenity for. If we truly search our soul, the answer will be "No." Serenity is one of the most valuable assets we possess. It is our road to God.

Hopefully we will find serenity and peace this holiday season. Better yet, let's carry it into the new year and throughout our journey. Nothing is worth sacrificing our emotional well being over. Life can be a joy. It is an opportunity to share love and happiness. It does not have to be so hard. We possess the tools to make our lives more beautiful. Let's start using them today!

⚜

DECEMBER 9

Sharing/Caring

We live in a greedy society. Many of us make decisions based on how they will affect us. We do not consider others. We work for the things we want. Sometimes we go overboard and get carried away. We place our wants above our inner needs. We make sure we get our fair share. But the more we take, the less we become. And we forget the most precious part of the journey, the reason we are here. It is not to fulfill our desires, but to enhance the lives of others. We have so much to give.

We all contribute to the good fortune of each other. As we give, we receive so much more. We do not have to give everything. We can have nice things too. It is okay to treat ourselves. And yet, there is a delicate balance. We can share our gifts with others and still have plenty left over. It is amazing. It is magical. It feels like we have even more than we did before. Our lives are blessed abundantly.

Giving opens the window of our soul. It is the eternal fountain of life. When we shift our focus away from satisfying ourselves and begin looking at how we can help others, our whole attitude and outlook change. We find the true joy of living.

What better time than the present to experience the joy and peace of giving! We will discover the awesome wonder and magic of caring for others. There is no greater feeling than the love that comes from sharing with a soul in need. This puts us face to face with God. When we reach out to others, we are spreading his light into a world of darkness. We are shining his hope on the shadows of sadness and despair. We are bringing about a better world.

❦

Walls/Surrender

Some of us feel dark and cold and empty. Our thoughts are blank. We are numb. It has been a long time since we have felt the light of the spirit. Perhaps we never have. During the holidays, the emptiness is magnified. We may have been getting by, but we are beginning to feel our pain more and more. It intensifies each time we see the hope and light around us. We want to plug in, but we are unsure how. There is a wall between God and us. We have put it there. He patiently waits for us to tear it down and surrender.

And so we begin, step by step, moment by moment. We turn to God in prayer. The tears fall like rain on a dry and thirsty land. They moisten our soul. We feel the infancy of life again. We are on the edge of rebirth. God immediately begins his healing work within our hearts. He wastes no time at all. He has been longing for our surrender. He dreams of the moment when we will take down our walls and seek his presence again.

The light of the spirit will surely fill us when we surrender in God's presence. We enter the garden of peace and happiness. Everything around us appears different. We are no longer jealous or resentful of those who have found true joy. Our pain and sorrow disappear. The wounds we have hidden are exposed as we lift our hands. God heals them. We feel whole again. We are content.

Let's spend time alone with God this Christmas season. We can surrender, cry, and be renewed by his great love and strength. What a gift!

❦

Receiving/Gratitude

It is hard for some women to receive. We are so used to giving. We work hard to support our families. We spend much of our time doing things for others. We try to make the people around us happy. We are kind and generous.

But what happens when it comes time to receive? We are so independent. We are not accustomed to letting others do for us. Somehow, when we receive a gift or favor, or even a compliment, we feel undeserving and, therefore, try to reject it. It is hard for us to be grateful—hard, but not impossible.

We can learn to let others help instead of always working so hard to do things on our own. We needn't fear. Our lives will not fall apart just because we are giving up some control. We will begin to feel a new ease. It is good to let others do for us. We cannot accomplish everything on our own. Even if things appear good on the outside, we are suffering on the inside. We can admit we need help.

Another part of breaking our self-reliance is learning to appreciate gifts. We do not have to feel guilty. Letting others give to us satisfies their need to love us. We have done much to help them. We have affected them in positive ways and really made a difference. It is not bad to accept gifts in return. Others need a way to express how they feel toward us. When we feel awkward, we deny them the opportunity to bless us.

Let's learn how to receive as freely as we give. God, please cleanse us of the barriers that prevent us from receiving.

◆━━━◆

DECEMBER 12

Anticipation/Patience

Christmas is a time of anticipation, but it is not the only time along the journey that we find ourselves caught in the excitement of what is yet to come. Some of us live our lives as if we are holding our breath. We want something so badly. Perhaps we long for the restoration of family. Maybe we want a promotion, a new home, or a change in location. Maybe we anticipate the day we will find that special someone who loves and understands us. We hope to discover a partner for life. Whatever our wants and desires, it is important for us to remember that all we really have is the here and now. Our best times are found in the moments at hand. This is why it is called the "present."

Some of us put our lives on hold in anticipation of what we hope will be in our future. We lose appreciation for the many blessings we have as our thoughts are consumed in what we hope for tomorrow. We miss so much of the journey. Little do we know that each and everything that happens along the way is preparing us for the joy we will encounter in our future. We need to experience it all, step by step. Our lives have been purposefully planned in a logical, miraculous order. We can trust in the sequence of events we face. We are right where we need to be.

We can learn the art of patience to fully appreciate each season of the journey. We can bring our focus back today. There is much to be thankful for. We will see many gifts that have been unnoticed until now. Wow! We are discovering that our lives are good just the way they are! Perhaps there will be a day when our greatest hopes and dreams will come true, but for now, we are satisfied. We have found peace in the moment.

DECEMBER 13

Control/Faith

Some of us are fixers. We like to control. We like to be in charge. We funnel a great deal of energy toward trying to change things. We manipulate situations to go our way. We try to change people. We try to make them do what we think is best. We want to help everyone who crosses our path, especially our loved ones. But not everyone is ready and willing for change. And who says we know what is best anyway? We are wasting precious energy. Things will be the way they are. We can relax and let go.

The bottom line is we cannot help everyone, and we cannot fix everything. Ouch! These words hurt. It is hard to accept there are things beyond our control. But we must. Until we do, we will find no serenity. As hard as we try, instead, we can turn our efforts toward trusting that God has a bigger plan in store, something that is far greater than we can plan or imagine, far more magnificent than we can fathom. He times everything perfectly, and each person and event we encounter will fit into place someday. We will see. And it will be divine!

Faith helps us let go. It helps us let people be who they are and situations be what they will be. We can know that God is working things out in others. We all have a unique journey. We are each created to discover and experience what it takes to bring us to our destiny. When we relinquish control, we join the natural flow of life. We are calm amidst the storms we face. God has laid a magnificent future before us. We can have faith and discover just how beautiful it is, day by day.

DECEMBER 14

Moderation/Effectiveness

It is hard for some of us to moderate. We get carried away. We find something we like to do, and we cannot get enough of it. We crave exhilaration. We chase accomplishment. We do not slow down. We are in trouble.

Our journeys become softer and brighter when we learn the art of moderation. We can step back and look at our behaviors and actions to begin the healing process. Are we getting carried away? After all, life is short and our days are precious. How are we spending our time? Are we helping others? Are we taking care of ourselves? These things are paramount.

Moderation helps us be more effective. We are free to flourish in many facets of life when we are not directing our energy into only one area. Our relationships are enriched. Our interactions become more meaningful. Life becomes beautiful. We see things anew.

We can learn to live more moderately through self-control. We can give ourselves limits and boundaries. This may feel uncomfortable at first, but in the long run we will be grateful. We love ourselves enough to practice balance. We are teaching ourselves to live life abundantly. What joy we are finding! What peace! We are truly satisfied.

DECEMBER 15

Self-Care/Selfishness

It is hard to distinguish between selfishness and self-care. Where do we draw the line? Some of us think tending to our needs is selfish. We feel guilty when we take time out for us. We are reluctant to rest and replenish ourselves. We are uncomfortable saying no to the requests of others, even when they do not feel right. It is difficult to accept that we have inner needs, and taking care of ourselves is one of the most important things we have to do. We not value this concept. It is hard to swallow.

Others go to another extreme. Some of us are selfish and place our needs and wants above everything else. We satisfy ourselves first and give others the leftovers. We do what we want, even though we may be hurting others or ourselves. We are in the danger zone. Selfishness is the opposite of love. The two cannot exist together.

What a blessing it is to discover the balance of self-care. This will happen as we continue to learn and grow. We develop inner confidence. We know deep down that our needs are important, especially our spiritual and emotional makeup. We devote time and energy to maintaining this precious part of who we are. At the same time, we surrender selfish behavior. We let others in. We truly love our neighbors as ourselves, and we can do this because we have found the inner peace that comes through self-care. Our spirits are rich and vibrant.

Let's begin the journey that leads to self-discovery. Let's care for ourselves in a way that will prepare us to care for others. Let's surrender selfish behavior.

DECEMBER 16

Resting in the Cradle

There is a special place where we can go to find peace and renewal. We can all rest in the cradle of God's love and care. No matter what is happening in our lives, despite our worries and fears, we can let go and give our troubles to the Creator of the universe. He will work things out. He has been healing and transforming people since before the beginning of time. We can trust in God's mighty power to care for us in ways that are sustaining and fulfilling. He has seen us through many dark valleys and helped us climb mountains that have seemed insurmountable. We see this when we look back across our lives. This gives us hope for the future.

And yet, so many times we turn away and try to do things on our own. We work hard to get our way. We think we know what is best. We don't give up. We can't give up. This would mean failure. The world would crash in upon us. Our attitudes are based on fear and delusion. We have no real power. Our best efforts will not affect the course of our future. God is in control. When we step back and rest in the cradle of his love, we become willing to leave chaos and destruction behind. And, we discover we have been moving backwards. Self-will has sabotaged our progress.

Our journey becomes incredible when we let go and turn our lives over to the care and protection of our Creator. When we rest in the cradle of his peace and soothing love, all is well. Our worst problems become faint memories. All that we have been through—the troubles we have faced—disappear. They melt in the compassion of the Lord of creation. Our spirits are soothed and reborn in divine illumination. We can rest here. It is safe.

DECEMBER 17

Trapped/Rescue

Some of us feel trapped in life. We are frustrated. We know what we want and we cannot get it. We know how we feel, but we are afraid to express it. We know what we want to do, but we are afraid of how others might react. Whose life are we leading? Is it ours or someone else's? It's all so confusing. We have lost who we are. We are unable to see our many choices and options. We cannot see our own destiny.

Thankfully, we can surrender doubt, fear, and insecurity, and ask God to come to the rescue. He will save us from our feelings of helplessness and discouragement. He will help us see that life is full of options, and we can make our own choices about how we want to live. He will show us the way to freedom and happiness. All we need to do is ask him. We can admit we have come to the end of our rope. We are tired and scared. We are sick of living our lives for others. We have reached that glorious time when we see the illuminant rays of our own journey. We see the light of tomorrow.

God rescues us here in a new reality. He picks us up and shows us how to live a new life, one that embraces our deepest desires and values. He helps us affirm the most beautiful part of our character. We are enlightened to see we are children of a mighty Creator, nothing more and nothing less. This revelation fills us to the point of overflowing. There is nothing more we need to know. This is enough. It is sustaining. It is lasting. It is fulfilling. It is a miracle!

DECEMBER 18

Lethargy/Strength

Life can be very difficult at times. The journey winds through rocky hills. We encounter one obstacle after another. After a while, we become lethargic. We have tried and tried and tried, and seem to be getting nowhere. We get discouraged.

It is only natural to become lethargic from time to time. We cannot continue combating challenges on our own indefinitely. We are human. There are limitations to what we can endure and how much we can accomplish. Without tapping into a greater source of power, we are bound to give up. Our own efforts fail us. It is time to find true and lasting strength. It is time to find God.

This fills us with hope. A renewed mind and spirit replace our negative thoughts of fear, failure, and self-pity. We are motivated once again to move forward. The bondage of dejection is broken. We see our future more clearly, and all the beauty and awe we are yet to discover. God has not brought us this far to let us down. He did not create us to journey in vain, but to reach a state of total ecstasy. He is trying to show us just how much hope and joy we can experience when we live our lives with him. This is our greatest gift.

We can be patient with ourselves when we feel lethargic. We can rest and replenish ourselves. Our spirits are exhausted. Then, we can turn our hearts and minds to God. He is working out a great destiny in us. He is leading us toward our purpose in life. We can journey in his presence. We will find the strength we need here.

DECEMBER 19

Grace/Miracles

Life presents challenge and heartache. We endure much pain and despair. We may think life is unfair, that the journey is one hardship after another. Our thinking becomes distorted. We let doubt rule our lives. We are ridden with guilt and shame. We have lost our faith in God. We have forgotten that he will not let us down. He holds us ever so carefully and lovingly in his tender arms of mercy. He provides the grace we need to make it through.

In fact, great miracles unfold from God's grace—greater miracles than anyone could ever imagine! His power to heal and change human lives is fascinating. We needn't ever give up. Just when we think all is lost, a miracle is at hand. We can hold on and believe. We can trust that God can restore anyone and anything. He mends broken hearts, heals torn relationships, and restores hurt souls. His mercy is endless. His grace is abundant. His love is eternal.

This Christmas season, let's deepen our understanding of just how awesome God's grace is. As the bells jingle and carols play, our hearts can sing a song of joy. We are discovering a peace we used to only dream could be. We are finding a happiness and freedom that will carry us through any challenge ahead. We see the true meaning of life and it is not at all what we once thought. It is deeper. We are awakening to a new understanding. We are embracing the gift of love.

DECEMBER 20

The Joy of Giving

The joy of Christmas is found in giving. There is no greater peace than that which comes from the feelings of satisfaction we get from giving. When we freely give all that we can, God blesses our journey abundantly. We are filled with happiness and gratitude.

Unfortunately, some of us hold back. We are scared to give too much. We might fear for our future. We question what tomorrow holds. But we can trust. God has good plans in store for us. We will be okay. We can turn our selfishness and insecurity over to his loving care and guidance. He will provide. He will protect us. We will not suffer any hardship beyond the trials we need to get where we are going. He sees our destination. He knows our destiny. He will see us through safely until the end.

And so we can give freely of what we find along the way. God has blessed us with success, good fortune, and many gifts. He hopes that we will share these with others. We are not all in the same place. There are others along life's path that need to see just how good life can be. We can show them. We can give them what they need to reach the next stage of their journey, whether it is love, food, clothes, money, or just a listening heart.

The choice is ours. We can retract or step up and serve God's great creation. This is the reason we are here.

This holiday season, let's give freely of what we have. Let's place fear aside and share God's blessings with those around us. We will be amazed at our reward. We will feel a peace that passes all understanding. We will experience joy like none we have ever felt before. It is ecstatic. It is fulfilling. It will be ours!

❦

DECEMBER 21

God Is Here.

There are times in life when we feel apathetic. We are worn out and tired. The year has brought many challenges. We have traveled across winding roads and may not even be sure where we have ended up. We might feel like we are on our way to nowhere. We slowly withdraw from life. We detach moment by moment. We have entered the danger zone. We have come to a place where our soul begins to die.

The good news is God is still with us, even when we are not responsive to him. He is here. He is everywhere. He is in the mighty creation that surrounds us and, at the same time, dwells right here in our hearts. His kingdom is within us. We can let go of whatever is causing us grief and reach in to find his holy presence. Our bodies are his temple. Our minds are filled with his inspiration, our hearts with his love and affection. Our spirits soar when we tap into the infinite source of love within. Our journey is illumined with happiness and peace.

This is the perfect time of year to find the joy of our soul—the tender feeling of freedom that comes when we connect to the power within. God is here. No matter how far we have drifted, he has remained close by our side, patiently awaiting our return home. He embraces us now. And it feels so good. We did not realize how dry and hard our hearts had become.

What a miracle it is to nourish and renew ourselves in the presence of God! His love transforms and heals. No sin or burden is too great for him to erase. Merry Christmas! It is the season of hope.

❦

DECEMBER 22

Soul-Searching

We are busy. Life is hectic. We bounce from one event to another. The beat goes on. We wake up, grab coffee, run out the door, go to work, pick up the kids, cook the family dinner, catch up around the house, and before you know it, start all over again the next day. We all have our own hectic routine. We can count on the rapid pace. Our lives are ticking like a time bomb. The question is when will we explode?

It is time for us to step away from our general routine, if only for a moment. We cannot continue at the same pace without something giving. If we do not slow down long enough to evaluate our lives, we will reach a point of spiritual bankruptcy. We are already heading in that direction. Deep down, we can feel it. It is time to search our souls and discover what is most important in our lives. Then, we can make a decision to place these things utmost in our journey. It may break up the routine. We may have to change our schedule. But as a result of this, we will find victory. We will experience a better life.

Soul-searching is an invaluable gift that helps us stay connected to God and our innermost self. It brings us to the core of who we are. We discover the best part of our creation, our moral fiber, our convictions and highest values. Without knowing ourselves intimately, we are like ships without a rudder. The winds of life blow us here and there, and we are unable to sail the course of destiny. We may not even know what our destiny is.

During this holiday season, let's take some time for soul-searching. It will be the greatest gift we will ever receive!

❧❧❧❧

DECEMBER 23

Our Heart's Treasure

It is said that our heart is where we keep our treasure. What kinds of things do we treasure? A simpler question might be, "Where do we spend most of our time"? Time is one of our most valuable assets. We dedicate time to things that we consider important. Do we treasure our family and friends, our homes, our relationship with God and our spouses? Or, are we spending the majority of our time and energy on less relevant things? The answer to these questions will help reveal where we place our treasure. This is where our heart is.

We can strive to keep our hearts above all the hustle and bustle of life. We can take time daily to meditate and pray. We can talk with our kids in a way that shows we are also listening to their needs and concerns. We want to do what is best for them. We can spend time with our spouses, showing them love and affection. We can be encouragers. We bless everyone we come into contact with in some way. We radiate God's light. We are all conduits of his love. It is amazing.

We begin storing treasures in heaven when we quit chasing the insignificant and petty. Life is so fragile, and so are the hearts of those with whom we come into contact. We can treasure our relationship with God, asking him for the courage and strength to be everything he wants us to be. This involves self- sacrifice. It might mean giving up some of our wants and desires. And yet, the rewards are incredible. The angels sing each time we reach out to love one another. They rejoice every time we take another step that leads us closer to caring and compassion. Let's begin the journey toward heaven now.

❧❧❧❧

DECEMBER 24

Old Habits

The journey has become burdensome for some of us. We have carried

208

old habits and negative behavior patterns into a life that could be fresh and new. It is up to us to change. No one is holding us back. We only hold ourselves down. The time has come to change. We possess the power of renewal. We can change our behaviors right here, right now. We can root out the thoughts and actions that no longer belong in our lives. The time has come for a new beginning.

But old habits die hard. We've heard this many times, and it is true. It is not easy to change the very substance of our being. We've behaved certain ways for so long that they are ingrained in our personalities. Thankfully, God will help us change our negative behavior if we surrender our defects of character to him. We can humbly ask him to remove the obstacles in our psyche that darken our path. We can earnestly seek healing and transformation. Our lives will change. We will see. We will begin seeing life anew.

This process requires patience and practice. We can be patient with ourselves as we learn healthier, more gratifying behavioral patterns. Then, we can practice, practice, and practice some more. Each time we feel like reaching back and using old mechanisms for coping, we can reach up instead. We can embrace the light of our new way of life. We have come so far. There is no turning back. We wouldn't want to, even if we could. We are finding a peace and joy that surpasses all understanding. We are beginning to discover a love that radiates and transcends anything and everything we have ever held dear. Hang in there! It is happening!

DECEMBER 25

A New Attitude

Let's give ourselves the gift of a new attitude this Christmas. We have been reluctant to surrender, but the time is here. We have reached that pivotal point along the journey where we can put wisdom into practice. We have discovered many things about ourselves this year. We have learned that we do not have to be afraid of our feelings. We realize that our thoughts and behaviors are choices that have consequences. We have seen how bright our future can be when we stay connected to God and in the center of his love. We can let these gifts permeate our lives now. We can change our attitude.

A new attitude will bring renewal and hope into our lives. Everything that happens to us is a direct result of how we think, behave, and react. Our attitude affects all of these areas. It is the core of our personality. It influences how we treat others and ourselves. It prepares us to succeed or fail, depending on whether it is good or bad. It is the driving force of our journey. It is an intricate part of all we do and become.

The best way for us to develop and maintain a new attitude, one that is full of hope and happiness, is to enter into a close relationship with our Creator. God is the greatest companion and friend we will ever know. He knows our thoughts and feelings even before we do. He is in a constant state of readiness, catching us when we fall and lifting us up to a place where we can resume our journey. We may slip for a time, but we will always find our way back if we remain open to God's love and mercy. He will continue to renew our attitude. He will refresh it time and time again to make it new.

DECEMBER 26

A New Journey

Some of us feel stuck. We feel helpless. We have tried and failed. We give up. We quit believing in the future. We find fault with the present. We regret the past. We are frustrated and fearful. We have lost hope. We have lost heart.

Little do we know we can make our lives whatever we want them to be. We can create a new destiny for ourselves. Our future will be as bright as we dare to imagine. Our present can be as wonderful as we dream. And we can let go of the past with peace and acceptance. We have done all we can. It's time to move on.

We can create a life we want to live. This is exciting and rewarding. It's amazing how our thoughts and actions can lead us to a better tomorrow. We leave pain and struggle behind. There's no more room for sorrow. We have spent plenty of time captive to despair.

We are turning the corner now. We are approaching the crystal clear dawn of a bright and glorious season. We can put one foot in front of the other and open our hearts to a new journey. God wants to show us the very best. We can step into the radiance of his love.

Today, I will begin a new journey. I will let go of pain, regret, failure, and despondency so that my heart can be illumined with the hope and fascination of the season just ahead. I will begin creating the life I have always wanted to live. It will begin today!

DECEMBER 27

Resentment/Freedom

Some of us are angry and resentful. We lash out at those around us. We are unhappy with life. We blame others for our circumstances. We think they are responsible for our misfortune. It is important to realize that nothing will change for us until we accept the reality that we are responsible for our own journey. No one else is to blame. We create our own grief and heartache. On a more positive note, we can also create a successful and joyous future. The choice is ours.

Hope begins by turning our attention inward. Instead of looking for mistakes in others, we can honestly and openly evaluate how we are living our life. What kinds of things are we doing with our time? Are we dedicating energy to our priorities? Have we even identified what means the most to us? If not, why? Is there something we are afraid of? Are we afraid of happiness?

The answers to these questions help us discover that whatever is wrong with our lives is within us. It is not the fault of anyone or anything around us. It's time for us to accept this and learn to live differently. We can stop blaming others for our problems. They are our own. Thankfully, the solutions are also.

God, please give us the courage to reach within and discover the root of our discomfort. Give us the strength to deal with it. We want to be free.

DECEMBER 28

Justification/Rationalization

We justify everything. We think we have to, for some reason. We feel guilty, deep down. People have shamed us in the past. Perhaps we have been told we are worthless. Maybe we grew up with parents who were hard to please. Some of us still live in families where we are not appreciated. Our ideas and beliefs are not valued. We regress. We begin justifying our every move.

What a relief it is to discover that we do not have to justify what we do or how we feel any longer. Our journey belongs to us alone. We are making it what we want it to be. We are intelligent, competent people. We do not behave negligently. We have worked hard to become who we are. The decisions and choices we make today are healthy and productive. Our actions are thoughtful. We can quit justifying our behavior and let go of guilt. Until we do, we will find no freedom.

This is not to say that we should rationalize unacceptable behavior. We know when we are wrong. There are times when we realize we have made a mistake, and we are headed down the wrong path. We may be tempted to rationalize what we are doing. We try to justify it, but it doesn't work anymore. It doesn't work because we know we must change. We can no longer live with the consequences we are experiencing. The cost is so much more than we can bear.

Self-confidence and self-discipline will help us quit justifying and rationalizing. They are priceless tools we can begin learning today. We will be led to inner freedom and happiness. We are already on our way!

DECEMBER 29

Honesty/Healing

The hardest person to be honest with can be ourselves. Some of us have hidden behind cloaks of pride, insecurity, fear, and shame for so long. We have been scared to come out of our shell. Even though it is dark and cold, it's familiar. We feel a certain comfort here. We are afraid of change. We dread the thought of revealing our deepest wounds. We would rather deny our feelings and ignore our pain a little longer.

But healing cannot begin until we become honest with ourselves. The first step is opening up. We can pray for the courage and strength to open our hearts for God to reveal our wounds. It is hard, but it is okay. Trust. Have faith. We are opening the door to a world we have never seen before. We are on the brink of a personal revolution, one that will set us on a new and brighter course toward our destiny. We are about to encounter a journey we only dreamed could be so good.

We may find things about ourselves that we do not like. There may be characteristics and behaviors we need to leave behind. This is part of the process of honesty. We can do a thorough evaluation of our strengths and weaknesses. We can praise ourselves for our strengths. We have worked hard and come a long way. We can surrender our weaknesses. There is no need to carry them into the future. Honesty is the cornerstone of hope and healing.

God, please help us search our souls and become honest about who we are and what really matters most. Help us stop hiding in fear and insecurity. Please help us begin living our lives this way.

DECEMBER 30

Defining the Journey

Some of us have felt ambiguous through life. We simply go through the motions. We do what we think we are supposed to do. We are lost in careless routine.

We now approach the dawn of a new year. Looking back, how long has it been since we've enjoyed the brilliant rays of a sunset, smelled a fragrant flower, or felt the tender morning breeze? How long has it been since we called an old friend or played with our children? We have not taken the time to do those precious things that mean everything to us. We have given ourselves to a creed that does not let us dance! Our soul is no longer breathing.

It's time to define our journey. We can make it what we have always wanted it to be. We can have courage and faith. We can carve enough space in our lives to make room for God, our loved ones, and ourselves. Our spirits will be rekindled. Our souls will be reborn.

In the new year, let's have the confidence and wisdom to define our journey. We do not need to live in fear and doubt. We do not have to live according to the expectations of others. Let's find our innermost needs and live our lives accordingly. God will help us. He already is.

DECEMBER 31

Surrender/Freedom

The year is quickly drawing to a close. We have learned much. We have come a long way. We have been through hard times. We don't only think we have, we know we have. We have had faith, doubted, and then had faith again. We have been strong and weak. And now, the time has come. It is here. In this moment, we can surrender. We can turn our faces into the light. We can embrace freedom.

We have held on tightly to so many things. It is hard to let go. And yet, until we do, we cannot truly receive. We do not control our destiny. There is a loving Creator, much wiser and more powerful than we who has held us in the palm of his hand as we have struggled. He has longed to show us an easier, softer path. We can let God begin guiding our thoughts and actions today. This will prepare us for a wonderful new year.

Surrender is the key to inner peace and deep satisfaction. It is the handmaiden of freedom. All we need to do is to let go one last time and trust.

God will see us through. He will carry us along the journey. He will help us climb steep mountains and lead us along quiet streams.

God, we surrender our journey to your care and protection. May we walk with you forever!

About the Author

Amy lives in Sioux City, Iowa, with her husband and two wonderful teenagers. She writes on the topics of personal discovery, spiritual growth, and recovery from addictions and abuse. She also owns and operates a corporation she began in 2004.

Amy lectures regularly and conducts seminars to help others find hope and healing.

To schedule an event, call 712-259-1956 or email her at alz@cableone.net.